The Long Ships Passing

The Fesler-Lampert *Minnesota Heritage* Book Series

This series is published with the generous assistance of the John K. and Elsie Lampert Fesler Fund and David R. and Elizabeth P. Fesler. Its mission is to republish significant out-of-print books that contribute to our understanding and appreciation of Minnesota and the Upper Midwest.

The series features works by the following authors:

Clifford and Isabel Ahlgren

J. Arnold Bolz

Walter Havighurst

Helen Hoover

Florence Page Jaques

Evan Jones

Meridel Le Sueur

George Byron Merrick

Grace Lee Nute

Sigurd F. Olson

Charles Edward Russell

Calvin Rutstrum

Timothy Severin

Robert Treuer

WALTER HAVIGHURST

The Long Ships Passing

The Story of the Great Lakes

Revised and Expanded Edition

ILLUSTRATED BY JOHN O'HARA COSGRAVE II
AND JANE CHAMBERLIN

University of Minnesota Press
MINNEAPOLIS

To
GEORGE A. MARR
Dean of Lake Men

CONTENTS

I. SEAS OF SWEET WATER

   1. Mirage and the Mapmakers   4

   2. The Five Sisters   22

   3. Panorama from a Graveyard   34

   4. The Big Sea Water   42

II. THE VANISHED FLEETS

   5. "In a Handy Three-Master"   56

   6. Golden Cargo   76

   7. Sawdust on the Wind   86

   8. I Hear America Singing   96

   9. Smoke Clouds Blowing   104

   10. Wagon Wheels in the Rigging   120

   11. Kingdom in Lake Michigan   146

III. A STAR TO STEER BY

   12. The Fleet That Sailed on Land   158

   13. Death in the Copper Country   166

   14. Log of the Independence   174

   15. The Iron Mountains   180

   16. Coming of the Scootie-nabbie-quon   186

vii

CONTENTS

IV. THE LONG SHIPS PASSING

17. Deep Voices at the Soo   196

18. Boom Years on the Ranges   208

19. Freshwater Ships   218

20. A Fleet Was Frozen In   226

21. Fathoms Deep But Not Forgotten   238

22. The Big Storm   250

23. Freshwater Men   258

24. From Duluth to Salt Water   268

25. Iron Is Master   284

26. Overlook at the Locks   296

27. The Long Ships   312

28. The Harbor Lights   332

Acknowledgments   342

Bibliography   345

Index   349

I

FIRST PART

SEAS OF SWEET WATER

CHAPTER ONE

Mirage and the Mapmakers

"SEAS OF SWEET WATER" the Jesuits called the linked lakes that opened the way from the St. Lawrence into the western wilderness. The *voyageurs* who found those waters had ño knowledge of their farther shores or what races peopled them. They stood, first, at the edge of Lake Huron, and then, having passed through North Channel and the St. Mary's strait, on the lonely shore of Lake Superior. Each time, they brought the water to their lips and were bewildered not to find the sharp salt flavor of the sea.

On a soft September day in 1634 Jean Nicolet, with seven Huron paddlers, entered the Straits of Mackinac. Beyond the portals of Round Island and the cliff-walled Michilimackinac the sea widened nobly, and Nicolet peered westward with the tumult of discovery in his heart. Out there, he thought, the sweet water mingled with the salt tides of ocean, and he was looking toward the coasts of China.

It is easy to recapture that scene and that tumult. Standing on the cliffs of Mackinac one can lose the geography of three hundred years in the strong spell of solitude and space. That sea and sky have not changed in any aspect, since Jean Nicolet's heart swelled under his deerskin jacket. The coasts of Michigan fade into blue distance. A vast light lies upon the waters. One might be looking at the ultimate sea. And then, in the silence that Nicolet knew, on the wind that fanned his cheek, comes a steamer's throaty call. The long lean shape grows across the water, her upper works flushed in the sunset light. A big ore carrier, in ballast from Chicago, swings into the straits.

Nicolet was peering toward a coast that had never been charted.

Jean Nicolet had come to New France in 1618 as a youth of twenty years. He was one of the early recruits sent by Champlain to live among the Indians. To spread their influence in the New World the French needed explorers able to travel unknown country and to subsist like savages. They required interpreters, able to communicate with the Indians and willing to live among them till their confidence was won. Such schooling could be provided only by the wilderness itself and the smoky lodges of the Indians. For sixteen years Nicolet lived among the tribes, learning their country and their language, living on their food, mastering their crafts, even assuming their movements and posture. His skin weathered dark and his voice, forgetting the quick syllables of French, deepened to the guttural tones of Algonquin. While he lived with the Nipissings he passed as a member of the tribe. The wilderness was a thorough teacher and Nicolet learned his lessons well.

Finally his great mission came. He was an expert in the Huron and Algonquin tongues and a veteran *voyageur* when Champlain ordered him to penetrate farther west than any white man had gone. There, Champlain had been informed by Indian messengers, dwelt a people who had neither hair nor beards and who lived on the shores of the western sea. Champlain hoped his *voyageur* would find the passage to China.

In his birch canoe Nicolet carried a robe of China damask, embroidered with poppies and birds of paradise, so that he could dress in fitness to arrive among the merchants and the princes of Cathay. Emerging from the Straits of Mackinac he studied his rude map and directed his paddlers across the northern end of Lake Michigan. When at last they drew near the shores of Green Bay he donned his mandarin robe and stood up ceremoniously with an upraised pistol in each hand. He must have made a strange sight. Beneath his oriental dress were the buckskin and moccasins of a man who had taken the ways of savages. The swarthy face, the seamed, discolored hands, the wary eyes that the wilderness had given him—he was a curious ambassador for France to send to the harbors of China.

As he appeared at the first village in the country Nicolet

6

fired a salute with his two pistols. When the natives had recovered from their fright he found them to be half-clothed,
copper-skinned savages like those he had dwelt among. Perhaps there was some relief at finding men in breech-clouts instead of silken robes, and exultation in the knowledge that the
New World wilderness began again beyond the western sea. He
put off his mandarin gown and the savages roasted a hundred
and twenty beavers in a feast of welcome for him. Nicolet
would have been a stranger in the courts of China but he was
at home among the Winnebagoes—"the stinking people" as
their name signified. No Indian was sweet-smelling, and one
of a *voyageur's* first lessons was to harden his nostrils to the
reek of smoke, dirt, bear grease, and fish oil.

The Winnebagoes told him about their country and spoke
of a great river in the west. So he was lured, by the passion
for new journeys, into the green valley of the Fox River flowing south and west from the foot of Green Bay. The Fox
widened, after thirty miles, into Lake Winnebago, and then
narrowed again. Nicolet kept on till the river shrank to a
creek choking with wild celery and wild rice, and the Indians
pointed to the portage path that led to a west-flowing river.
Perhaps Nicolet portaged there, over the mile-wide strip of
land, as the Indians had done for generations. Some historians
believe his moccasined step was printed in that ancient trail
(where now a highway parallels an unused canal) and that he
saw the Wisconsin River on its way to the Mississippi.
Whether or not he crossed the low and narrow height of land,
he was the first white man to sense the far country of the
west, with the great loom of its forests, its flowering prairies
and its broad rivers flowing.

Nicolet left no records but told his story to the priests when
he went back to the churches and the trading compounds of
Quebec. He was a forerunner of pioneers. He went ahead of
the missionaries who carried portable altars to the wilds and
the men who pushed their trade in French guns and knives,

beads and cloth, tobacco and brandy. His zeal was not for trade or evangelism. It was purer and simpler, a passion for the wilderness itself. After him came the priests and the trading companies. They followed his route up the St. Mary's and to Lake Superior, and through the Straits of Mackinac to the far shores of Lake Michigan. They passed over the Fox River portage and sailed down the Wisconsin till they found the great river rippling and rolling in a mile-wide flood toward an unknown sea. It was a solemn river, Father of Waters to the Chippewas—such a stream as could rise only in a continent's midlands.

So the French began to comprehend. There must be leagues and leagues of wilderness before the salt tides of the western ocean broke upon the land. This unlooked-for country, that lay like an obstacle in the way to the Orient's riches, unfolded in their minds with a new vastness.

The explorers learned the lakes by a groping, widening experience, by their own voyages and the tales of the Indians. They saw marvels—floating islands adrift on Lake Superior, cloud banks moving like gray cliffs across the sea, and from impossible distances the columned smoke of Indian fires. Isle Royale, mysterious with Chippewa legend, sometimes appeared inverted, with its base among the clouds and its pine ridges pointing at the water. Sundogs hung on the horizon and there were nights when two moons rode together through the sky. The lakes have always been a region of mirages. Their shining distances and crystal air have played with men's beliefs. But the most stubborn and haunting mirage was the Northwest Passage, the mythical strait of Anian that the British searched for, and Nicolet's narrows that would open on the China sea. When that mirage faded the mapmakers drew their outlines with a firmer hand. Reluctantly they closed the western shores of Lake Michigan and Lake Superior, and wrote "Wilderness" across the untraveled country beyond. Then, they had no

Passage to India but a shining waterway, intricate and spacious, into the continent's heart.

Though that waterway did not lead to China, it led to other wonders. It led Radisson and Groseilliers up the Fox River and across the Indian portage to the Wisconsin River and so down to the mighty river that the Chippewas called Mee-zee-see bee. It led Marquette and Joliet a thousand miles down that river to the swamps of Arkansas, and it led that brown-robed wanderer Hennepin to the Falls of St. Anthony in the dark wilderness beyond the head of Lake Superior. It led Alexander Mackenzie to the rugged northern shores of Lake Superior and to a fur empire that ended in the Arctic wastes. It led young Douglass Houghton to one of the world's great copper ranges, and it led William Burt and Philo Everett to the iron hills.

The French entered the Great Lakes by a wilderness route that has remained to this day a route through wilderness—up the Ottawa River and the Mattawa, through Lake Nipissing and French River and so into Georgian Bay. They learned Lake Huron first and mapped it accurately while Lake Superior was still a mysterious sea and Lake Michigan (the Lake of the Illinois) was but vaguely known. They followed the northern route for two reasons: the Iroquois along the lower lakes were hostile to the French, and the Falls of Niagara thundered at the head of Lake Ontario. So the paradox of the lakes—history came first to the remote northern shores. That country, which has remained a wilderness, has a record of exploration, trade, and evangelism as old as Massachusetts. The missions and trading posts were planted on the shores of Lake Superior and the Straits of Mackinac and at the mouths of northern rivers. Nicolet died believing there were four lakes; Lake Erie had not been discovered when he drowned in the numbing waters of the St. Lawrence in 1642. The towns of St. Ignace, Sault Ste. Marie, Mackinaw City, and Green Bay had a history of two hundred years before Cleveland grew up at a river mouth on Lake Erie and Fort Dearborn was raised among the wild onions that the Indians called "Chicago."

The first white man over that Ottawa-Lake Nipissing route, preceding Nicolet by some ten years, was hardly more than a boy. Etienne Brulé was a French lad who had spent two winters in Quebec, looking up the great interior river and feeling the tug of unknown regions. Soon he had his desire. He was seventeen years old when Champlain sent him to live with the Algonquins, to learn their language and their country. He went to the wilderness in 1610 and from that time he was no longer a Frenchman but a savage. Briefly he returned to Quebec the next year, clad like a native, speaking their tongue, filled with the lore of wild country and restless to be back in it again. In 1612 he accompanied the Hurons to their home on Georgian Bay and before many seasons were past he had seen the rushing rapids of the St. Mary's and the shining waters of Lake Superior. He was the first white man to reach the northern lakes.

For twenty years Brulé carried on perilous missions and a savage life. On one occasion he was captured by a band of Senecas who tortured him in their fiendish ways and prepared to burn him at the stake. But in the west the clear summer sky suddenly darkened. Daggers of lightning jabbed earthward and thunder crashed around. In a loud voice Brulé, tied to the stake with the fires ready for lighting, began to call upon the heavens to destroy his tormentors. He used the Seneca language, for his captors' benefit. As he spoke a blast of wind toppled a forest tree and the rain swept down. The Senecas fled from him in terror. After the storm had passed a chief crept back humbly and severed his bonds.

So Brulé was spared to continue his career of adventure and violence. Before many years among them he became more savage than the savages. He used his French pay for rum and brandy and while still in Champlain's employ he sold his services to the English invaders of the Huron country. For that treason Champlain disclaimed him as a Frenchman and Brulé lived on, fearless, brutal and dissolute, among the Hurons. But not for long. In 1632, two years before Nicolet breasted the Straits of Mackinac, in a quarrel over an Indian woman he was clubbed to death and eaten by the Hurons at their palisaded town of Toanchi on Georgian Bay.

But Brulé had found the way into a savage empire. He was followed by Champlain and Nicolet, by Allouez and Marquette, and countless others. For the next two hundred years the Ottawa route supported the trade and communication between the St. Lawrence and the upper lakes. Over this way, hard and hazardous, the Recollets, the Jesuits, and the Sulpitians carried the cross to the savages, and the canoe caravans brought the peltry of the wilderness to the warehouses of Three Rivers and Quebec.

Bancroft wrote, "Not a cape was turned, not a river entered, but a priest led the way." The missionaries followed the Indian to his hunting ground, threading forests, swimming rivers, reading their Testaments by firelight, building their bark chapels on the lonely shores. Always journeying "in weariness and pain, in watchings often, in hunger and alone, in fastings often, in cold and nakedness." One of them, after having lived for six days on rock moss and a moccasin, wrote in his journal, "I thank God I have this day saved from the burning an infant who died of hunger . . ."

They went out with altars strapped to their backs, with a flask of communion wine and a packet of colored pictures of the saints. Their task was to consecrate a wilderness five times the size of France, and it called for long, hard and repeated journeys into savage country. The story of those journeys fills a whole shelf of books (seventy-one volumes of the Jesuit *Relations*). With it the recorded history of the Great Lakes begins.

SEAS OF SWEET WATER

It is a crowded, intricate and dramatic story, revealing a country of darkness and grandeur, a furtive and reluctant people, and above all other things the patience and valor of the men who wrote it. Far from people of their kind, far from gardens and cloisters, from stained glass and stately music, they lived alone in the wilderness or with flies, fleas, dogs and dirt in the noisy confusion of an Indian camp. Their story is made up of notes and records, letters and diaries, rude tracings of rivers and fragmentary maps intended only to guide one man out of a tangled forest or through a sinking swamp. The pages were written by firelight or in darkness, with numb or bleeding hands, by men hungry, diseased, wounded, lost, but never disheartened or complaining.

I know not whether your Paternity will recognize the letter of a poor cripple who formerly when in perfect health was well known to you. The letter is badly written, and quite soiled because in addition to other inconveniences, he who writes it has only one whole finger on his right hand; and it is difficult to avoid staining the paper with the blood which flows from his wounds, not yet healed: he uses arquebus for ink, and the earth for a table.

It is difficult to imagine a harder and more hopeless task than theirs—making the half-naked, painted-faced savages understand the mystery of the Trinity and the symbolism of the cross. Sometimes the native tutor tricked them into using the foulest words of Indian language so that when the priest spoke earnestly of spiritual matters he was greeted by guffaws from the men and gigglings from the squaws and children. The Indians grasped enough of their magic to blame the black-robes for storm, famine or pestilence, and they tortured some of their missionaries to death. But the priests kept on with their journey. Picture any one of them patiently learning the Algonquin language while Indian children swarmed around pulling off his shoes and trying on his hat, bribing an unwilling tutor with a string of beads or a piece of tobacco, with numb fingers in a winter wigwam writing his Algonquin exercises, eating boiled corn and fish entrails or fasting in a hard season, sleeping on the ground. They shared the savages' hunger, cold and filth for the peculiar glory of their mission. Their lot was solitude, suffering, privation, and death.

Here are three of them, out of many—

Father Menard was a man of delicate constitution who experienced in full measure the hardship and peril of the western wilderness. On his last mission he was a gray-haired veteran, already worn by years of service in that hard country. But his hardest season was coming. He spent a winter in a surly Indian camp on the windswept shores of Lake Superior at Keweenaw, living in a hut that he wove out of fir branches and concerned above other things that the wine for the Mass should not turn to ice in that poor shelter. In the spring he set out to baptize a tribe of starving Hurons. But his Huron guides abandoned the frail man on the wilderness trail. His last mission ended there, in the dark forests below Lake Superior, with the wind moaning through the pines. Only his breviary, cassock and kettle were ever found.

Claude Allouez left the pleasant scenes of central France for a savage country. He took a world of dark woods and mysterious waters for his parish. He was not a man to write in scholarly French of his journeys among the tribes, but he had courage, hardihood and zeal. Beneath his black robe were tireless legs and powerful shoulders, his hands were calloused from canoe paddles and his skin was weathered dark. For twenty-five years he was the life and soul of the missionary enterprise on the upper lakes. In 1665 he landed his canoe in Chequamegon Bay at La Pointe, the ancient Chippewa capital, three hundred miles west of Sault Ste. Marie. He remained there, weeks' journey from his nearest countryman, until Marquette succeeded him in 1669. Relieved of that lonely post he set out for another and founded the mission at Green Bay. Before his death on the western shores of Lake Michigan his calloused hands had baptized ten thousand savages.

The prince of the Jesuits, a man of distinguished birth and endowments, was Jacques Marquette, who planted his devotion and compassion over all the country of the upper lakes. Back in France, his father enjoyed wealth and honors and the high favor of Henry of Navarre, but young Jacques chose a life of poverty and toil. At seventeen he entered the Society of Jesus in his native city of Laon, and there he learned the repose, endurance and self-control that marked the Jesuits in the golden age of their power.

Every year there was published in Paris a volume of the Jesuit *Relations*—the letters and reports sent out by missionaries in New France to their superiors across the sea. Here were accounts of trade, of the Indians, of wilderness life, brief, uncomplaining notes on hardship and persecution, appeals for funds and entreaties for new missionaries to join them in their far country. Young Jesuit priests read the pages with deeply kindled eyes and dreamed of being chosen for that hard task.

In Laon Jacques Marquette read the *Relations* and waited for the call. It came in 1666, when he was twenty-nine. Joyfully he sailed for the New World. Soon he was in the wilderness, founding a church for the two thousand Indians who lived beside the loud rapids of Sault Ste. Marie. After a few seasons he went on, following the bold wild shore of Lake Superior, to succeed Allouez at La Pointe. Here, while the winter raged and the savages hugged their sullen fires, he learned from an Illinois captive of a great river, five days' journey to the west. That river haunted his thoughts.

A Jesuit scholar, a man of reflective mind and cultivated tastes, Marquette shared the hunger and the cold of the Chippewas. When they were driven out of La Pointe by their enemies, the Sioux, he made the miserable journey with them across wild land to St. Ignace on the Straits of Mackinac. There he built another chapel, beside the wind-streaked waters of Lake Michigan. Patiently he toiled at his task, learning

six Indian languages and slowly winning the confidence of
surly and suspicious tribes. He tried to keep himself clean
without offending his charges and he practiced the mercies of
simple medicine among their wailing children. In the cold
winter moonlight, away from the stench of their wigwams,
he read his breviary. Then, with a serene spirit he baptized his
converts and distributed colored pictures of the saints. For
years he lived among primitives, half-breeds, squaw-men,
renegades—hard-living, irresponsible, willful, often violent
men. He took their wilderness for his world but he never
yielded his tranquillity of spirit, his dignity and gentleness of
heart, and his devotion to a cause that must often have seemed
alien in that savage country. What he had to overcome was
thousands of years of ignorance and indifference, the whole
weight of a barbarous tradition; and the miracle is that he
succeeded, nearly. If he did not win his savages to Christian
doctrine, at least he won them to himself, and like good Chippewas they reverenced his bones after he had died in their
service.

At St. Ignace his mind kept turning to the fabled western
river, and in the fall of 1672 Louis Joliet, the son of a wagon-
maker of Quebec, arrived from Montreal to join him in his
greatest journey. The following spring, on the seventeenth
of May, they set out, traveling south to Green Bay, up the
Fox River and across the historic portage into the wide-curv-
ing Wisconsin. On the seventeenth of June, "with a joy I
cannot express" Marquette saw the majestic river rolling between bold shores. That was the supreme moment of his life.

They journeyed down the Mississippi a thousand miles to
the mouth of the Arkansas, which flowed from the unknown
west. There, fearing that they might fall into the hands of
the Spanish along the lower reaches of the river, and anxious
to report their discovery, they turned back. Their return to
the lakes was by a new route, up the Illinois and Des Plaines
Rivers and over the portage, on the site of a great city then

unfounded, to the Chicago River and so into Lake Michigan.

Exploration was not so significant in Marquette's eyes as the finding of new tribes for his ministry. *Had this voyage caused but the salvation of a single soul I should deem all my fatigue well repaid, and this I have reason to think. For when I was returning, I passed by the Indians of Peoria, where I was three days announcing the faith, in all their cabins, after which, as we were embarking, they brought me on the water's edge a dying child which I baptized a little before it expired, by an admirable providence, for the salvation of an innocent soul.*

In the following year he obtained consent to return to that prairie country and found a mission among the Illinois tribesmen. With his party he sailed down the west shore of Lake Michigan and into the Chicago River. On the portage trail they built a hut and passed the winter, and Marquette, enfeebled by illness, feared that he would never travel again. All through the month of January he lay burning with fever and racked with chills, but in the spring, though weak and emaciated, he was able to proceed to the Indian town of Kaskaskia. When his illness returned, the party was compelled to turn "homeward"—to the bleak and lonely mission of St. Ignace. They passed over the Chicago portage, steered their canoes into Lake Michigan and followed the eastern shore toward Michilimackinac. But Marquette did not live to reach his post. He died near the site of Ludington, just below the river that now bears his name, where today the Pere Marquette railroad ferries steam in from the broad waters. He was thirty-eight years old. Later, the Indians exhumed his bones and took them back to that wilder northern country. They buried him again at St. Ignace on a little hill overlooking the storied Straits of Mackinac and the blue leagues of Lake Michigan.

One other priest—a gray friar this time, a man more marked with human failings, an adventurer rather than a martyr. Early in his life Louis Hennepin confessed to an overruling passion for adventure and the fascination of strange lands. Although an evangel in the New World, he was free as the wind, not serving any sedentary mission but traveling the waterways and the forest trails. Unlike many, he did not die in the wilderness but in a European city. He spent just six years in the New World but they were as crowded with adventure as even he could wish.

Hennepin acquired his taste for roving from the sailors on the wharves of Calais and Dunkirk, where he was sent fresh from the Bethune monastery in the province of Artois. He went to the fishing ports in the time of herring-salting and he found the quays and taverns crowded with seamen just returned from long, eventful voyages. Those sailors made a more zealous convert of the young friar than he ever made among his charges. He could not have enough of their stories, and by his own account he often hid behind disreputable tavern doors to hear the talk of strange lands and the sea's peril. Perhaps it was there that he acquired his notorious gift for enlarging upon history.

He arrived in New France in time to accompany LaSalle on the historic voyage of the Griffin, the first commercial vessel on the lakes, from the Niagara River to Green Bay. That was an epic in itself, but Hennepin's adventures were just begun. He went on, by way of the St. Joseph River and the Illinois, to the Mississippi, and he later claimed to have descended that river to its mouth. In truth he was captured by the Sioux, before he had a chance to conduct his explorations, and was carried to their hunting grounds along the Upper Mississippi. On the way north Hennepin named Lake Pepin, that beautiful broadening of the Mississippi under Wisconsin's bluffs, the Lake of Tears, because, as he reported, on that shore his captors cried all night when their chief refused to let them kill the French prisoners. Arrived in the Sioux domain the restless friar could not indulge his passion for traveling, but he taught the Indian children to chant and repeat the Ten

Commandments, bribing them to that empty lesson with beads, raisins and prunes. He had a way with children; he could soothe a crying infant or charm a restless one. After five months he was released from captivity, through the graces of Sieur Dulhut, the prince of *coureurs de bois*. He returned to tell his saga in Quebec and to write it, with considerable embroidering, in Europe.

Evangelism was but a part of the French scheme for their Great Lakes empire. Already, while the missionaries went about establishing their stations, the upper lakes were growing busy with trade. Great as the Jesuits' zeal for baptizing was the traders' zeal for beaver.

In 1654, Radisson, a youth of eighteen years, set out from Quebec with his brother-in-law, Groseilliers, on a two-thousand-mile canoe trip—a journey that was to take them up the fabled Mee-zee-see-bee and to the unmapped western shores of Lake Superior. Now the Gooseberry River, threading through the iron hills, marks that exploration: no Englishman could pronounce the name Groseilliers. When they turned back to the St. Lawrence they traveled at the head of three hundred and sixty canoes laden with peltry.

This was the first of the great brigades that for a hundred and fifty years journeyed from Lake Superior down the Ottawa route to the St. Lawrence.

Behind Radisson and Groseilliers came Nicholas Perrot, a small man of great eloquence. He had a mysterious fascination for the Indians, and quickly the fame of the little man with the big voice spread among the tribes. To trade with him came distant Illinois and Miamis, three thousand of them led by a chief. Perrot entertained them with feasts, celebrations, ceremonies. The little man stood on a stump and prophesied the doom of the Iroquois, traditional enemies to the Algonquin tribes. Three thousand voices shouted "Ho! Ho!" in approval. When Perrot returned to Montreal he was at the head of nine hundred men in a great caravan of canoes laden to the gunwales with beaver skins.

Soon the traders on the St. Lawrence were shipping whole cargoes of fur to France, and the French Company was paying dividends of forty per cent. Back in the wilderness the posts grew—Green Bay, Grand Portage, Sault Ste. Marie, Michilimackinac. With the spring race of water came the Indians and *voyageurs*, anxious to exchange their winter's catch for the guns, traps, blankets, knives, and whisky of the trading posts. The rivers echoed with old Norman songs, songs from a hill country, whose rhythms curiously fitted the stroke of canoemen. In those first lake ports the fur yards were full of French and Scottish clerks, sorting packs at their long tables (first, second, third, fourth quality) and the compounds were bright with the plaid mackinaws, scarlet sashes and beaded leggings of the Chippewas and half-breeds.

It was a rich and far-flung trade, and it grew to enormous proportions. In the year 1798 the North West Company received:

106,000	beaver skins
2,100	bear skins
1,500	fox skins
4,000	kitt fox skins
4,600	otter skins
17,000	musquash skins
32,000	marten skins
1,800	mink skins
6,000	lynx skins
600	wolverine skins
1,600	fisher skins
3,800	wolf skins
700	elk hides
1,950	deer hides
500	buffalo robes.

For two hundred years the furs of the upper lakes were a source of wealth, as their forests and mines became in a later century.

There was nowhere in the world a geographical phenomenon like the linked great lakes that permitted the French to penetrate fifteen hundred miles into the interior while the English and the Dutch were hacking out their little settlements on the loud Atlantic shore. Over that water road the fur trade became the first chapter of a continuing commerce. When the forests were felled from Lake Huron to the Mississippi, when the mine shafts rose in the hills of Michigan and Minnesota and the grain fields spread over the great plains, the canoe caravans were replaced by fleets of ships, at first sail-borne over blue water and then steam-driven with their smoke staining the bright skies. From the first it was a commerce that linked the people of distant places and carried the richest products of the New World.

Father Hennepin was an unscrupulous liar when a feather quill was in his hand, but he was a prophet also. He saw the lakes when forests lined their shores and the infrequent smoke of Indian villages was the only sign of man in all that country. But he had another picture in his mind. *It were easy to build on the sides of these great Lakes, an Infinite Number of considerable Towns which might have Communication one with another by Navigation for Five Hundred Leagues together, and by an inconceivable Commerce which would establish itself among them.*

That was a bold prophecy, in 1680, to come from a man who was a captive of the Sioux, who saw only the warring tribes and a trade in peltry at the scattered posts. But the lakes gave men a sense of the future. From Nicolet to the St. Lawrence Seaway project those shining waters have kindled men's imaginations.

CHAPTER TWO

The Five Sisters

WHEN CHICAGO ROSE, sprawling and huge on the marshy shore of Lake Michigan, the lakes brought the lumber that built the city. Fleets of schooners delivered fish, whisky and tobacco, and carried away grain, dressed pork and pigs of lead. And for fifty years the immigrant boats discharged a continuing stream of Irish, German and Scandinavian settlers on its wharves. Chicago is the greatest in that string of cities that Hennepin had foretold and that the lakes brought into being. It is fitting that Chicago's sculptor, Lorado Taft, should have symbolized the lakes in his memorial fountain.

That fountain, looking over the terraces of Grant Park to the wide blue distance of Lake Michigan, shows the lakes in the imagery of five gracious sisters who proudly hold their vessels of flowing water. Lake Superior, remote, virginal, majestic, stands high above the rest, pouring the crystal stream from her scalloped vessel to the basin of Huron. Lake Michigan stands beside her sister, Huron, the two receiving the descending water and sending it on to the gentle figure of Erie who stoops to fill the basin of Ontario. But Ontario has turned, heedless of the flowing waters' source. She looks away with a hand lifted, half-pointing, because her currents and her commerce are not contained in the midlands but are directed toward the tidal flow of the St. Lawrence and the wide ocean lanes beyond.

The mapmakers gave up their myth, in time. Michilimackinac became a strategic gateway, not to China but to the rich lands of Wisconsin and Illinois. Sault Ste. Marie then marked the barrier rapids that isolated the greatest of the lakes from the others. But a commerce grew to include them all, and to build their cities. They were five lakes, linked by three rivers and a deep, island-studded strait. And the head of Lake Superior was fifteen hundred miles inland from the mouth of the St. Lawrence where the cold sweet waters at last mingled with the salt Atlantic tides.

As the symbolical fountain suggests, Lake Ontario never

23

belonged to the others. It was cut off from their commerce by two reasons: Niagara Falls, with less than one-third the six-hundred foot height that Hennepin claimed for it, presented a barrier to all navigation until the Welland Canal was opened in 1832, and the Erie Canal became a by-pass carrying the lakes trade to the Hudson River and a nearer ocean outlet at New York harbor. Though the Welland Canal opens Ontario to the other lakes it still remains apart, linked closer to Canada's commerce and to the St. Lawrence than to the American trade that stains the skies from Duluth and Chicago to Buffalo.

More than a century ago the Chippewa chief Kichiwiski paddled a canoe from Duluth to Buffalo, and then walked on to Washington to attend a Congressional conference on Indian affairs. When the conference was over he walked back to Buffalo, pushed his canoe out of a screen of willows and paddled the 988 miles back to Duluth. He found the lakes a convenient route to travel. They were a highway, unique in the geography of the earth, linking widely separated regions, ready to carry an Indian on an errand or the bulk commerce of the age of steel.

Today the route that Kichiwiski paddled, through three lakes and two famous rivers, is a panorama of American fields and forests, towns and cities, fishing villages and fashionable resorts, industrial plants and wilderness ranges of timber and iron. At the foot of Lake Michigan the skies are angry with the glare of blast furnaces, and two hundred miles north the lake winds carry the fragrance of orchards blooming on Traverse Bay and Door Peninsula. On August nights clouds of sand flies ("Canadian soldiers" to everyone on the lakes) make a windless blizzard over the harbors of Sandusky and Toledo, and every November sees the white fury of snow-laden gales that sweep down the long lake lanes. There are dreaming old lumber ports and noisy young steel towns, the plashing of an illuminated fountain in Grant Park and the roar of Beaver Falls into Lake Superior. Two days away from the clamorous Detroit River the land is aloof and wild. Even a lake man who has known this for thirty years feels it. So the Chief Engineer steps out of his cabin. The winy wind of Lake Superior is blowing off the dark northern shores. "It's wilderness," he says, making the slow circle with his eyes. "It's all wilderness. No roads in there. No people. Not even Indians. Nothing." Four days later, with the clamor of Cleveland in his ears, he is walking up Euclid Avenue to make a report to the fleet engineer.

The Great Lakes are many things—the gleaming at the end of a long street in Chicago, the smoke blowing across the Johnny Walker sign at Windsor, Ontario, the long red docks at Ashland, the excursion steamers jammed to the rails on a Sunday morning in Detroit, the flashing towers of Spectacle Reef and Rock of Ages, the red sunset over Lake Erie from its tranquil shore, the water slapping at a crumbling lumber wharf in Cheyboygan, the moon shining on the rock face of Neebish cut, Perry's monument dreaming of an almost forgotten victory at Put-in-Bay, a lightship rocking at the mouth of Lake Huron, the fishing boats chugging into St. Ignace with a web of gulls around them, a freighter creeping up to the Soo with a deckload of automobiles while the sunset flames in all those windshields. But most significantly, they are the long ships passing through the busy rivers and over the wide seaways.

Industrially the lakes are a highway linking the materials that have produced the age of steel. Three-quarters of the iron ore in the United States is in the old blunt hills around Lake Superior, a thousand miles from the deep coal beds of the Alleghenies. Only water transport could bring the two together in the enormous volume and with the economy that heavy industry requires. The big freighters passing—one every twelve minutes past Windmill Point at Detroit where the patients in the marine hospital can hear hoarse voices signaling for the channel—carry the commerce with an efficiency that few Americans realize. They transport a ton of coal from Lake Erie to Duluth, eight hundred miles, at less than it would cost to have it wheeled into a basement window from the curb.

For hundreds of thousands of immigrant Americans of the last century the lakes began at Buffalo, where the Erie Canal poured its commerce into the wide waters of Lake Erie. For fifty years the people of Ireland and Germany, of Holland and Denmark, of the Baltic and the Slavic countries thronged the wharves of Buffalo. Famous lines of "immigrant boats," wood-burning steamers with household goods crowded on deck and wagon wheels lashed like life-buoys up and down the rigging, carried them to Detroit, Milwaukee and Chicago. They sent back the harvests of the prairies and the ore from the hills, and Buffalo became one of the world's great ports.

It is a misnamed city. There were never any bison in the forests at the end of Lake Erie. "Beaver" was its proper name; its swampy flats were a place of beaver for centuries before the first schooners fired their signal cannon at the harbor entrance. But an interpreter mistook the translation of the local Indian name and the town became Buffalo. The original beavers did not make it so busy a place as the immigrant boats and the grain schooners of a century ago and the long freighters of today. The lakes created the city and they still sustain it.

The long straight shore of Lake Erie is dotted with cities. There is a port at every inlet, at every Ohio creek mouth where a ship can swing in to an unloading dock. Conneaut, Ashtabula, Cleveland, Lorain, Sandusky, Toledo—they receive a greater tonnage than many storied seaports of the world. So the procession of freighters breaks up on Lake Erie, heading in to the coal and ore ports. The greatest of them is Cleveland, marked far out on Lake Erie by the granite shaft of the Terminal Tower, flood-lighted in darkness and sun-lighted

26

in the day. Under that soaring tower, into the smoky twisting channel of the Cuyahoga come the long deep-laden ore boats. They creep through the tortuous channel with their whistles crying.

Once the Cuyahoga was a meandering prairie stream where foxtails and milkweed blew in the wind. But the Ohio and Erie Canal brought it the commerce of the inland towns and the harvest of unnumbered fields of grain. The channel was dredged and the shipping of the lakes met the canal barges at its wharves. A hundred years ago it was a crowded harbor. For miles it was filled with lumber scows and grain schooners, tugboats churning through the current, strings of canal boats towing in. The masts of sailing vessels were a thick and leafless forest along the river banks, and the docks were laden with cargoes of flour and lard, of fish and cheese and grindstones. Stevedores sang as they rolled the grindstones down the gangplanks and trundled barrels on the wharves. Today the trade still clamors in the Cuyahoga. But now it is the big, long ships maneuvering the bends, with tugboats fuming, of a tortuous and smoky river. On the docks are millions of tons of ore, coal, limestone, cement, and sulphur. Night and day the cargoes pass through that haze-veiled river that few Clevelanders ever see. But it is the pulse, deep-tied to the great fresh seas, of the city's industry. Hills of red ore lie in the basin under the towers of Cleveland. Raw iron makes steel and steel makes cities.

Conneaut, Ashtabula and Cleveland mean ore. Toledo and Sandusky mean coal. A dusty thunder hangs over the docks where the big gondolas are tilted, one every seventy seconds, into the yawning holds of up-bound freighters.

Toledo was once called Vistula and another time Swan Creek. Its first steamboat was built in 1832 by Captain David Wilkeson, whose neighbors, relatives and crew took stock in the vessel. So Joe Langford, the colored cook, boasted that he was "one of the owners." To insure a safe launching Captain Wilkeson stripped himself and examined the bottom of the Maumee before he let his vessel take the water.

Now the historic Maumee is lined for miles with oil refineries, coke ovens, stone crushers, and coal docks. Originally called the "Miami of the Lakes" the river's name was changed because Ohio already had two Miamis, the Great and the Little Miami Rivers that empty into the Ohio. And Maumee has come to mean coal, the biggest coal trade on the continent. The gaunt rigs rise above the black acres of the switching yards. Coal dust settles on the river. The Maumee runs black to Lake Erie.

Erie is the shallowest and most treacherous of the lakes. Sudden storms lash the shallow water, flinging mud-dark waves along its sandy shores. To make its passage doubly treacherous there is the maze of islands at its western end, all of them fertile, some of them storied (where Commodore Perry lurked with his fleet at Put-in-Bay till he could engage the British, with the famous outcome "We have met the enemy and they are ours"). Now the islands are tranquil and the shores lie in a golden haze after the heat of an Ohio day. Along the mainland are farms and vineyards. The level land is patterned with tasseled corn rows, burnished plains of wheat and dark fields of soy beans, growing lush in the rich earth of the Firelands and the Western Reserve.

Detroit was named for navigation. The fairway of Lake Erie closes in, at its northwestern end, to a narrow river, and at "the strait" a navigator steers for the magnetic north. Now the river is cut into a two-lane channel past Bob-Lo Island, where the Canadian Mounted Police in their scarlet coats tediously patrol the amusement park and supervise the roller-skating rink. Above Bob-Lo the channels come together, up- and down-traffic passing closely, and the smoke grows in the north. Twenty-eight miles from Bar Point to Peach Island, the Detroit River is the shortest river in the world, and the busiest. Mud scows biting bottom, pleasure boats surging by, tugboats hooting in the basins of Ecorse and River Rouge, and always the long freighters plodding through the channel. Around a bend the towers rise dimly and the great weight of Detroit is on the land. The bluff bows of freighters loom through the haze of Wyandotte and River Rouge. The once green shores are mounded now with the many colors of industry—ridges of red iron ore, tall black cones of coal, pyramids of pulpwood, rusty hills of scrap iron and white hills of limestone and bright green hills of sulphur.

Under the firm arc of the Ambassador Bridge the traffic moves, and past the landing wharves of the excursion steamers beneath the Fisher and Penobscot towers. Belle Isle, once a hog range infested by rattlesnakes, now has its beaches and lagoons, and beyond it the river opens to the tranquil waters of Lake St. Clair. But Lake St. Clair is a false opening; after twenty miles the waters close again at the fan-shaped delta of the St. Clair flats. Like a canal the St. Clair River threads through the level land. A hundred years ago Thurlow Weed, editor of the Albany *Evening Journal*, traveling to Chicago in the splendid side-wheeler Empire, said another barrel of water would overflow the fields. But the land remains, unflooded, flanked now with cottages and quiet towns and salt works and shipyards and the homes of lake captains with verandas that face the river and the long ships passing.

The Blue Water International Bridge links Sarnia to Port Huron, and beyond it is the open water. Lake Huron is a deep blue sea leading into the north—leading to the Ojibway country, the Thirty Thousand Islands, and the great woods.

For a hundred miles the shores are farmland, where once a white pine forest stood. Saginaw Bay opens deeply into the west, and at this point the land changes. Draw a line west from the upper point of Saginaw Bay, across the state of Michigan and across the lake beyond; it will lead to the lower end of Green Bay, that narrowing western arm of Lake Michigan. That line is where the North begins. Below lie the great cities and the fertile land, and trunk highways carrying a never-sleeping traffic along the lake shores. Above are fishing towns and Indian villages, the mining ranges and the timber lands, and lonely shores that face the aloof cold waters.

The De Tour Reef radio beacon signals in the ears of navigators, and a vessel bound for Lake Superior steers for the St. Mary's river mouth at De Tour. Two hundred years old, it is still a northwoods village, supported by fishermen and a coaling dock. The place was named, no one knows how long ago, Giwideonaning, by the Indians, but the French translated the Chippewa word into their own equivalent of "the turning." For again, at the head of another lake and a river's entrance the channel turns north.

De Tour was named two centuries before there existed any idiom of highways and motor travel. But the automobile caught up with De Tour and an old word became suddenly meaningful to a new people. Many drivers at the lonely junction of M-129 and M-48 read the highway sign "Detour 32 miles" and believing the road ahead closed they detoured to Detour. That confusion led to spelling the name as two words, and now the highway sign reads "Village of De Tour, 32 miles."

Past De Tour the channel of commerce follows the wild and beautiful St. Mary's River, passing close to the varied islands and the devious shores. So a sailor crossing the spar deck waves to a family in a summer cottage on Neebish Island and a Finnish farmer looks up from his hayfield to the freighter steaming around Shingle Point.

At the head of Sugar Island, after forty miles of intricate channel, the river makes a grand crescent curve, with the Laurentian hills a bold horizon on the north. Under that granite ridge lies the Canadian "Soo" and on the near side of the river is the town of Sault Ste. Marie, Michigan. The channel swirls with the current of water released by the Michigan Northern Power Canal, and a wheelsman keeps his hands alert on the big spokes. The captain rings down his engines; the ship creeps in toward the locks. Here is one of the oldest and most famous points of North America, the "Soo."

The whistle sounds and a signal shows at the lockmaster's station. The big gates open to discharge a vessel, laden to the water line, bound down to an ore port on Lake Erie or Lake Michigan. The up-bound ship glides in. The gates swing together. Twenty feet of water lift her to the level of Lake Superior. The upper gates open. With a short blast of her whistle she glides out. The smoke streams behind her between the wooded shores that open into Whitefish Bay.

Lake Superior is a highroad now, but the distances are still vast and the water is still shining, and it is possible to feel in the bold contours of the shores and the great clear depths of the lake the quality of legend that made it Gitche Gumee to the Chippewas, the mysterious and mighty sea. Its waters are deep, thirteen hundred feet at deepest sounding; the lake's bottom lies three hundred feet below sea level. Its numbing depths seldom give up their dead.

Out of sight of the main steamer lane are the cities of the southern shore: Marquette, the pioneer iron port, Ashland, iron and lumber port, and the copper cities, Calumet, Hancock and Houghton, which lie halfway out the bold promontory of Keweenaw thrusting its seventy-mile length into the lake. Out of sight to the north, beyond the portals of Thunder Cape and the Sleeping Giant, are the twin grain cities of Canada, Port Arthur and Fort William, with their miles of grain cars from the western plains and the gray cliffs of their loading elevators.

Isle Royale is primal wilderness and to the south the Apostle Islands keep their ancient Indian villages. As a group the Apostles still bear the religious name the Jesuits left there, thinking them twelve islands in that lonely sea. Actually they are nineteen islands, and they are curiously named. The largest, Madeline, bears the name of a half-breed trader's wife.

Two others kept the names Schoolcraft used in 1820 when he mapped them roughly in his canoe on General Cass's expedition to the headwaters of the Mississippi. He found them a symbol, not of religion but of his country's history, and called them the Confederated Islands. Though the collective name never adhered, two of the islands now are York and Michigan. The rest are natural north-country names, Outer, Oak, Basswood, Raspberry, Bear, and so on, with a mysterious Hermit among them.

Lake Superior narrows to a point, like a blue and shining arrowhead. At its tip, where ninety years ago the surveyor George Stuntz lived in his solitary cabin, rise the two cities of Superior and Duluth. Superior occupies the level ground south of the St. Louis River that comes curving out of Minnesota's forests. And Duluth rises, tier on tier, along the great northern hillside. It is one of the dramatic cities of America, in its history, its setting, and its trade.

The commerce moves between Duluth's channel piers, under the aerial bridge and into the dredged harbor of its river mouth. Above, far back along the lake the streets of Duluth climb against the north. At night the hillside blazes with its chains of light.

On one side Duluth gives way to water and on the other sides to woods. Forest fires have driven deer into the city streets, and it is the boast of the Hotel Duluth that a full-grown black bear, straight out of the woods, smelled the breakfast bacon and made his way into the hotel kitchen on a crisp morning in 1933.

The streets of Duluth rise sharply, and every one tugs the mind up to that lifted northern skyline. Beyond lie miles of cut-over forest and muskeg swamp and the great iron ranges. And below lies the young city (there were cedar stumps in most of the streets in 1890) with its harbor supporting a tonnage second only to New York. Day and night the freighters' whistles drift over Superior Street and up the hill. You may remember then, with the endless trains of iron ore coming down from the north and the long grain trains from the Dakotas, that ninety years ago George Stuntz looked around him at the unpeopled hills and the empty water and said, "This will be the heart of the continent."

He saw it even then.

CHAPTER THREE

Panorama from a Graveyard

GEORGE STUNTZ WAS the kind of man that people around the lakes like to remember. Part bushwhacker, part builder, part dreamer, he belonged to the wilderness and yet he saw the nation's commerce coming. Most of his life was devoted to getting that commerce started. He was as tough as a juniper bush and as stubborn as muskeg. He lived at the head of the lakes where there was nothing to see but miles of tangled woods and sinking swamps, the old blunted hills of the Chippewa country and the vacant water. But there were times when his smoke-gray eyes filled up with pictures of flourishing cities and fleets of ships carrying a momentous trade in grain and iron.

He came north from the Mississippi River town of Davenport and the Wisconsin prairies where he had been running the section lines of Juneau County. But he liked the Lake Superior country better. The tamarack swamps, the old worn granite ridges, the gloom of the woods and the gleam of the water all had a spell for him. Not that he saw it as a picture. He crossed hundreds of miles of it on foot, with a pack on his back and a surveyor's instruments pulling at him. A surveyor had to travel a straight line, through swamps and over blow-downs, with no thought for easy contours and open country. He saw it the hard way, wading through muskeg and slapping mosquitoes and bleeding from the fierce little wounds of the black fly. But still he liked the country. In fact he made up dreams about it and spoke prophecies that rocked sane men with laughter.

In the summer of 1852 he reached the head of the lakes, running the Wisconsin-Minnesota boundary line. At the end of the season he went out to make his report to General George B. Sargent, who was in charge of the Wisconsin survey. But the next spring he was back—to stay. At that time there was just one other settler in the whole wild country thereabouts. That was Stephen Bonga, the American Fur Company trader, with his broad nose and grisly goat beard, his fur cap and pine staff, who claimed to be the first "white man" at the head of the lakes. He was half Negro and half Indian.

George Stuntz liked the woods and he liked the water, so he built his shack between the two, on the spit of land that curved out into the lake from the future site of Duluth. Confident of the future he ran some township lines and pictured the inrush of life to that remote place. In Washington, Henry Clay had called the Soo, when the canal was first projected, "a place beyond the remotest settlement of the United States, if not in the moon." George Stuntz was four hundred miles beyond that.

He was a patient man, as all pioneers must be. But not a passive one. In 1854 there were seven shanties where Duluth now stands. To reach the land office, to get mail and provisions, they needed a road. With axes and crowbars and fourteen men George Stuntz cleared a road for fifty-seven miles, through country that had not even an Indian trail, from St. Louis Bay to the St. Croix River. He brought back three yoke of oxen and two cows. These were the first cattle ever to forage for a living on the sand grass and deer moss and hazel thickets beside Duluth harbor.

Duluth's first flurry came in the sixties with a report of precious minerals up in the Canadian Border country. Stuntz tramped north in '65 and looked for gold on the many islands of Lake Vermilion. He discovered iron and brought a chunk of it back with him. No one showed any interest in the heavy stuff or considered that Duluth might rival the older iron ports of Marquette, Escanaba and Ashland.

But George Stuntz thought otherwise. He traveled all the way to Astoria, Long Island, to see his old field boss, General Sargent, and half persuaded him of Duluth's future as an iron and grain port. Sargent gave him a letter to Jay Cooke of Philadelphia. There Stuntz found a man who could see visions as clear as he. Jay Cooke came up to Duluth in a silk hat and cloth-topped shoes and saw the heady prospects for himself. With Cooke's backing Stuntz hired eighteen men and two ox teams and built eighty-five miles of road to Lake Vermilion, through a rough and savage wilderness that had never had a wheel mark in its billion years of being.

Then the panic of '73 wrecked the iron business and deflated Duluth's first boom. With Jay Cooke wiped out, Stuntz hunted up another Philadelphia financier, Charlemagne Tower, and spoke his persuasive piece again. With Tower's millions behind him he at last located the Duluth and Iron Range Railroad, which did not come within twenty miles of Duluth but ran by easy grades from Lake Vermilion down to Two Harbors. So George Stuntz heard the trains tooting up through the wild hills where he had dreamed and cursed and frozen and sweated. And on a cloudless day in July, 1884, he saw the steamer Hecla, with a barge behind her, clear Two Harbors deep-laden with Vermilion ore for Cleveland.

Stuntz lived for eighteen years after that. But he had no part in the development of the Vermilion range or the incalculably greater range of the Mesabi, the Giant, that was to follow. He was a landlooker, not an owner. Perhaps that explains why his vision never dimmed and narrowed. He kept on dreaming, while the lakes trade caught up with all his wildest prophecies.

Now George Stuntz lies buried in the Oneota Cemetery, overlooking Duluth and the long blue seaway of Lake Superior. Aside from his surveying he didn't show much interest in figures. He never bothered to figure out, as someone has done, that the Great Lakes contain half the fresh water in the world, enough to cover the entire continental United States to a depth of fifteen feet. He just knew, like Chief Kichiwiski, that they provided a convenient way to travel. Before he died the lake fleets carried a greater volume of maritime trade than the entire foreign commerce of the United States.

As his gray eyes looked down the lakeways he saw many nations coming. In the raw woods town and lakeport that was Duluth there were Cornishmen and Finns, Swedes and Germans, Irishmen and Scots, along with the restless Yankees from the settled shores of Lake Michigan and Lake Erie. The lakes are still cosmopolitan. Though the men in the ships are ninety-seven per cent American, the names in their discharge books represent all the migrations of Europe. In one crew there may be names from a dozen nationalities—English, German, and Scandinavian, Irish, Slavic, and Italian. The same variety is present along the shores. There are the Poles of Detroit and Buffalo, the southern Slavs of Cleveland, the Germans of Milwaukee, the many nations of Chicago, the Scandinavians of the Lake Superior cities, Indians on the Straits of Mackinac and the Soo, and a community of Icelanders still fishing and farming on Washington Island at the entrance to Green Bay. Buffalo has its bulbous church spires straight from Warsaw, and along upper Lake Michigan Scandinavian maypoles rise in the meadows. There are the German mansions of Milwaukee and a big Dutch windmill slowly turning at Holland, Michigan. The immigrant boats brought multitudes of new settlers to the midlands. The lakes are still colored by their many nations.

At present there are a few more than three hundred bulk freight steamers in the trade. A few carry limestone. The rest carry iron ore and coal, with some traffic in grain at the end of the season. They are a famous fleet around the world—famous for the skill with which their men handle them in winding rivers and narrow harbors, famous for the speed with which their cargoes are loaded and discharged, and famous for the fresh meats and vegetables, fruits and pastries that go onto the tables in their mess rooms.

Life aboard those vessels is half marine, with the hazard and movement of any sailor's lot, and half like life ashore. Mostly they call their big ships "boats," and at mealtime a porter goes along the deck in a white apron ringing a dinner bell, like a cook in a construction camp. The officers wear straw hats and street clothes. The only way to tell them from business men in Chicago or Cleveland or Duluth is by their weathered faces and the fine lines around their eyes. They stand on their own decks and wave to their families on the veranda at Marine City or Port Huron. Many a mate carries a megaphone for a bit of conversation with his wife as the ship sweeps past. As his voice grows louder the deckhands wink and snicker. He drops the megaphone and waves a handkerchief till they round the bend. Then he says, a little sheepishly, "Beats writing a letter, anyway."

Beneath their twenty, thirty, thirty-five hatches those vessels carry ten, twelve, fourteen thousand tons of cargo. Across Ohio the long coal trains are always moving on the C. and O., the B. and O., the Norfolk and Western, the Pennsylvania. Their roadbeds are sanded black with coal dust and the switching yards are gritty underfoot. The swaying strings of gondolas labor over the gradual height of land and then coast down to Toledo, Sandusky, Cleveland, Ashtabula. At the docks the coal rigs turn them over. The black fog drifts up while the thunder rolls in a steamer's yawning hold.

At the same time in the rough wooded country that rims Lake Superior other trains are coasting down to blue water. They are smaller gondolas, heaped with the dull red rock and sand of iron. The Duluth, Mesabi and Northern, the Lake Superior and Ishpeming, the Great Northern, the Soo Line— their roadbeds are sifted red with ore dust and the cement docks are red as brick. The engines toot and the trains creep out like toys on the red-stained trestles. They stand against the blue northern sky at Escanaba, Marquette, Ashland, Duluth, Two Harbors.

There are red pits in the earth of Minnesota and black shafts in the West Virginia valleys. Red hills of ore line the Ohio waterfronts and black hills grow on the coalless shores of Lake Superior.

So a big freighter steams out of Toledo filmed with coal dust. The long deck is gritty underfoot. The black tracks into the crew's messroom and through the companionways and onto the thick rug in the observation lounge up forward where the captain is shaking hands with the company's guests. The deckhands are closing the hatches and a watchman drags a hose behind them, washing down. Four days later it is a red cargo coming aboard, and a red iron dust tracking into the companionways and messrooms and finding its way, like a subtle, creeping stain, down the ladders and onto the oiled steel decks of the engine room. With a hoarse blast echoing the ship pulls away. The pumps begin to throb. On deck the hatches bang shut and the hose is washing down. Another red cargo heads for the harbor mouths of Ohio.

George Stuntz lived all his life beyond the sounds of commerce. But he surveyed the roads it would follow and he pictured the life it would bring to regions that were wilderness. From his grave above the blue and shining road of Lake Superior, it is easy to remember the movement that has been the heartbeat of America, and to hear the sounds of transportation, changing but persistent, through the land. The watery rhythm of canoe paddles in Georgian Bay, the ear-splitting axle-creak of Red River carts piled with peltry, the bells of Conestoga wagons, the horns blowing on the Erie Canal, the crack of bull whips over strings of oxen on the freight trails in the prairie dust, the whistle of river steamers on the Ohio, the Mississippi, and the far-away Columbia, the clank and rumble of trains across the continent, the steady drone of rubber tires on cement, and last the high hard snore of motors and a silver bird-shape in the sky.

The Great Lakes have their own sequence and it is all movement: Indian canoes, mackinaw boats, sloops, schooners, sidewheel steamers, whalebacks and bulk freighters with their long, clear, up-tilted decks. For three hundred years the sounds of travel have drifted over the lakes, from the *voyageur's* song to the deep-throated whistle of the steamers. The seas of sweet water became one of the great trade routes of the world.

CHAPTER FOUR

The Big Sea Water

FOR TWO HUNDRED YEARS Sault Ste. Marie was a one-street town, straggling along the portage trail beside the mile-long rapids in the St. Mary's River. Now that vanished trail is Portage Avenue, and it runs from the Country Club at the great bend of the St. Mary's to the railroad station opposite the Soo locks. On Portage Avenue, just beyond the bridge that spans the deep swift current of the Power Canal, stands a rambling gabled house, unexpected among the severe plain buildings of an outpost town. A curving drive, shaded by cottonwoods, runs in from Barbeau Street and Portage Avenue. In June the cottonwoods make a faint snow on the grass. The house has ten gables, large and small, and its lines are further broken by bays, dormers, and arched windows that look out now on the grim stone façade of the Michigan Northern Water Power Plant.

This was the home of Henry Rowe Schoolcraft, who from 1822–41 held the semi-diplomatic office of Indian Agent on the Northwest Frontiers. He saw to its building in 1826, in a grove of spruces on a river bank that he called "one of the most magnificent prospects in the world." Then the stone that was to go into the long walls of the power plant lay at the bottom of the unbuilt ship canal, and the house fronted the nobly curving river. The sound of the rapids was a constant voice and for miles the shore was dotted with the camps of the Indians. Their fires gleamed at the water's edge and constant as the rapids came the drone of Indian drums.

There was a permanent village of Chippewas who lived by fishing and making sugar on the maple islands. But in the spring thousands of other Indians gathered there to trade their furs at the big warehouses beside the portage trail and to gorge on whitefish from the river. Two men in a canoe could obtain five thousand pounds of fish in half a day. They dipped them out of the rapids—big, rich whitefish, weighing six to fifteen pounds—with a scoop net on a pole. They feasted then around their campfires and for miles the wind carried the savory odor of roasting whitefish. A Chippewa defined a good time as "fine weather and plenty to eat." They had both at the Soo when the ice had gone out of the river and the shy northern spring stole over the land.

The French and British had quickly learned the succulence of whitefish and they ate it in that country four times a day for years on end. Alexander Henry after a long season of the diet still declared its flavor "beyond any comparison whatever." In time whitefish vied with fur as a commercial product. Great quantities were cured in birchwood smoke and shipped to the markets of the lower lakes and the St. Lawrence.

Henry Rowe Schoolcraft was an unexpected man in that wild country. Mild of manner, reflective, studious, he read Johnson's *Lives of the Poets* between obsequious and threatening visits from the Indians. He wrote poetry in his journal and often meditated on the strangeness of the destiny that had planted him in a wilderness outpost. Yet he was by nature an explorer as well as a man of books. Already, he had been with General Cass to the headwaters of the Mississippi, and after a second expedition under his charge his own name was left on an island in Lake Itasca that marks the true source of the great river. His home at the Soo was a center of many operations. He traveled to convocations of the tribes at remote wilderness points and signed treaties that brought the United States vast and rich territory. He followed trails through unmapped forests. He canoed down dark rivers and along the wild shores of Lake Michigan and Lake Superior. For twenty years he knew the country of the upper lakes like a *voyageur*.

As a scientist Schoolcraft carried on investigations of many kinds. He was a geologist who saw that the land that rimmed Lake Superior was very old and his observations helped Agassiz to establish it as "the first shore washed by the ocean that enveloped all the earth beside." He was also an ethnologist who saw the primal nature of the Indian lore. Though far from the world's centers of learning, he carried on an eventful correspondence and sent his findings out to kindle many minds. His repute in scholarly circles was so established that a diploma of membership in the Royal Geographic Society of London was addressed to "Henry Rowe Schoolcraft, United States of America." The diploma was missent to St. Mary's, Georgia, and only after months did it find its way to the cold St. Mary's fronting the Canadian hills.

There was an equally strange destiny in the lives of two of his associates. Sub-Indian Agent at the Soo after 1837 was James Ord in whose veins ran the blood of English kings. The son of King George IV of England, and his lawful wife Mrs. Fitz-Herbert, James Ord had been brought to America in 1790, at the age of four, and reared without knowledge of his paternity. A restless, obscurely gifted man, he lived for thirteen years in the outpost town beside the St. Mary's, listening to Indian complaints and issuing rations of beans and tobacco.

The Indian interpreter at the Agency was John Tanner, a white man with the language, habits and temperament of an Indian. His story had been widely told in England and it excited unfailing speculation and wonder. Kidnaped somewhere on the American frontier as a boy, he grew up among the Chippewas. Afterward he returned to civilized life, relearned the English language and took up white men's ways. But only briefly. After a few years he abandoned his own race for the savages that had reared him. He returned to the Chippewa campfires, married an Indian woman and lived there in contentment.

Schoolcraft himself came to the Soo in 1822, a young man not quite thirty, and he soon was married to the granddaughter of Wabojeeg, a Chippewa chief. His wife was the daughter of an Indian princess and an English trader. Educated in Montreal and in Europe, she was a beautiful and accomplished woman who possessed the best qualities in both racial strains. She had the dignity and reserve of the Chippewa and the unclouded, discerning mind of the European. Deeply devoted to the traditions of her grandfather's people, she helped Henry Schoolcraft to an understanding of their mind and their mythology. So the Indian Agent came closer to his charges as he worked futilely against the whisky of the traders and the shiftlessness of their own natures. His heart was involved in his profession, and that must always bring pain.

See the wistfulness in his definition of an Indian—"A man spending his time painfully to catch a beaver, or entrap an enemy, without stores of thought, without leisure, with nothing often to eat and nothing to put on but tatters and rags, and withal, with the whole Anglo-Saxon race treading on his toes and burning out his vitals with ardent spirits."

He spent twenty years issuing rations of bacon and beans and tobacco, and making gifts of axes, traps and kettles. To a chief there went special gifts, a large medal from the President, silver wristbands, a black hat for himself and his son. He found the Chippewas addicted to gambling, using colored beans or wild plum stones, which they shook onto a blanket from a wooden bowl. In an ecstasy of suspense they gambled away their knives, blankets, weapons, canoes, clothing, even their wives. Then they turned to the Indian Agent. They came to him on all kinds of errands, begging, wheedling, gossiping, quarreling, in grief and anger and need, asking him to satisfy their hunger and settle their disputes. Finally he refused to see them on the Sabbath, and refused to see any intoxicated Indian, explaining that "the President has sent me to speak to *sober* men only." With patience and ardor he came to know them and their country—the great cold sea of Lake Superior that never left him unmoved, the busy Straits of Mackinac, the portages and rivers.

But he was busiest in his own mind, and in his study when winter came. For four months the straits were quiet; the St. Mary's River was locked tight and Whitefish Bay above it was frozen from shore to shore. From December to May the little northern town was cut off. The cold dropped far below zero and while the maple logs burned in his fireplace Henry Schoolcraft was busy with his long projects. He was another explorer then, making his way through the unknown world of Indian myth and legend and along the hard road of their language. The Chippewa tongue was to the Lakes country what French was to Europe—the language of trade and diplomacy, understood by tribes with whom it was not vernacular. He worked for years on a lexicon of their language, and on his *Algic Researches*. His light burned late those winter nights while he filled his notebooks with legends of Gitchee Gumee, stories of the West Wind, fables of the forests and the islands and the cliff-lined shores with their pictured rocks.

He was a man cut off for long seasons from the life of his time, but his lonely studies were to kindle the imagination of all America. Before his death the school children of his nation were repeating

> *By the shores of Gitche Gumee,*
> *By the shining Big-Sea-Water.*

A Cambridge poet found the riches of the *Algic Researches* and made a song that all Americans could cherish.

Schoolcraft never lost the Indians' own wonder at Lake Superior; he saw it with their eyes and in the light of their legends. No Algonquin had ever been to the end of that sea; to them it was the mysterious border of the world. Living on the islands and peninsulas, canoemen and fishermen more than trail-makers and hunters, they saw the Big Sea Water as the dominant setting of their lives. Even their story of Creation came from its depths. In the beginning of all things their tradition pictured Michoban (Manitou) floating on a raft with the animals. Michoban wanted land brought up for a domain of men and beasts. He asked the beaver to go down through the deep sea and bring up land. The beaver dived deep and came up breathless, but he had not reached bottom. So Michoban sent down the otter. He stayed down much longer and when he rose to the surface they dragged him onto the raft exhausted, but he had not found the floor of that profound sea. Michoban was ready to give up, when the little muskrat volunteered. He dropped overside, and as time went on a few bubbles broke the surface. All through the night Michoban and the animals waited and watched, and in the daylight again they knew the muskrat must be dead. Then they found his body floating on the water. They lifted him onto the raft and saw his little paws locked tight. They pried open three of the paws and found nothing in them; but tightly clutched in the fourth they found one grain of sand. The little muskrat had done it; he had brought up land. And out of that single grain of sand Michoban made the world, the dark forests and the lifting mountains, the upthrust islands and the rocky shores.

Munising Bay, long before the whine of sawmills or the whistle of excursion boats, was a Chippewa camping site beside the Big Sea Water. Here lived old Nokomis, Daughter of the Moon, who nursed the lad Hiawatha and taught him the lore of woods and sea and sky. Just beyond that campsite were the Pictured Rocks, with their colored cliffs and echoing caverns, and the surf of Superior breaking high. There the gods of thunder and lightning had their abode. Sailing their birchbark fleets past Grand Portal, the Chippewas threw gifts of venison and deerskin into the mysterious grottos.

Even the French, bringing shrewd trade and new gospel to the savages, felt the power of that mythology. Many a *voyageur* crossed himself and tossed a twist of tobacco into the great portal as his canoe passed under the cliffs of legend. Some of them carried snakeroot, the Chippewa charm to keep one safe on a journey. It was not a land that civilization could take over easily. The *voyageurs* became more Indian than

French. The wilderness invaded them and the savage mind became in measure their mind. The half-breeds that they left as posterity are a symbol as well as a sign of the power of the dark land and the shining waters.

The Jesuits left their names like a patina of evangelism on the country—St. Mary's, St. Joseph's, St. Ignace, De Pere. The *voyageurs* left other names—Bete Grise, Grand Marais, Bois Brule, L'Anse à la Bouteille, picturesque and living beside the staid names from English nobility, Fort William, Port Arthur, Lake George, Drummond's Island. But the Indian names still held on stubbornly, the hard strong Chippewa names that will last as long as history in the upper lakes—Michipicoten, Escanaba, Ontonagon, Manistique, Michilimackinac.

Schoolcraft loved those names. He saw in them the long hold of a people on the land, the fitness of the native tongue, the strong claim that men make upon geography. The federal Congress had gravely selected a list of names for the lake states: Assenispia, Metropotamia, Polypotamia, and Pelisipia. Schoolcraft lived to see those conglomerates forgotten. He served on a commission that gave Indian names to Michigan's northern counties. But Charles O'Malley of the state legislature, having a quarrel with Schoolcraft, attacked him by changing Indian names to Irish, and so a tier of counties bear the names Clare, Roscommon, Emmet, and Antrim. It was a blow to Schoolcraft, and a loss to the map of Michigan.

Though trade was coming to Lake Superior in Schoolcraft's time the North remained a fabulous country. The *voyageurs* told tales of gold and silver and the Indians repeated their legends of hills of copper and regions of mysteriously heavy stones. Schoolcraft himself touched their copper legend at Ontonagon, near the old Chippewa capital of La Pointe.

Nine miles up the Ontonagon River was a rock mass that had been venerated as a sacred object by many generations of Indians. Vaguely known, marvelously rumored, at last out of legend the "Ontonagon Boulder" went to the halls of Congress and the Smithsonian Institution.

In 1667 Father Dablon, Jesuit missionary, confirmed the Indian stories of a mass of copper in the bed of the Ontonagon River near its mouth. A hundred years later a party of Chippewas led the trader Alexander Henry to the spot. He estimated its weight at ten tons and found it so pure and malleable that he hacked off a chunk of it. As time went on other explorers heard of its existence and saw the rock mass in the riverbed and kept reports of it alive. In 1819 young Henry Schoolcraft stood on the spot. He found the rock scarred by chisels and axes and estimated its copper content at one ton. Douglass Houghton, Michigan state geologist, wrote a final account of it in 1841; after that the rock passed from Indian legend into American enterprise. In the summer of 1843 a Detroit prospector, Julius Eldred, paid the Indians $150 for the rock. But the federal government, acting on the reports of government explorers, declared itself to be the owner of the rock and sold it to Eldred for $1365. At great toil Eldred hauled the rock, on skids and rollers, to the river mouth where he was met by the War Department. Those officials were prepared to seize the rock and ship it off to Washington. They hesitated long enough for Eldred to get his twice-purchased treasure aboard a schooner and down the lake. It was dragged across the Soo portage and shipped on down to Detroit. There he put it on public view, charging a cash admission from the curious. But the government caught up with him again and ordered that the rock be shipped to Washington. It is now on exhibit in the Smithsonian Institution. But Julius Eldred had an unquitted claim on the boulder and in 1847 Congress allowed him the sum of $5644.98 "for his time and expense in purchasing and removing the mass of native copper." Its copper content was found to be just $600 in value.

Meanwhile Douglass Houghton's guarded reports brought men swarming into the Keweenaw country. Trading vessels appeared on Lake Superior, having been dragged over the Soo portage on rollers, and settlements began on the lonely shores. It was a remote and difficult country. Oxen and mules fed on imported hay at $55 a ton. "There is not a spear of grass in the entire eternity of this country," a traveler wrote to the Buffalo *Morning Express* in 1846, "and an ox or an ass, turned out, would starve unless he could feed on pine shadows and moss." The same was true for men, and when they ranged the rough country without finding quantities of loose copper their disillusionment was deep. Hundreds of them drifted to another fabled country when the electric news from Sutter of California swept across America in 1848.

But there was copper on the Keweenaw. Fabulous lodes of it. Actual mining operations began at the Cliff Mine in 1844. And for the next fifty years copper stocks were traded in New York and Boston by men who could not pronounce "Ke-wee-naw" and did not know where to find it on the map. Calumet, Houghton and Hancock grew to swarming cities on that remote tongue of land that thrusts into Lake Superior. The shafts multiplied. Tunnels honeycombed the hills. Copper went down the lakes in schooners and barges and freighters. It left the north country gutted and poor. But it made fortunes for the Boston copper men.

The same year that saw copper mining begin was marked by an even more prophetic discovery. William Burt, a government surveyor in the rough country between the Carp and Dead Rivers, could not run his lines for the spinning of his compass needle. Around him in those old, worn hills he found iron outcrop. The next year Philo Everett, hearing the story at the Soo, came up with Indian guides and located the Marquette range.

That was 1845. With copper in the Keweenaw and iron ore in the Marquette hills the projected canal around St. Mary's rapids could not much longer be delayed. Ten years later

Lake Superior was open to the trade and the fleets streamed up from the lower lakes into the Big Sea Water.

It is fitting that Schoolcraft did not see the commerce come to that great lake of legend. He had moved his quarters from the Soo to Mackinac Island in 1833, and in 1841 he left the north country permanently. But first he made a final journey up the beautiful St. Mary's. Returning from a business trip to Detroit he was met at De Tour by a canoe-caravan of his friends and together they paddled up the autumn river where the maple trees were bannered with gold and the oaks were red as wine. They sang the old boatmen's songs, their paddles in unison and their voices echoing along the colored shores.

II

SECOND PART

THE VANISHED FLEETS

CHAPTER FIVE

"In a Handy Three-Master"

IT WAS SEVEN HUNDRED MILES from the Chippewa portage path beside the loud rapids of St. Mary's to the Seneca trail around Niagara's thunder and the whirlpools below the solemn Falls. Niagara was an everlasting voice in that country. But in the summer of 1679 a new sound echoed in those forests—the clatter of hammers and the thud of the ax on oak timbers. There, above the rapids of Niagara, the first commercial vessel in the New World was taking shape.

La Salle, more than any other empire-dreaming Frenchman, had a vision of the vast inland domain and its strategic waterways. Only a primitive trade could pass up the Nipissing canoe route with its treacherous currents and back-breaking portages. Even with the big French canoes, thirty five feet long, manned by seven skillful paddlers and mounded with bales of peltry, that trade was limited and uncertain. La Salle's dream called for a commercial vessel, with raised quarterdeck and emblazoned sails, riding the free winds of open waterways and carrying the furs of the distant country in her deep holds.

But such craft could not be portaged around the limestone cliffs where the water of four great lakes plunged down to the level of Lake Ontario and the St. Lawrence. Father Hennepin had reported the Falls six hundred feet high and their thunder audible for ninety miles. Nature never suffered in his accounts. But a cataract only a third as vast as his could still be an effective obstacle to navigation. So La Salle portaged his materials around the Falls and built the Griffin at the mouth of Cayuga Creek above the headlong water.

She had two square sails, a high poop, and a silhouetted griffin (taken from the arms of Count Frontenac) springing from her prow. A gilded eagle with spreading wings perched above the quarterdeck. From her jack staff floated the great white flag of France with its golden lilies. Five small cannon looked out from her portholes. She was sixty feet long, of forty-five tons burden.

When she was afloat her cannon thundered a salute. The

Indians staring along the shore were struck with awe. After the crew bared their heads and sang *Te Deum*, the Indians were given a cask of brandy to celebrate an event beyond all Iroquois comprehension. For with that prophetic vessel was launched the vast commerce of the inland seas.

On the seventh of August, 1679, she sailed with thirty-four men from the river mouth into the wide fairway of Lake Erie, laying her course West Southwest with a favorable wind. Three men in that company would go down in history. Standing on the Griffin's quarterdeck was Robert Cavelier de La Salle, a bold and clear-eyed man with an empire in his mind. While his vessel traversed Lake Erie his thoughts ranged from the St. Lawrence to the valley of the Mississippi and from Hudson's Bay to the southern gulf. He swept the horizon as though he could see the future. Before him were great explorations and honor for the flag of France—and an assassin's bullet and a miserable grave. At the rail, his iron claw hooked in the rigging while his good hand held a telescope to his dark eyes, stood Henry de Tonty. He was a man of great hardihood and endurance. On a battlefield in Spain he had hacked off a maimed hand with his own sword. Now he wore a hand of metal, useful in the wilderness to clean a fish or rake up a reluctant fire or split the head of an unruly Indian. To the savages he became a legend—the man with the iron hand. They surrounded him with mystery and credited him with more than human powers. He was to make incredible journeys and to survive many perils in country beyond the range of the telescope trained on Lake Erie's shores. The third immortal was an adventurer in a friar's robes. Louis Hennepin had long dreamed of new lands; now he was going to a country never seen by men of Europe. Fresh from France he had a shrewd, sharp eye and an expectant spirit. He was the historian of the expedition, and a graphic one. Zealously he entered his observations, the ship's progress, the plans of the leader, the bickering among the men. Whether his subject was wild turkeys feeding on wild grapes that festooned the forests along the Detroit River or the Griffin floundering through wind-torn waters in Saginaw Bay, he surrounded it with the feeling of discoverers. He had the excitement of history if not its sobering responsibility.

They crossed Lake Erie in good time and sailed into the Detroit River with high praise for "one of the finest prospects of the world." When they stopped for a day's hunting, flocks of turkeys and swans circled the vessel curiously. With fresh fish and bear meat they crossed Lake St. Clair on the day of the festival of St. Claire (from which they gave the tranquil lake its name), but in the river above a head wind compelled La Salle to send his men ashore with towlines. Their backs bent and their feet dug in. Slowly the high-pooped Griffin edged along the St. Clair flats. They reached the blue sea of Lake Huron on August twenty-third.

Two days later a gale blew loud across Saginaw Bay and they found a grateful shelter in the lee of the Charity Islands. A fair wind drove them through the Straits of Mackinac, where Nicolet had passed with his seven Huron paddlers half a century before. They crossed the Lake of the Illinois, as La Salle's map described Lake Michigan, and early in September, when the first autumn hues were bannering Wisconsin's forests, they sailed into Green Bay. Here La Salle found his agents, sent from Fort Frontenac the preceding year, waiting with a great quantity of furs.

To satisfy his impatient creditors La Salle had his ship laden immediately and dispatched her back, under her headstrong pilot, to the Niagara. Firing a parting shot the Griffin sailed away on September eighteenth—and was never seen again. A storm lashed the Straits of Mackinac the next day, perhaps overwhelming the small ship in deep water, or casting her on the sharp land. Whatever happened, the Griffin was the first of a great lost fleet of vessels that never came to port.

THE VANISHED FLEETS

It was more than a hundred years before another vessel of the Griffin's size raised sail on the lakes.

La Salle, unmindful then of the Griffin's disaster, led an expedition south into the country of the Illinois. He carried on his dreams of conquest and commerce for nine more years, until, wounded on the shores of Texas, he was assassinated by his own quarreling and rebellious men. Tonty, after long search for the body of his leader, became a fur trader at Fort St. Louis, established by La Salle at Starved Rock on the Illinois River. The third famous member of the Griffin's company, Father Hennepin, was taken prisoner by the Sioux. He was carried up the great river where he saw another Falls, which lost nothing in his description, the Falls of St. Anthony —though even his prophetic mind could not see there the great mills of Minneapolis, the white cliffs of her elevators and the long grain trains moving on to Duluth for shipment down the lakes. Hennepin, with his two companions, was at last rescued by the man whose name was to mark the head of the lakes. Daniel de Grosolon, Sieur Dulhut, was the prince of *coureurs de bois*. In the Indian country he heard rumors of French prisoners among the Sioux and he went to deliver them. In his blanket coat, leggings of deerskin, crimson cap and sash, he appeared among the Sioux and found there Louis Hennepin. They were not strangers. Their acquaintance went back five years to the battlefield of Seneffe where Hennepin in his long robes aided the wounded and confessed the dying. Now in the New World wilderness, five thousand miles from the battlefields of Flanders, the two met again. Always a persuasive man among the Indians, Dulhut persuaded the Sioux to release their captives.

After the loss of the Griffin there was no attempt to replace the canoe as the chief instrument of fur commerce, though for heavy hauling the plank bateau was developed. This craft, propelled by four long oars and carrying a square sail when the wind was right, came into wide use, transporting hides

60

and wool, flour and furs, all the way from Michilimackinac to Detroit and from Detroit to Niagara and the St. Lawrence.

Gradually, with the growth of Detroit as a commercial port, the lower lakes began to eclipse the canoe route through French River and Lake Nipissing. Sailing vessels appeared on Lake Ontario and then on Lake Erie, to aid the traffic between Detroit and the St. Lawrence. Cadillac, founder of Detroit and commandant of its garrison, himself owned a sloop of ten tons that plied between Detroit and the Niagara. During the British occupation Detroit became, as it is now, a shipbuilding center, with nine vessels on the stocks beside the Detroit River. By 1776 the traffic was entirely British, only the king's vessels being allowed to navigate the lakes. But after the Revolutionary War, with the transfer of the trading posts to American authorities, new ships began to appear.

Fortunately the lakes have a meager naval history. But there was one dramatic day when the cannon roared over Lake Erie and an American commander sent a memorable message of victory.

The War of 1812 was begun with surprising assurance among the American strategists that Canada would fall victim to their first attacks. In setting up their campaign they gathered three small armies on the Canadian frontier. One was to defend Detroit, the key to the fur trade and the upper lakes. Another was to cross the Niagara River, and with reinforcements from Detroit was to capture Toronto (then called York) and march on Montreal. At this point the third army should advance from Lake Champlain, and the combined forces, after the capture of Montreal, were to lay siege to Quebec.

The strategy looked fine, on paper. But General Hull at Detroit, having trouble with supplies, delayed his attack on Fort Malden, across the river. When he did attack he found that the British had assembled a larger force than he had counted on. On learning that Fort Mackinac had fallen and his lines of communication were broken, he retired to Detroit. The British followed him and soon compelled his surrender.

The entire campaign had fallen flat and General William Henry Harrison was hard pressed to hold his line of defense on the Maumee River. He could not hope to recapture Detroit unless the British naval control of Lake Erie was overcome.

Early in the season of 1813 Oliver Hazard Perry was ordered to leave his patrolling operations in Lake Ontario and prepare to engage Captain Barclay's British squadron on Lake Erie. In those days of simple warfare a commodore might build his fleet as well as sail it. Perry went to Presque Isle (now Erie, Pennsylvania) and hastily launched a fleet of nine wooden vessels. He mounted a total of fifty-four guns, which though of heavier caliber were of shorter range than the cannon of the British fleet. He would need boldness and quick movement when they joined battle.

On September tenth the two forces met at the west end of Lake Erie near Put-in-Bay. With superior range Captain Barclay concentrated his fire on the Lawrence, Perry's flagship. That vessel was hit hard before her own guns could reach the enemy. Under heavy firing Perry shifted his flag to the Niagara. From her quarterdeck he brought the rest of his fleet into play. Maneuvering them boldly, despite the British fusillades, he sailed in close enough to let his heavy, short-range cannon find their mark. The American guns spoke like thunder. They struck fairly. Soon the British had taken such punishment that four vessels lowered their flags in surrender while the remaining two dodged through the islands in an effort to escape. Perry overtook and captured them. Then he sent his famous dispatch to General Harrison: "We have met the enemy and they are ours—two ships, two brigs, one schooner and one sloop." The battle had lasted three hours and fifteen minutes.

That victory gave the Americans control over Lake Erie and ensured the recapture of Detroit. But there were lingering engagements in the north. One of them involved the Nancy, the finest schooner of her time.

The Nancy, built at Detroit in 1789, spent most of her life in the service of the North West Fur Company. Her floor timbers, keel and stem were made of Michigan oak. Her stern post, top timbers and beams were of red cedar. She was built to carry 350 barrels. From her prow leaned a figurehead maiden dressed in the current mode with a feathered hat, fashioned by the carver Skilling of New York. She voyaged from Detroit to Fort Erie and then sailed with full cargo for the Soo. So that carved face under the feathered hat looked across the wilderness river where the Chippewa wigwams stood among the birch trees on Neebish Island. For a dozen years the Nancy gracefully carried furs and merchandise, salt, whisky, flour, corn and lard on Lakes Huron, Erie, and Michigan.

Lord Bathurst, with the strategy of the great interior country in his mind, wrote to his superiors concerning Mackinac Island: "Its influence is felt among the Indian tribes at New Orleans and the Pacific Ocean; vast tracts of country look to it for protection and supplies, and it gives security to the great establishments of the North West and Hudson's Bay Companies by supplying the Indians on the Mississippi." In the interests of holding this commanding station the Nancy was armed in 1812. She made a light-footed, daring man-of-war. Time after time she got in her punch and then, with her tall sails filling and her cutwater cleaving the sea, raced out of the enemy's reach. She was too graceful and too living to deserve the grim pay-off of war. But she was cornered at last by clumsier ships, and destroyed. That carved face under the feather hat went to a shallow grave at a rivermouth on Georgian Bay.

Another vessel that met a violent end, perhaps the most violent in all the history of the lakes, was the schooner Michigan. She was a double topsail schooner, a big ship for her time, built in 1816 for the new trade that followed the war. After eleven years of profitable service she was condemned as unseaworthy and bought by a party of speculators. They announced by sensational handbills: "The pirate ship Michigan with cargo of furious animals will pass over the Falls of Niagara on the 8th of September, 1827." Apparently, their scheme was to collect cash for the spectacle from the thousands who would come.

Under direction of her Scotch captain, James Rough, the schooner was fitted out in Buffalo with an assortment of living animals: a full grown Arabian camel, an elk, a bear, and a variety of dogs. Then she was sailed cautiously down the Niagara toward the growing thunder of the Falls.

Beside the cataract thousands of people, from miles around, watched for the bizarre and terrible travesty of Noah's ark. The schooner appeared, swaying in the rapid current. Captain Rough, in his zeal to leave everything shipshape, withdrew only at the last moment. He and his crew, pulling frantically against the swirling river, beached their yawl on the Canadian side just above the cataract. Out in midstream, with her rigging strained and the abandoned wheel spinning on her afterdeck, the schooner hurried to her doom. The animals roamed about her waist, a dog barked sharply, the topmasts swayed against the sky. Then, while the watchers caught their breath, the Michigan made her fearful plunge. In the whirlpools below a mangled menagerie swirled amid the driftwood and the wreckage.

In the second quarter of the century the sailing fleet grew rapidly. Vessels took shape in the yards at Cleveland, Detroit, St. Clair, and Bay City on the Saginaw. Fish and furs went down to Lake Erie and the Ohio canal system; cheese and flour, corn and lard, whisky and tobacco went up to the north country. This freight they called "Ohio fur." With kegs and cases beneath their hatches the schoonermen carried a deck load of white oak staves and barrel heads. For this was the barrel age.

Meanwhile the Erie Canal was depositing multitudes of immigrants on the wharfs at Buffalo. They crowded the early steamboats to Detroit and the cities of Lake Michigan. So the forests were felled and the midland farms were settled and then a growing stream of grain went back down the lakes to Buffalo. For fifty years the sailing vessels carried the great bulk trade of grain and lumber.

At first there was a variety of rig—sloops, barques, brigs, barquentines and the fore-'n'-aft schooners, two-, three- and four-masters. But in time these schooners replaced the square-rigged craft, because the square rig required larger crews and would not swing clear to work the hatches. Shallow rivers and harbors limited the size of the sailing vessels, but as the channels deepened the vessels grew. Until the 1880's, though the lakes steamers made enormous strides, it was the wind-driven fleets that carried the big freight commerce and gave color to the lakes. Their white sails dotted the open seas and filled the rivers with a busy life. The sloops carried oars for propulsion in the rivers; the sailors bent their backs and provided an "ash breeze." At Black Rock, near Buffalo, a string of oxen drew vessels up the rapids by a hawser attached to the foremast. This was a "horned breeze." In the St. Clair and Detroit Rivers steam tugs towed the vessels through in strings, the squat little tugboat snorting and the tall ships moving in a graceful line. At the river mouth the towlines were cast off and the crews made sail.

> *The mate was a shellback from way down below below—.*
> *Hurrah boys, heave 'er down!*
> *He'd rave and he'd roar as he walked to and fro—*
> *Way down, laddies, down!*

Many a summer night the residents of Port Huron or Amherstberg heard chanteys chorused under the sky, and daylight found white sails spaced across the water.

The crews of the fleets came, in lake parlance, from "down below." They were Atlantic Ocean sailors, American, British, Scandinavian, German, attracted to the lakes by high wages and the shorter voyages. The bulk trade, grain from Milwaukee and Chicago to Buffalo, and ore, after the middle of the century, from Houghton, Marquette and Escanaba to Detroit and Cleveland, required voyages of two or three weeks. They had plain fare, salt pork or beef, hard bread, potatoes and beans, but the crew were allowed twelve shillings a month to buy extras from the ship's stores. Each man was rationed a half-pint of whisky, dealt out by the mate every day. Altogether it was an attractive life to men accustomed to the long lonely voyages and the hard conditions of deepwater sail. So the swaying step of sailors was familiar on the waterfront streets of a dozen inland cities.

In those years the harbors were filled with the precise forest of ships' masts and the taut web of their rigging. They were beautiful craft and under their curving fantails they bore romantic names: Felicity, Northern Light, Evening Star, Valhalla, Zephyr, Silver Spray, Frolic, Seaflower, Magnolia, Dawn. Most of them had hard fortunes. Some killed their captains and maimed their mates. Men fell from aloft to their pitching decks and other men went overboard in the sea's fury. Good men died in their fo'c'sles and strong men limped down their gangways carrying the scars of struggle and with broken bones. Their cargoes shifted; they took the pounding of the sea and were driven ashore in hard places. They knew danger and distress and violence—as well as a fair wind and a gently dipping bow and the moon making white cliffs of their canvas on a summer night—that was the life of sailing vessels in those years. They lost spars, listed, suffered collision on dark nights; they went aground and were lost. There were many hundreds of them, and they are all gone. But they had a grace and hardihood that men remember. A few of them left stories that were not forgotten, even after the big steam freighters, bearing the names of directors of the steel corporations, took over the commerce of the lakes.

The story of the Augusta, a trim, well-built topsail schooner, includes the tragic wreck of the steamer Lady Elgin, a flight to sea, a return to the lakes under another name, and an obscure end. It involves a one-eyed captain, a memorable lakes master in the years of sail, and a blue-eyed girl of ten whose life was to be curiously linked with the Augusta's wanderings, and another captain famous for having taken the first ship through the Soo canal. It even includes the political strife of 1860, when Abraham Lincoln was one of four men in a fervid and momentous campaign for the presidency of a divided country.

The story begins with politics. In the summer of 1860, the last summer of an era that would never return to America, Stephen A. Douglas, John C. Breckenridge, John Bell of Tennessee, and Abe Lincoln, the prairie lawyer, were engaged in their contest for the presidency. While the campaign grew toward its pitch of feeling, the Irish boys of Milwaukee's Third Ward banded together in a military company and held parades and rallies to support their favorite, Stephen A. Douglas, the Little Giant. It never took the Irish long to feel at home in American politics. Many of these boys had come to Milwaukee in the immigrant boats of the forties and fifties, and already they were ardent party followers. But because of the political exigencies of his office, Governor Randall of Wisconsin was embarrassed by these demonstrations within his own militia. Consequently he disbanded the Third Ward Company and called in their arms. But Governor Randall didn't know the Irish. They promptly designated themselves a volunteer company, the Union Guard, arranging to supply their own arms and equipment. Their political feelings were fanned by the Governor's opposition.

In September, Stephen A. Douglas, at the height of his campaign, was swinging through Illinois. At Chicago a great rally was planned for the seventh of September, when the Little Giant would address a mass meeting of his western supporters. This was an event to the liking of the Third Ward boys in the Union Guard. They chartered the finest steamship in Milwaukee, the Lady Elgin, and planned an excursion to Chicago.

The excursion was a great success—until the festive, crowded steamer was rocking back to Milwaukee. It was a black night, with Lake Michigan shrouded in an early autumn fog. In the lighted saloon the band played Irish airs and the boys of the Union Guard danced with their Third Ward girls. But out in the lake's darkness, with her running lights dim in the fog, was the schooner Augusta, heading obliquely across to Chicago with a load of west Michigan lumber. The lookout on the deckload must have seen the blurred lights of the Lady Elgin, but he did not judge their distance. With the wind in her sails the Augusta drove on. She thrust her sharp bow square into the steamer's midships section. Both vessels recoiled from that blow. A megaphoned voice came through the fog as the schooner swung alongside the Lady Elgin. "Shall I stand by? Will you need help, Captain?"

Captain Jack Wilson was proud of his big new steamer. Five years before, he had taken the first vessel through the Soo locks, the side-wheeler Illinois, and he had no reason to think that a steamboat needed help from a lumber-laden wind bag. He supposed the schooner was worse off than the Lady Elgin, and he told her to keep going if she could. The Augusta kept going. Little realizing what disaster she was leaving, she sailed on to Chicago. When she arrived there in the gray dawn her men discovered her damage—she had lost her jib and all her headgear—and they heard that the Lady Elgin had gone down, taking three hundred victims with her.

Just ten miles off the shore, abreast of Winnetka, Illinois, the excursion ship had foundered; she sank so rapidly that her lifeboats could not get away. The ardent Third Ward Company never cast their ballots for the Little Giant. For many weeks there was mourning in Milwaukee.

At the end of the season, four months later, the Augusta pointed her blunted bow into Milwaukee harbor. A big fleet wintered there and the Augusta, when her sails came down and her lines were secured, was one more lifeless vessel with ice silvering her rigging and the snows drifting on her deck. As spring came round a crew went aboard to fit a new jib boom and recondition her for another season. Even before the dark night of her meeting with the Lady Elgin the Augusta had carried a shady reputation; men over the lakes called her a bad-luck ship. Now her owners hoped to change her luck and cast off her reputation. They painted her hull black and lettered a new name on her bow and under her fantail. When she was ready for sea she was the Augusta no longer, but the Colonel Cook. In her cabin was a new captain, a veteran Milwaukee shipmaster. He had lost an eye in the service of the lakes but had lost none of his skill as a navigator. He was Captain Jasper Humphrey.

On the first day of May the Colonel Cook stood under the tipple of a grain elevator taking on cargo. But the Third Ward Irish had not forgotten the Lady Elgin and the happy lads who had gone down with her. Word of the Augusta reached them, how with a new name and a new master the murdering vessel lay in Milwaukee harbor loading grain for Buffalo. The more they thought of it the uglier their feelings grew. They agreed to burn the schooner, thoroughly and forever, before she could begin another vicious season on the lakes.

But mob plans are a poor secret. Before the Irish touched brands to the unlucky craft, their plot was reported to the owners. In great haste they got the vessel ready and gave Captain Humphrey his orders. "You must sail before night.

Take her to the Atlantic and sell her to the first man that makes a decent offer. Don't bring her back to the lakes."

Captain Humphrey waited only to summon his wife and his ten-year-old daughter, Emily. Once they were aboard he ordered his gangplank in and his lines cast off. "Cast them off! Lively!" The tugboat churned white water and the towline tightened. Through the old Ferry Street bridge the Colonel Cook passed, and out to the safety of blue water. The men sang together as they got sail on her. The renamed Augusta had escaped the anger of the Irish.

Captain Humphrey sailed down the lakes and the St. Lawrence, with a stop at Montreal. A few weeks later, with salt spray drying on her sails, he docked his schooner in the mast-lined slips of South Street in New York. From there to Boston, and then down the summer coast to Baltimore, where he loaded mixed cargo for Mobile. There were new voices in the fo'c'sle, deep, soft voices, and new songs at the capstan and the halyards.

> Oh, Shenadore's my native valley,
> Away, you rolling river!
> Shenadore's my native valley.
> Ah-way we're bound to go,
> 'Cross the wide Missouri!

In the fo'c'sle was a crew of Negro sailors, big black fellows who walked the deck in bare feet and rolled their eyes at fascinated little Emily. Captain Humphrey could pick up cargo and tramp from port to port. But he could find no buyer for his vessel. The hazards of merchant shipping in 1861 didn't help him any.

To Cuba the Colonel Cook voyaged, and then to the coast of Texas. Little Emily was a taller girl and her blue eyes had looked at many shores and waters when the schooner berthed again in the mast-lined docks of South Street. There Captain

70

Humphrey found a buyer for his ship. He took his family back to Milwaukee and himself back to the quarterdeck of lakes vessels.

But Emily Humphrey had not seen the last of the schooner which had become as familiar to her as any home. Years later she was the wife of a Great Lakes master, Captain Edward Thompson. She often made voyages with him when he commanded the big new passenger steamship Minnesota. One night in the harbor of Marquette a schooner slipped in from the wide waters of Lake Superior and tied up under the Minnesota's stern. In the morning Captain Thompson's wife, taking her turn on deck before breakfast, looked over the curving green hills of Marquette harbor and the pale clear waters of the bay. Then her eyes dropped to a trim little schooner in the dock. She looked sharply, at its deckhouse, the line of its cabin, and its jib boom once shattered but showing where a new boom had been stepped in. She did not need to look at the name on its bow. The Augusta's banishment was over, she had been forgotten. And the Colonel Cook lay there innocent upon the waters, with a sailor singing as he crossed the deck.

The crews of the windjammer fleet developed a body of lore that the men in the modern freighters have not maintained or duplicated. The longer runs, the dependence on wind and weather, the natural hazard of their life bound the old-time crews together and produced songs and stories that reflect their common mind and experience. They were proud of their craft and derisive of the barges, scows and gradually lengthening freighters that were destined to carry the lake commerce of the future. One of their songs derides the tow barges of the "Old Mont Line," the Montmorency, the Montcalm, the Monticello, the Montpelier, and the Republic, all strung out behind the tug Niagara on their way to Lake Superior for ore.

THE VANISHED FLEETS

There's one Mont, two Monts, four Monts in a row
And you come to the old Republic, the end of the rotten tow

Oh, maybe you don't believe me, lads,
And maybe you think I lie;
But ship in this starvation tow
And you'll see the same as I!

Ore and grain were handled on the sailing fleet by man power. The crews worked with wheelbarrows, and that was an indignity that a sailor could not forget.

> *Oh, we're bound down from Marquette*
> *My two hands are sore;*
> *I've been pushing a wheelbarrow*
> *And I'll do it no more.*

It was hard work, handling heavy ore and trucking pigs of copper. Captain Eber Ward's fleet carried Negro deckhands who put their blues into a many-versed work-song.

> *Her smokestack's black and her whistle's brown,*
> *And ah wish de Lord ah'd a stayed in town.*

The wind blew loud from Lake Superior and a ship's hold was a hot place in an Ohio harbor. But that cargo was back-breaking in any weather. It was a life of toil, interspersed with the sea's misfortune.

> *De Ward's boun' up, de Moran's boun' down,*
> *An' de John M. Nichol am ha'd agroun'!*
> *An' de William H. Stevens's a-lyin' roun' de ben,*
> *An' all she's a-doin' is a-killin' good men!*

Before many years new machinery was developed, culminating in the mammoth elevators and the great ore docks with their electric scoops and dippers. Then the labor of hand loading was ended, but the era of sailing ships was ended too. The cargoes went to the steamers with bigger capacity and faster schedule.

One cargo remained for the windjammer fleet. There were no machines for handling it and it had to be loaded in forty different harbors and river mouths where there was no deep-dredged channel. It was lumber.

It is a familiar story through the middle states how the pioneer sawmill was set up in the woods and began to turn out building lumber. The history of every town begins that way. But in the lake towns of Michigan and Wisconsin the sawmills multiplied and yellow dunes of sawdust grew along the shore. Then the landing wharfs were lined with lumber, waiting for the schooners to carry it to the great lumber markets, Chicago, Detroit, Cleveland, Buffalo.

The lumber trade reached its peak in the 1880's, and the wind-borne fleets reached their peak in the same period. In those years there were eighteen hundred sailing vessels on the lakes, five times as many as the big freighters that now carry the enormous commerce in ore, coal, and limestone. Their canvas whitened every seascape and their tall masts fretted every harbor from Buffalo to Chicago and Duluth.

These vessels sailed the intricate waterways of the lakes without the aids to navigation that exist today. They rounded dark promontories and skirted unmarked shoals. They fought gales of wind and the hazard of rocky shores. Then there were no channel markers, only an infrequent light at a harbor mouth, no government weather forecasts, no Coast Guard service. So these masters and their crews developed a remarkable seamanship. They were as skillful and resourceful, as hardy and bold as any salt-water sailors. They sailed in fog and the blinding smoke of forest fires, along ragged coasts and upthrust islands, through snowstorms and ice-menaced rivers. They did not always survive.

A veteran lake man, Captain Edward Carus of Manitowoc, listed more than 350 sailing vessels lost on the lakes. There were hundreds of others cast up on the rocky shores or beached on the sands or disabled after collision. There were many that ended in mystery, sailing away and never appearing again. The old schooner crews had stories of underground channels that connected Lake Erie with Lake Huron, and that led down deep and dark from Whitefish Bay and came up at the point of De Tour. They had stories of great winds that blew a ship out of one lake and into another. There were mysteries enough in the years of sail.

Few sailing vessels were broken up, or moored in retirement. Some were converted into steamers, their topmasts sheared off and engines braced in their framing. Others had their masts yanked out and were used as barges. But most of the 1800 windjammers of sixty years ago were lost on the lakes. They were beautiful ships and they went the hard way.

When the whalebacks were being built in Duluth and the long freighters were growing longer in the yards at Detroit and Cleveland, the end of the schooners was at hand. They continued to carry lumber while the big ore carriers grew to five hundred and then six hundred feet. In the 1920's an occasional topsail schooner could be seen on the upper lakes. So the crew of a big freighter lined the rail to watch an old-timer with the wind in her sails. Sometimes they watched her out of sight.

The last surviving full-rigged schooner was the Lucia A. Simpson, built at Manitowoc in 1875. She was wrecked in Lake Michigan, near Sturgeon Bay in 1929. With her went the last of those fresh-water crews that bent their backs at the halyards and raised their voices together.

"IN A HANDY THREE-MASTER"

In a handy three-master I once took a trip
Hurrah boys, heave 'er down!
And I thought that I was aboard a good ship
Way down, laddies, down!

CHAPTER SIX

Golden Cargo

In 1820 the entire marine of the port of Buffalo Creek comprised three small boats, a skiff and a canoe. Its swampy flats were threaded by a creek, deep enough at its mouth for the early schooners and navigable by canoe for some ten miles. But a shifting sand bar lying across the creek mouth made its entrance troublesome and uncertain.

Two miles north lay the settlement of Black Rock, sheltered behind Bird Island, at the head of the Niagara River. This was the port of call for the thirty vessels that plied Lake Erie, and it promised to become the chief commercial city at the foot of the Lake. But in 1820, with the Erie Canal approaching across the Mohawk valley, the citizens of Buffalo began to move their sand bar.

The three boats in Buffalo Creek, manned by local crews, were sailed across to the Canadian side to load stone from the shelving shore. The men worked waist-deep in water, ready to throw their cargo over if a squall blew up. By driftwood fires on the shore they cooked their meals and dried their clothing, and they slept there under the stars. They boated that stone to the newly dug channel and filled the timber cribs that would keep their entrance open. Then Buffalo had the first artificially improved harbor on the lakes.

In the summer of 1822, in a room of Benjamin Rathbun's Eagle Tavern on Main Street, near Court, the commissioners of the Erie Canal met to locate the western terminus of the rapidly advancing canal. They heard General Porter argue for Black Rock and Samuel Wilkeson present the claims of Buffalo. Black Rock boasted a natural harbor and a completed pier. But Samuel Wilkeson unrolled a map and pointed out the action of wind and currents, along with Buffalo's newly opened channel and its protecting cribs.

After the rival pleas were made Canal Commissioner De-Witt Clinton summed up the case, deciding in favor of the most persuasive claimant. In the name and authority of the state of New York he chose Buffalo as the terminus of the canal.

On the twenty-sixth of October, 1825, the canal was opened. Signal cannon, relayed from the hills and across the valleys, carried the news to Albany and thence down the Hudson to New York City, a distance of five hundred miles in ninety minutes. A fine swift packet boat, built of Lake Erie red cedar, the Seneca Chief, with DeWitt Clinton, Samuel Wilkeson, Myron Halley and other notables aboard, set out from Buffalo to Sandy Hook. At Rochester, with multitudes cheering from the embankments, the Young Lion of the West swung in behind the Seneca Chief. The Young Lion was as good as a circus parade, for on its decks were a pair of eagles, a pair of wolves, a fox, a fawn and four raccoons. Soon the packet Niagara joined the procession, and behind it came the Noah's Ark, carrying among its passengers two Indian boys and a restless black bear. Through the Mohawk cities and down the broad Hudson the procession passed, with cannon booming, bands playing triumphal music and church bells ringing night and day.

Aboard the Seneca Chief was a brass-bound cask of Lake Erie water. After the music and the oratory in New York harbor that cask was emptied into the salt sea. Along with it went vials of water from the great rivers, the Thames, the Seine, the Elbe, the Rhine, the Orinoco, the Ganges, and the Nile. So was symbolized the union of all the waters of the earth.

There were parading and fireworks in Manhattan while the Seneca Chief laid her course back to Buffalo with a cask of salt water to pour into Lake Erie. The Great Lakes were joined forever to the ocean highroads.

Immediately Buffalo began to grow. It spread out over the flats and reached along the shore. As the canal brought its endless traffic and the lake fleet put in to transfer cargoes, its harbor was thronged with life. Day and night the horns of the canal boats and the schooners' signal cannon sounded over the town. In 1850 more than half the commerce of the lakes was concentrated at Buffalo. Before many decades the once-rival town of Black Rock became a small corner of the expanding city.

In Cleveland during the 1820's no craft drawing more than three feet of water could enter the Cuyahoga River. Vessels anchored offshore, discharging goods and passengers into small boats. But Cleveland was destined to grow. Across the rolling lands of Ohio, winding through the valleys to Portsmouth on the Ohio River, went the Lake Erie and Ohio Canal. It was completed in 1832, and it brought to Cleveland's newly improved river basin a varied and vital commerce. With lake and canal traffic Cleveland became a crossroads of water-borne trade.

Incorporated as a city in 1836, Cleveland grew rapidly but with order. Standing on a plain eighty feet above the lake, it made an impressive picture. Over the roofs of the well-planned town rose the white dome of the courthouse, four church spires and the turrets of two hotels. On the roofs of the hotels, the American and the Franklin, were sentry boxes where lookouts kept watch, day and night, for the approach of steamers. At every arrival runners hurried down to the wharves to meet prospective guests.

An early citizen, Levi Johnson, was responsible for much of Cleveland's architectural dignity, and he was also its pioneer shipbuilder. He constructed the first frame house in the city, the original courthouse, and many of the early business structures. As evidence of his versatility and of his foresight when the lake trade was still limited to such commodities as grindstones, salt and whisky, he built the schooner Pilot in a yard on the site later occupied by the Cleveland Opera House. This was some distance from the Cuyahoga, and there were men who thought Levi Johnson would never get his vessel into water. But when the Pilot was ready for launching Levi Johnson hired fourteen teams of oxen. With much urging and straining, and half the population of Cleveland standing by as spectators, the craft was hauled to the Cuyahoga.

Far in the west, on the shore of Lake Michigan, two towns took shape in the 1830's. The Black Hawk War opened the southern part of Wisconsin to settlement in 1832. Three years later the first white settlers built their homes at the weedy mouth of the Milwaukee River. That year saw the first hectic fever of land speculation. Land values soared, trade suddenly possessed the quiet waters of Milwaukee harbor and the first rush of immigration crowded the boat landings and thronged the dusty streets beside the river. In the summer of 1836 sixty buildings went up in seven months, ferries plied the busy river, and Byron Kilbourn, dreaming of the city's future, established a newspaper to hasten the dream. On its bluff above Lake Michigan, Milwaukee began to rival Cleveland, the growing city above Lake Erie.

At the lower end of Lake Michigan the Indians had ceded to the white men "one piece of land six miles square at the mouth of the Checagau River." This was a real concession, for the spot had been an important gathering place for Indian tribes and fur traders. But after the treaty the Indians remained in the vicinity, and it was the opportunity to trade with the tribes that brought the first settlers to Chicago. In 1830 twelve families lived there beside the garrison at Fort Dearborn. Three years later the population numbered nearly five hundred. The town then established a free ferry across the river, enlarged the log jail and at a cost of twelve dollars built an estray pen for lost animals. Thus began the city of Chicago, and immediately it saw an inrush of merchants and settlers. Land speculation, the sudden tide of immigration, and the beginning of the Illinois and Michigan Canal multiplied the population ten times within three years. In 1837 Chicago had five thousand residents.

These four ports, Chicago, Milwaukee, Cleveland, and Buffalo, were quickly to be linked in the first bulk trade on the lakes, the trade in grain.

In the 1830's, long before the age of rubber tires and machine tools, Ohio was a grain state. Canal barges brought quantities of wheat and corn to Cleveland, where it was loaded into vessels for the eastern market. In the first two weeks of September, 1839, sixty thousand bushels of wheat and over five thousand barrels of flour were shipped from that port. Some of this grain went to Buffalo; much of it went through the Erie Canal and down the Hudson, or through the Welland Canal to markets on Lake Ontario. By 1840 Cleveland was receiving two million bushels of wheat annually and sending the bulk of it on east in the growing fleet of grain schooners.

But the immigrant boats were carrying multitudes of ardent settlers to the lands beyond Lake Michigan. Before the end of the eventful 1830's a new grain country had appeared; wheat fields were spreading, green in May and golden in mid-summer, across the prairies of Illinois and southern Wisconsin. In 1839 Newberry and Dole built a combination grain dock and elevator on the Chicago River, and in October of that year the historic brig Osceola loaded the first bulk cargo of grain for Buffalo. It was a primitive process. Two men on the upper level of the commission house poured the grain into a chute which opened on the dock. There it was caught in a deep, four-handled bin. Two men, carrying this load like a stretcher, walked up the gangplank and poured it into the open hatchway. The Osceola loaded 1678 bushels of wheat. At Buffalo seven days were required to unload that cargo. Today Buffalo's elevators would unload it in precisely seven seconds.

In 1842 an elevator was erected at Buffalo and that port was on its way to becoming a general market for western grain. Oswego and Kingston, on Lake Ontario, were receiving ports second only to Buffalo, and all of these ports dispatched goods to the western cities. The vessels engaged in transport of wheat, corn, oats, and barreled flour brought back cargoes of coal, salt and general merchandise. By 1840 the tide of commerce had shifted from East to West; from that time the preponderant volume came down the lakes, from the new states beyond Lake Erie.

The Lake Michigan cities had phenomenal growth in the middle years of the century. In Milwaukee, despite a serious outbreak of cholera, the population jumped from 21,000 in 1850 to 46,000 in 1851. Such growth was made possible by lake shipping. The Milwaukee River, fifteen years earlier a tangle of wild rice and water grass, was teeming with commerce, and the masts were thick as forest trees along her waterfront.

To Milwaukee came throngs of Irish settlers after the potato famine of 1845, and the German "forty-eighters," men of intellect and culture, came in great numbers after the unsuccessful rebellion against the German monarchy. With these streams of settlers the roads into the new country saw a continual procession of families on foot, in wagons, and on horseback, seeking the pre-emption lands of the prairies and the oak openings. Quickly the fields that had known only waving grass were patterned with the ribboned green of corn and the ripening gold of wheat and barley.

Out of Lake Michigan's ports that grain went in ever increasing volume. By 1850 Chicago was shipping fifty million bushels of wheat annually and was the greatest grain shipping point in the world. In 1856 the steamer Dean Richmond carried Milwaukee's first European consignment of grain direct to Liverpool.

Between Milwaukee and Chicago was the town of Racine. Located at the mouth of the Root River, it still suffered for want of a harbor because cross-currents from Lake Michigan kept a sand bar building across the river's entrance. In 1842

Congress rejected a bill to improve Lake Michigan's ports and the citizens of Racine were deeply disappointed. However, they still had their own efforts. Five years earlier they had yanked 120 oak stumps out of their Main Street. Now they set to work cutting that sand bar and pulling the roots and snags out of Root River. Without the aid of Congress they got their channel open.

Trade did not appear at once. There was a slack season, with scores of vessels waiting in Chicago and Milwaukee while farmers refused to unload their wheat for the sixty-five cents they were offered. When the price dropped even lower many farmers returned home with their heaping wagons. On the farms harvesting stopped. Farmers would let their grain rot in the field rather than sell it at that price. Finally Captain William Burton left his schooner at the dock. He took his crew ashore and led them over the prairie roads where the wheat stood bronze across the land. He offered to thresh grain for every tenth bushel in order to obtain a cargo and leave port.

But the slack season passed and grain schooners whitened the long lanes of Lake Michigan. Then in the middle fifties the Crimean War and the loss of Russian harvests sent the price of wheat beyond two dollars a bushel. Wheat spread like a prairie fire over the upper Mississippi valley. Farmers drove a hundred miles with their grain wagons to lake ports, and sometimes waited all day and all night to unload at the docks. Where railroads fed the ports long trains of grain cars rolled under the new warehouses and the ponderous elevators. Those were prosperous years for the prairie farmers and for the vessel men who carried the wheat and barley, hides and flour to Buffalo and the Atlantic. Immense grain shipments went over the lakes at high rates. Warehousemen made fortunes and a grain schooner could earn her cost in a single season.

So the golden harvest of the prairies poured like dull gold

rivers into the holds of the grain fleet. By 1870 the Lake Michigan trade was declining, but a new grain trade was beginning on Lake Superior. Through the Soo Canal came the first cargoes of wheat from Minnesota, and in a few decades the vast wheat lands of the great plains sent an enormous commerce down the lakes. The old grain schooners were forgotten then, when six-hundred-foot carriers could load half a million bushels, the harvest of thirty thousand acres in a single freighter's hold. But it was the trim little schooners that began the trade between the infant cities on Lake Erie and Lake Michigan.

CHAPTER·SEVEN

Sawdust on the Wind

FOR SOME HUNDREDS of years to the Indians Saginaw meant "Sauk-town," but to all America from 1850 to 1900 it meant lumber. Vessels swinging in from Lake Huron and approaching the river mouth were met by the smell of sawdust, and if the wind was right that resinous air carried far out onto the wide waters of Saginaw Bay. In fog a keen-nosed captain could steer his ship into the river by the sharp, sweet sawdust smell.

That was in the 1880's, at the height of the lumber trade out of Bay City and Saginaw, the twin brawling towns that straddled the winding Saginaw River. In those years, at the peak of the valley's production, there were sixty big mills cutting over a billion feet of lumber annually. There was lumber to build with and lumber to burn and lumber to ship in the holds and on the decks of the hundreds of lumber hookers that caught the wind coming down from Thunder Bay. With spreading sails they rolled down to the Detroit River and the distant port of Buffalo.

Those towns were built on sawdust fill, acres and acres of it on the low land along the river. Genesee Avenue in Saginaw was a plank road, following a crooked Indian trail through the vanished woods. The first pavement in Bay City was made of pine blocks that floated away during high water after a winter of deep snow. The duckboard sidewalks were of heavy planking and a plank road connected Saginaw with Flint— thirty miles paved with three-inch clear white pine. For the Saginaw country was a pine country, one of the finest in the world.

The riches of that pine were not early understood. The town began in 1816 as a fur-trading post. When the treaty with the Chippewas was concluded three years later, Fort Saginaw was built, a pine stockade on the west bank of the river near Louis Campau's small post. In 1822 the commander of the garrison, after a bitter winter, a spring flood and a summer epidemic of fever, wrote to the War Department, "Nothing but

87

Indians, muskrats and bullfrogs could possibly exist here."
Fifty years later the Saginaw River was the busiest harbor on
the lakes, and the first lighthouse on the shore of Lake Huron
was built at the river mouth to guide its commerce in.

Early in the century timber grew scarce around Detroit
and Port Huron, and by 1830 "timber lookers" were scouting
the Saginaw valley. They marked out their tracts and bought
them for $1.50 an acre from the Detroit Land Office. Then
Harvey Williams came up from Detroit and built the first
steam sawmill on the Saginaw. He brought with him, on a
schooner's deck, a famous steam engine. He trundled it
ashore and set it up in the shadow of the vast pine tracts. The
hissing of that boiler meant the end of Saginaw pine.

Harvey Williams' engine was a pioneer. Nearly twenty
years before, in 1818, it had been installed in the lakes' first
steamboat, the storied Walk-in-the-Water. For three busy
seasons it drove those paddle wheels from Black Rock to Detroit and from Detroit to Mackinac. But on a stormy autumn
night she sank to the bottom of Lake Erie, a few miles from
Buffalo. When the ice was gone next season her hulk was
raised and her engine salvaged. It was installed in the Walk-
in-the-Water's successor, the steamboat Superior, and served
for ten more years until the Superior was broken up. Then
Harvey Williams bought the veteran engine.

He was a skilled blacksmith and mechanic. On his own
anvil he forged the ironwork for the mill and succeeded in
adapting the old marine engine to sawing machinery. So the
engine that had driven two pioneer steamboats turned out pine
lumber on the banks of the Saginaw. It cut two thousand feet
a day for twenty years and sent hundreds of loads of cork
pine down to Lake Erie towns. Finally the old engine was
destroyed with the mill when it burned on the Fourth of July,
1854. It was the victim of a celebrating mill-hand's firecracker.

By that time there were more than thirty mills on the
Saginaw and miles of lumber seasoning along its banks. Four

rivers flow into the Saginaw, like twigs on a maple branch, the Shiawassee, the Cass, the Flint, and the Tittibawassee. Each one brought down its separate flood of timber in the spring and the boom-works of Saginaw and Bay City were jammed with a solid mat of pine logs. Year after year the enormous business grew, until the river was spaced with saw mills for twenty miles and walled on both shores with cliffs of drying lumber.

Along with the mills were shipyards, building vessels to carry the pine to market. Saginaw became an important ship-building center because of the excellence of this timber. There were oak stands up the rivers, and ponderous oak logs came down with the hurrying pine in the spring drives. For flexibility, durability and toughness that Michigan oak was equal to the best English oak and superior to ship timber found elsewhere on the lakes. Saginaw built its own fleets.

When the industry was at its height, in the early 1880's, the Saginaw lumbermen had eight hundred camps and 25,000 loggers at work in the woods. To Saginaw in April the "red-sash brigade" came in a rush like the logs in the five rivers. In their plaid mackinaws, crimson sashes and tasseled caps they swarmed over the town. But Water Street, from the Depot to Sears and Holland's mill, was their stamping ground, and the Riverside House, at the corner of McCoskry and Water, was their favorite hangout.

Quickly they forgot the bitter winter in the woods, the long day's work in the frozen swamp, and the camp ringed round by desolation. There were thirty-two saloons on one side of Potter Street, between Washington and Third Avenue. They scuffled, fought and skylarked in the streets and spent their winter's wages like water at Warren Bordwell's show-house and in the row of ever-open resorts on Franklin Street.

When the ice went out of Saginaw Bay the shipping season could begin. For thirty years an immense fleet of schooners wintered at Bay City. With the warming winds of April other schooners crowded in to the lumber docks. In the spring of 1883, at the height of operations, three hundred million feet of lumber waited on the river banks for the opening of navigation, and there were acres of logs waiting in the booms to be rafted down Lake Huron and through the rivers.

In those years the Saginaw River was one of the wonders of the West and a showplace for all visitors. During the seven-month season the winding channel was literally jammed with shipping. Over a thousand vessels a month were tallied at the Genesee Avenue bridge at Saginaw, and there were other thousands of craft in the twenty miles of river below. Now the drawbridges are seldom open, but when Saginaw was the lumber and salt capital of the nation vessels in the river held up land traffic for hours at a time. Night and day the commerce was moving, the schooners and steamers, the scows and barges, and long rafts of logs towing from the upper sorting gaps to the bull ponds beside the mills. Paddle wheels churned and towboats hooted and the echoes rang back from solid walls of lumber along the shores. A scum of sawdust floated down the river and onto Saginaw Bay. To the rhythms of *We'll Say Farewell to This Old Town* the lumber hookers made sail. Then the snarl and clang of the mills faded to the wide blue silence of Lake Huron.

Back in Saginaw the lumber barons knew the trade would not last forever. The lumber kings who met in the Bancroft House, Miller, Grant, Estabrook, Loveland, Hardin, Bliss, were mostly New England men who had seen the forest stripped off the valleys of Maine and New Brunswick. Some others were Michigan men to start with. Bill Callan, well known through the Saginaw valley, began as a boy in Wellington R. Burt's big mill, bundling lath, fifty staves to a bundle. Another self-made man was the salty and eccentric old pine king Curt Emerson, who called his famous home on the site later occupied by Saginaw's city hall, "The Hall of

Montezuma." When the first steamer was launched in the Saginaw River, the Buena Vista, there was an all-night celebration at Montezuma Hall, and a good deal of debris was carried out next morning. A still bigger operator was David Ward, who as a boy carried the surveying chain for his father on the shores of Saginaw Bay. He was a cousin to Eber Ward, the largest vessel owner in the lakes at the same period. There was intense hostility between these cousins. David Ward followed the lumber business up the Huron shore from Saginaw to Cheboygan and then around the Lake Michigan shore to Charlevoix and Manistee. Eber Ward built big lumber mills at Ludington, perhaps to stir up his always angry cousin. But no man could have his fingers in all the profits of the expanding lumber boom. In 1875 there were thirty solid miles of logs in the Au Gres River, north of Saginaw, with three hundred men working on that drive. The same year eleven million feet came down the Tobacco and fifty-five million feet down the Upper Muskegon on the western shore of the state.

Another figure in boom-time Saginaw was "Little Jake" Seligman. He was not a lumber king, but only a clothing merchant. Still he made his fortune and erected a memorial to himself on the top of a business building on Saginaw's most conspicuous corner. Little Jake stood only four feet four, and the copper figure is life-size, though a long coat and a stovepipe hat give it a false height. When visitors to Saginaw mistook it for the figure of a military hero or a mid-west statesman, Little Jake, in order to be recognized, took to wearing that garb himself.

In the logging days he was well enough known. He was a friend of all the lumberjacks from the camps and the sailors from the mast-filled river. He hired an eight-piece band to play outside his shop while from an upper story he threw vests down to the crowds of men in the streets, promising free coat and trousers to every man who brought in a vest. He kept his word; but the vest was torn to shreds before a winner got into the store, and Jake replaced the vest—at the price of a suit of clothes.

The great age of lumbering in Michigan began shortly after the Civil War. The Saginaw valley felt the boom first, and it was first to see the decline. The climax of its operations came in 1882. By 1885 the masts of lumber schooners were thinning along the river, and the mills were closing, one by one. But the boom years had left acres of slabs and sawdust, and this refuse became the basis of a new industry. Discarded slabs and edging became fuel to pump the brine out of Saginaw's sands and to evaporate salt. So while the sawmills grew quiet, vessels waited at Saginaw wharves to load salt for a dozen cities.

Meanwhile the lumber industry moved north along the Huron shore. The lumber fleets sailed past the stump lands of Saginaw to the Tawas, the Au Sable and the Black Rivers, and to Thunder Bay River and the new boom town of Alpena.

Alpena means in Algonquin "good partridge hunting," and that is about all that Lewis Clason and his surveyors found when they ran the Alpena County township lines in 1839. Finishing their work, and glad to be out of the cedar swamps and the mosquito-infested pine lands, they reported the country worthless. Clason and his men refused a deed to any township of the survey in lieu of their summer's wages. They settled in cash for three dollars a day.

It was only five years before the first sawmill came. Jonathan Burch and Anson Eldred found only one white man living at the mouth of the Thunder Bay River. He was a simple, illiterate fellow named Walter Scott, who had a shanty on the river bank. Burch and Eldred looked at the timber thereabouts and built their mill in 1844. The beginnings were slow; nothing much happened for fifteen years. But after the Civil War the boom years brought a roaring life to that river mouth. At the peak of production in 1889 the Alpena mills cut over two hundred million feet of pine and Thunder Bay was white with the sails of the lumber fleet.

By the end of the century the pine was exhausted and the decline set in. Cedar and spruce went through the mills. Then birch and maple. One after another the mills shut down, the Island mill, the Thunder Bay, the Oldfield and the Broadwell. Finally in 1921 the whistle of the Gilchrist mill, the last of them all, was allowed to die on its own steam, and the sawdust days were over.

When the decline began there were ten thousand people in Alpena and their streets were named for lumbermen: Trowbridge, Chisholm, Broadwell, Miner, Oldfield, Potter, Lockwood. They had no hopes for the town. They knew what becomes of a sawmill town when the timber is gone, and they did not know then that under their feet was a deposit of the richest limestone on the continent. But a grocer, John Monaghan, found limestone and marl at the edge of town, on the flats that border Lake Huron. He brought some home to the back room of his store. Using an old cookstove as a kiln he succeeded in making Portland cement, though the heat nearly melted the old stove to the floor.

That was the beginning of the big cement business on upper Lake Huron. Alpena, that shipped sawed lumber to lay the plank roads of the last century, now ships Portland cement to build the high-speed highways of the Middle West.

But there were other beds of limestone along that shore. Forty miles north, over the pine barrens, lies Rogers City, home of an enormous industry. The quarries lie on the edge of a primitive, unpeopled, nearly roadless country. But the harbor is busy with the big gray freighters, powdered with a dust of limestone, loading under the great elevators and carrying their 14,000-ton cargoes to the steel mills down the lakes.

A few old-timers are left along Thunder Bay River, men like Lem Defoe, Lon Loomis, and Eular Thorne. They remember when the river was jammed solidly with white pine logs all the way from Alpena to the Long Rapids bridge. They remember Paulette Cicero, "the roaring lion of Thunder Bay," a man of Herculean strength who lifted an ox off the ground so its four feet pawed the air. He was the terror of Alpena when loaded with forty-rod whisky, but otherwise gentle as a child. In those days the Columbia and the Forest Queen sailed regularly into Thunder Bay, bringing, among other things, smuggled Canadian whisky with duty unpaid. But the real life of Thunder Bay was the white-sailed fleets and the steam barges, with raised fo'c'sles and elevated poops, called "rabbits" on the lakes, and the great rafts of logs behind a tooting towboat. The boys of Alpena had a favorite pastime, "running lumber"—racing along the drying lumber piles on the river banks, leaping the gaps, sometimes bringing a whole cliff of lumber down into the river. Then they ran for dear life.

Now where the lumber hookers once stood in the river, fishing tugs unload their daily catch of Thunder Bay trout, perch and whitefish, and express refrigerator cars hurry off to market in Detroit, Chicago, Cleveland, and New York.

A century ago the clang of the cross-cuts moved north through the woods and the lumber fleet put in at Cheboygan. With eight big mills running day and night the town reached its peak in 1890, when it sent 127 million feet of lumber down the lakes in schooners and "rabbit" barges. Now Cheboygan has its tourist trade, its Indian curio shops and a fleet of forty fishing tugs. It also has, across the State Street bridge, its famed mountain of sawdust, a long yellow dune that covers twelve acres and rises higher than the tall masts of the vanished topsail schooners. It has a remnant of the old fleets, wooden ships moored to the decaying piles and slowly rotting in the river, while the long smoke pennants of the steel ships lie low on the sky over Lake Huron.

Bay City, Saginaw, Alpena, Cheboygan and twenty lesser towns on the Huron shore sent Michigan lumber to build the growing cities of Ohio and New York state. In 1890 Buffalo had 132 lumber firms, dealers in finished lumber and millers who sawed the logs that were rafted down the lakes. Above Buffalo, on the Niagara River, the Tonawandas were even greater centers. In the 1880's, with their waterfronts lined with vessels and miles of lumber along their shores, North and South Tonawanda were the greatest lumber receiving ports in the world. To those wharfs came the lumber from Lake Huron's forest shores, while the forests that lined Lake Michigan were going down to Chicago and the growing prairie towns.

CHAPTER EIGHT

I Hear America Singing

Down the west shore of Michigan in ages gone by, ice fingers, spreading out from the glacier that lay in the bed of the great long southward-looping lake, reached into the sandy shore to form sheltered waters and river mouths. Muskegon, Pentwater, Ludington, Manistee, all wrote their names with lumber. They were sawmill towns that sprang up on these "lake fingers." So did geology cooperate with the lumber kings who aeons later found that country.

Muskegon was west Michigan's great lumber port. At its height, with fifty-two mills on Muskegon Lake, it was "Lumber Queen of the World." The river drivers and the mill men and the sailors of the lumber fleet collaborated to make it also the Red Light Queen, the Saloon Queen, and the Gambling Queen. This queen city produced forty millionaires and in the roaring eighties its fleets carried nearly a billion feet of lumber annually out of the Muskegon River.

Most of this lumber went across Lake Michigan to build Chicago and the prairie towns. Chicago, rising dramatically from the ashes of its great fire, was already setting records. Among other records Chicago had the greatest horse market in the world. Percheron, Clydesdale, and Belgian animals had been introduced on the prairie farms when a John Deere plow and a McCormick reaper required a stout span of horses in those long fields. From the Chicago market came the loggers' horses. Many a lumber schooner came back to Muskegon with horses stamping in its holds. The next winter, when the swamps were frozen and the log roads coated with ice, those magnificent Percherons and Belgians hauled pyramids of logs down to the river landings.

No other west Michigan town could match the famous mill hands' boarding houses at Pentwater. Father Marquette had seen that timbered country first, but it remained for a Chicago industrialist, Charles Mears, to bring commerce into Pentwater River. Charlie Mears, the "Christopher Columbus of the West Coast" (of Michigan), deepened the river, built a battery of sawmills and put up model boarding houses for the Swedish mill hands who came to work for him. He built his own vessels and operated them, sending lumber down to Chicago where he marketed it in his own yards. Now his mills are gone and his vessels have vanished, and a thrifty colony of Mennonites ship cherries, apples, pears and berries down the old route of the lumber hookers.

In the 1870's the Grand Rapids and Indiana Railway sent an immigrant agent to Scandinavia to recruit settlers for western Michigan. He promised free land, work for all, and religious and political freedom. Promptly a thousand families came to the Grand Rapids region, and others came to the country north, along the Manistee Rivers. So the town of Manistee was developed largely by Swedes and Norwegians, many of whom, with the Viking tradition behind them, joined the crews of lumber schooners that loaded Manistee pine. Down the Big and Little Manistee Rivers in the eighties came some of the biggest log drives in all of Michigan. Sawmills lined the waterfront and Manistee's long harbor was a forest of tall ships, hurrying away with the harvest of a denuded country.

There is a familiar and troubling paradox in the history of Great Lakes lumbering. There were riches, then ruin—the vast timber resources and the feverish, short-lived trade. It began, in volume, after the Civil War; it was virtually ended in 1900. By that time all of Lower Michigan was logged off, and much of Wisconsin, Upper Michigan and Minnesota. The boom trade out of Wisconsin ports came a decade later than the great peak at Saginaw, Alpena and Muskegon. And it was not a lake trade primarily. Much of that timber went down the Mississippi to be milled in river towns all the way from St. Paul to St. Louis. In the later years a great volume of it went out on railroads. But still the lake fleet carried lumber from a dozen Wisconsin towns, and a dozen others in Upper

Michigan and Minnesota. All the old harbor prints of Manitowoc, Sheboygan, Oconto, Menominee, Escanaba, Manistique, Ontonagon, Ashland, Superior show a background of terraced lumber.

One of the new boom towns was Manistique, in the shadow of the deep woods at the head of Lake Michigan. Down the Manistique River came logs from the interior wilderness, and down to Manistique came tales of the lawless camp of Seney. Seney never had but a few hundred population, but they made more stir than many cities. Stub-Foot O'Donnell and Pump-Handle Joe were a committee that met all trains to their village. They stood newcomers on their heads, shaking the silver out of their pockets, and then sent them on their way. Stuttering Jim Gallagher put the mark of his hobnail boots on the face of any man who snickered at his speech. Snap-Jaw Small lived on the fees he collected for biting the heads off living frogs and snakes. He met his end, they said, by biting the head off a lumberjack's pet owl; the lumberjack knocked him out with a peavey handle. The best fighter in that town of hard cases was Big Jim Keene, the big push of the woods, who was at last wounded in a knife-fight and ran half a block with a sheath-knife in his heart before he died.

Manistique itself was a rough and ready place, and a boom town for twenty years after the Chicago fire. Docks and saw-mills bordered the river for five miles. At its mouth the lumber schooners set sail for the long run down to Chicago and tugboats hooted ahead of their sluggish rafts of logs.

A dozen different towns claimed to be the greatest lumber center, and in each case it was true. The timber went so fast that the peak of production shifted, almost from season to season. In 1890 it was Menominee, on the west shore of Green Bay. Down to Menominee came logs from the Brule, the Sturgeon, the Paint, the Iron and Little Cedar Rivers on the Michigan side, and from the Sausaukee, Pike and Pembine on the Wisconsin side. This great territory along the Wisconsin-Michigan boundary was a natural pine country. In 1890 three-quarters of a billion feet of logs passed through the works of the Menominee River Boom Company. The Norwegian mariners of Wisconsin ports steered down Lake Michigan with high deckloads under their billowed sails.

The long dark shores of Lake Superior were clothed in timber. As soon as the government surveys were completed, in the middle of the century, lumbering began. Marquette was an early center. Before the Marquette docks were built, horses and oxen, brought up to work in the woods, were put overboard from the trading schooners and left to swim ashore. Soon the Carp and Dead Rivers were bringing down logs. The Cleveland sawmill, at the mouth of Dead River, was for many years the biggest and best equipped mill on Lake Superior. In the nineties it cut fifty million feet annually. By that time at Ashland, Ontonagon, Superior and Duluth the mills were snarling, with lumber banked high around them.

Ontonagon turned to lumber only after the hectic copper fever had died down. In the early forties prospectors ranged the entire wilderness of the Porcupine Mountains. They passed through rich stands of pine and spruce, maple, birch and hemlock. But they were looking for copper. Legends of Ontonagon copper carried far—to Boston and New York, to the clubs of London and the courts of snowy St. Petersburg. At Victoria, twelve miles up the rocky Ontonagon River, the mines were financed by European royalty who sent agents into the fabled country. The Empress of Russia developed one mine and the Duke of Gloucester controlled another. But copper was thin in that valley. The mines closed, one by one, and it was lumber scows and log rafts that kept Ontonagon alive.

Millions of feet of Lake Superior lumber went down the lakes unfinished, in raft tows. Gulls from their breeding place on Gull Island in the Apostles flew over the lake in thousands. They lighted like a summer snow on the big slow-moving rafts. Some of the birds rode for a week at a time across Lake Superior. During the early 1900's those immense log rafts were locked through the Soo. In places they filled the St. Mary's River from bank to bank. Ahead of the long creeping raft the tugboat kept up a continual tooting to clear the hidden channel. Some of the settlers on Neebish Island still remember the terrifying siren of the Tom Dowling. One inland farmer, miles away, rushed to the house for a gun when he heard through the woods that fearful cry. Those logs from the wilderness shores of Lake Superior were milled in the cities down below.

So the schooners, the "rabbits," the scows and the towboats carried the forests of the upper lakes to build America's cities. There was zest in that trade that rose and fell in forty years. Even after it was gone it left echoes drifting over the lakes.

> *'Twas the timber drover Bigerlow*
> *A-hailing from Detroit—*

She carried a couple of mules on the fo'c'sle deck to haul timber aboard, and all through the ship you could smell the condensed mule feed.

> *You'd swear that whiff of D.C. feed*
> *Came clear from Buffalo.*

But Buffalo was still a long way off and the wind was whining in her shrouds.

> *You should a heard her howling*
> *When the wind was blowing free*
> *On that voyage down to Buffalo*
> *From Milwaukee.*

THE VANISHED FLEETS

The sailors looked over the waters and the many shores. They saw a country growing into greatness, and yet they saw it lonely and large. They heard its names out of the past, Indian and French and British names—three epochs of history before the American destiny began to unfold. They passed Ile au Galets and Waugoshance Reef and their lusty voices rang:

> *We made Shilagalee and Wobbleshanks*
> *The entrance to the straits,*

and laughing at their own calling and the peril that was in it they sang:

> *Oh, the Erie was a-rolling*
> *The rum was getting low,*
> *And I hardly think*
> *We'll get a drink*
> *Till we get to Buffalo.*

In those years of the nation's growing Walt Whitman said "I Hear America Singing." Some of the haunting voices came from the crews of the lumber hookers, heaving their anchors or making sail at a river mouth where the blue waters widened.

CHAPTER NINE

Smoke Clouds Blowing

On a winter night in 1837 the steamer Caroline was set on fire and sent over Niagara Falls. Down the swift current she came and she was burning fiercely. Trailing sparks and embers she hurried toward the brink. With her decks ablaze and flames running up her masts she lighted the whole gorge of Niagara as she made her final plunge.

That was the biggest and briefest blaze ever seen on the lakes. But there were many others. In 1834 the handsome side-wheeler Washington burned in Lake Erie on her maiden voyage. In the 1840's two big passenger steamers burned, the Erie on Lake Erie and the Phoenix on Lake Michigan, with more than four hundred dead between them. On a fine June night in 1850, while she was jogging along twenty miles east of Cleveland, fire was discovered below decks in the steamer G. P. Griffith. As she was just three miles off shore, her captain thought he could beach her and save all his passengers. But half a mile out she struck a sand bar. While three hundred people fought for their lives the ship burned like a torch. The sky over Lake Erie was a lurid tent until the sunrise came. It dawned over a tranquil lake and a lifeless, slowly smoking hull.

Fire was a common hazard in the old wooden ships with their cargoes of grain, lumber, coal, tanbark, and in the early steamers with their ricks of fuel wood beside the pounding boilers. But there were even bigger blazes on the lake shores.

Frontier towns burned like tinder. The board streets and sidewalks, the open frame buildings, the lack of water pressure and of fire-fighting apparatus made them terribly vulnerable. Nearly every American city has had a great fire in its brief history. Often the lumber towns had a series of them. The very ground they rested on, built up of sawdust, slabs and refuse from the mills, was inflammable. The drying yards, with lumber stacked and open to the air, could quickly roar into acres of flame. There were always sparks from the big consumers and the straining boilers of the steam engines to start the disaster. Sawdust towns lived violently, with the rumble of logging, the snarl and scream of the buzz saw, and the tumult of the loading wharfs. And mostly they died violently. A sawmill town could not expect a peaceful end.

Even schooners were a fire hazard in the lumber ports, for with schooners there had to go tugboats, puffing smoke and sparks over the river. When steam barges shared the lumber trade the hazard grew. In the eighties a law required all steam craft to carry a spark-catcher, as locomotives were required to screen their stacks in logging country. At least one stubborn steamer, the Odd Fellow, was seized at Saginaw for violation of this ordinance. She was sold at auction, and her new operator promptly put a muzzle on her gaunt black funnel. She was a small propeller steamer, good for about three miles an hour.

In the seventies the Saginaw River boasted two steamboats plying on schedule between East Saginaw and Bay City. They were the L. G. Mason and the Evening Star, and they competed strenuously for the commuting trade. Regular fare between the two towns was ten cents and neither steamer chose to undercut the rate. However, as an inducement to ride the Evening Star, her passengers were furnished with a copy of the Daily Enterprise or, if they preferred, a glass of whisky.

These two craft did not long have the trade to themselves. When the roaring eighties brought a climax to the lumber business a new fleet of steamers appeared on the Saginaw River. They were the famous "Boy" boats: Handy Boy, Plow Boy, Post Boy, News Boy. These new vessels were equipped with fire pumps and reels of heavy hose. In their regular trips up and down the river they provided an efficient fire patrol. Many a passenger down to Bay City had his trip interrupted by a cloud of smoke from the busy river bank. The "Boy" left her course in midstream, hurried to a blazing mill or lumber yard, started her fire pumps and poured arching streams of water ashore. When the fire was out the pumps were shut off, the hose coiled, and the steamer went on.

These steamers were well built, sturdy craft. Two of the "Boy" boats remained in use around Saginaw Bay until 1920.

Other lumber ports were not so well equipped. Alpena had a series of disastrous fires, five of them within ten years. When the dense gray smoke billowed out over Lake Huron, schooner mates knew that Alpena was burning again. On a hot July day in 1862 fire raced through the slash, left tinder-dry in the cut-over lands behind Alpena. It roared along Thunder Bay River, wiped out the big sawmill of Lockwood and Minor and left most of the village in smoking ruin. The rebuilt town was swept again by fire in 1863, and 1867, and 1869. Each time the mills turned out new timber and the town was built again. But in 1871 a fire bigger than all the others leveled the whole town north of the river. That was the year of fires, of the great Chicago fire and of vast searing forest fires that swept four counties along the Peshtigo and Oconto Rivers in Wisconsin and burned swaths across the whole state of Michigan. Some towns might have given up, but not Alpena. They rebuilt the town, and after a vote of 82 to 82 (half of the leading citizens were fatalistic) they bought a steam fire engine from the city of Port Huron down the lake. That was a famous old engine, named Sahgonahkato for an Indian chief. It had done valiant service up and down the St. Clair River. In October, 1871, when the dreadful news *Chicago is burning!* came across the prairies, the Sahgonahkato was loaded onto a steamboat's deck and rushed to Chicago, where it fought the stubborn flames. Now it came to Alpena, and for years it lived an amphibian life, part of the time in Alpena and part of the time at sea. For it was freighted up and down the Huron shore, fighting fires at Harrisville, Hillman and Mackinaw City.

The Sahgonahkato was a sturdy old engine, but despite its

faithful pumping Alpena had another fire in 1888 that left 1500 people homeless and acres of smoking ruin.

Fire engines had considerable standing in those lumber towns. At every celebration the fire engine, freshly shined and painted, looking like a circus wagon while the horses fidgeted proudly and the smoke puffed up from the boiler, led the parade. Now a superannuated old fire engine stands like a monument in the village park at Harrisville, fronting the blue waters of Lake Huron.

The autumn of 1871 was a dark season in the lakes country. The same wind that fanned the flames in the stables and warehouses beside the Chicago River spread fire in the dry woods of Wisconsin and Michigan. While the smoke of the Peshtigo fire rolled across Lake Michigan, the town of Manistee was rimmed in a crescent of burning forest. Flame swept into the village and along the river until vessels were blazing beside the flaming wharves. The whole town crowded into one steamer, whose captain steered her past two fiercely burning lumber yards. From that heat the steamer took fire. While men fought the flames the captain saw his way blocked by a burning bridge. He rammed the bridge but failed to break it. He reversed his engines and drew back for another try. Three times he rammed it before the burning bridge broke through. Then with smoking embers on his decks he steered for the open water of Lake Michigan.

Along the shores of Lake Michigan and Lake Huron town after town went out in flames. At Saginaw sawmills and salt blocks were swept away. At Lansing, in the interior of Michigan, students of the Agricultural College fought forest fires that threatened to devastate the capital city. And out on the lakes ships groped day and night through a choking, blinding pall.

In that strange, remembered autumn of 1871 there were many dramas on the lakes. One of them is the story of

Menominee, the busy lumber port on the pine-dark shores of Green Bay.

From Green Bay and Bay de Noc the woods stretched north over a wild country, marked only by tote-roads, a few scattered logging lines and an occasional sawmill settlement beside the rivers that run down to Lake Michigan. The summer of 1871 was a hot, hazy season, with brush fires burning in the cut-over sections and miles of slash smoldering beside the newly completed railroad lines. An occasional shower kept them from spreading, though there was not enough rain to put them out. As autumn came on, the ground baked dry and the fires grew larger. Still it was not alarming. Forest fires were no novelty, in that country. People got used to hazy sunsets and a sharp smell in the air. But when September passed with a succession of hot, windless days and not a drop of moisture, the weatherwise old settlers began to look puzzled. There had never been a season like this before.

During the first week of October Menominee's narrow harbor was glassy still, under slow-drifting curtains of smoke. Schooners groped in to anchorage, and before they became visible there was the sound of sailors coughing on their decks. At midday the sun was a dull coin that men could stare at steadily; there were no stars at night. Rumors came down the river—of inland camps wiped out in a sudden spread of fire, of people standing all night in the streams, of farmers walking over their blackened fields and eating potatoes that had baked in the ground.

There was nothing to do about it. Work went on in Menominee. The logs came snarling through the mills, the smoke from the consumers thickened the haze that hung around, and people scanned the sky thinking of a long, deep autumn rain.

Young Charlie Ingalls, son of a Menominee lumberman, was getting out cedar posts on his father's Hay Creek farm a few miles up river from the town. He had a schooner in the river and a crew of fifteen men working in the woods. On Sunday morning, the seventh of October, most of his crew had gone to town to chat with sailors on the docks. But Charlie, feeling uneasy about the thick gray air, had stayed at the farm instead of going to his mother's house in Menominee for a good Sunday dinner. He was thinking of the dry woods, the miles of pine needles like a floor of tinder, and acres of slash piled up along the railroad where the swampers had gone through. All through the country wells and cisterns were empty and the rivers ran low in their banks. A fitful west wind brought a hot smell and waves of heated air from Oconto and Peshtigo, where the swamps were burning. At times he heard a low and distant sound, softer than thunder. In the quiet Sunday, under the heavy sky, there was a kind of premonition. Even the hens in the barnyard wandered abstractedly, forgetting to scratch for grain.

In mid-afternoon people appeared on the road to Menominee, carrying baskets and bundles. The woods along Birch Creek were burning, they said, and the village was doomed. At that Charlie Ingalls looked grim. There was fire on two sides of them now. He got his few remaining men to work with spades and shovels, digging a trench around the farm buildings.

That evening a color like sunset edged the woods, but it was in the wrong direction. Soon half the horizon was tinged with light and waves of smoke passed over. The mutter rose to a roaring.

There was no darkness that night. There was a fierce sky and a land terribly illumined. At Hay Creek farm the fire struck suddenly, not with a wave of flame but with a rain of sparks and embers. The dried fields took fire like scattered haycocks, flowering up in many places and spreading quickly. When the barnyard was smoking Charlie turned out the cattle and horses, except one team that he hitched to a light wagon, quieting them with his voice as he hooked the traces to the double-trees. He called to his men, but they had crowded into the dry cistern and would not come out. He had to leave them there. Before the night was over squirrels, rats and rabbits were huddled with them in that pit.

Charlie turned his team toward Menominee and the harbor. The horses needed no urging. Their hooves pounded the dust, the buckboard rocked like a rowboat. On the road ahead were cattle and horses, running wildly, sometimes plunging into the woods or racing over fire-patched fields to escape the blowing smoke. Deer and wolves fled together across the dried swamps. Ahead, under the lighted sky, Charlie Ingalls saw that Menominee still stood. His team plunged on through the town and into the harbor. They did not stop till the wagon bed was floating.

Charlie waded ashore and met Ed Byers and Nate Nickerson on their way to the docks. They looked at the water running out of his clothes.

"Where you been, Charlie?" Nate asked.

"Tying my horses." Charlie grinned as the puddle collected under him. It was the first time he had smiled that day and it was gone quickly. "Any fires in town?"

"Yes, a couple on the west side. Come on over to Jones Dock with us. The Northern City is coming in. We'll get the captain to take the women and children aboard."

Out at the harbor entrance a big passenger steamer was swinging. She came up cautiously, with men stamping out sparks that fell on her decks. In the river mouth two schooners began to blaze. Small boats jerked away from them over the polished water. Slowly the steamer crept in.

Before his lines were ashore the captain heard men calling him from the dock. He leaned over the bridge rail.

"The town may go before morning, Captain. Can you stand by?"

"Yes. I'll stand by till it gets too hot to hang around."

"Will you take the women and children aboard?"

"All I got room for."

"Thank you, Captain. How are you fixed for fuel?"

"Got plenty." He breathed the acrid air. "It don't take much to get up steam in this weather."

Soon women were streaming up the gangplank, women with babies in their arms and wide-eyed children around them, grim-faced women lugging baskets of food and bundles of clothing, trembling old women with bright distracted eyes, carrying a gilt clock, a big black Bible with a metal clasp, or a porcelain lamp with a shattered chimney.

While the steamer stood by there was a way out of Menominee. But that could not help the neighboring settlements. Stragglers came in, smoke-blackened and exhausted, from Birch Creek and Peshtigo. A few had left those burning towns before the fire closed them in. The women went aboard the steamer; the men threw themselves down on the harborside and when they got their strength back they went to join the citizens throwing water on Menominee's smoking buildings. Even the streets were taking fire. Sawdust streets, they flared up in sudden bright patches that went on smoking after the blaze was trampled out. The whole town was ready to burst into flame.

In the lighted fitful night people brought out their treasures, carrying them to the water's edge or burying them in the ground. George Horvath, the dry goods dealer, hurried through the streets with a big gilt mirror that gave back the lurid color of the sky. Old Frenchy Theriault, who fiddled for all the dances in Menominee, trotted down to the beach with a box of his fine cigars. He clawed a hole in the sand and covered it so smoothly that he never found the cigars again. The rest of the night he spent marching up and down Main Street with his fiddle under his arm. A distracted old man was found feverishly burying a hammer and a lighted lantern in his garden.

Back on the steamer at Jones Dock under the mate's watchful eye a consignment of fine furniture was going ashore. A team of restless horses pawed the wooden wharf while it was loaded in Charlie Fairchild's dray. At last he drove through town toward E. L. Parmenter's big new house on State Street. That house was the show place of Menominee in 1871.

It was two A.M. and the bright sky gleamed on the polished mahogany.

"Where you taking the furniture, Charlie?"

"Taking it to Parmenter's. It just came in on the steamer."

The big house stood untouched and impressive, but no house in Menominee was a good bet that night. A little shift of wind and E. L. Parmenter's mansion could burn like any mill shed.

"Better take it back to the boat. The hills are all on fire up Kirby Creek."

"Nope," said Charlie Fairchild. "It's got to be delivered to Parmenter's. They'll get th' insurance if it's in the house, but not if it's in the boat."

The fire reached its height three hours after midnight when a strong west wind blew up. All at once the dry swamp along Kirby Creek was blazing. It threatened the whole town. There was but one good road across the swamp, Pengilly Street, which led to a row of mills on the creekside. Over this road Charlie Ingalls hurried a troop of weary townsmen. Their only hope was to make a firebreak of the road. Working without words, the breath grunting in their throats, they threw up a trench. The wind was scorching in their faces and it was like breathing pain to inhale that fiery air. But the town depended on them. Sparks streamed across the road, lighting up the brittle reeds and grasses beyond. Men beat out the fire with their own shirts and raced with pails of water from the sinking well on Oscar Saxon's place. They worked till their legs buckled. Then they lay flat, scooping out holes for their faces and gulping the air. They got to their feet and fought the fire again. They plunged their shirts into pails of water, they pounded and trampled the spreading flames. Fire scorched their arms and feet and faces and the smoke was tightening in their throats. But those were things they would remember later; now it was only the fierce struggle, fighting the foe that licked hungrily toward their homes and their people.

When daylight came, a dull, ash-colored light, the men of Menominee stood in a smoking grassland with blistered hands and blackened faces. But behind them their town was saved.

Charlie Ingalls went to his mother's house on Menominee Bay. Inside the house children were stretched out everywhere; he counted eight babies sleeping in one bed. He found the back yard filled with refugees from Frenchtown, up the river. His mother was in the kitchen making two big kettles of coffee. They had a breakfast of bread and coffee for forty people. Suddenly a lake breeze blew in, cool and clean and reassuring. They put their coffee down and breathed the air like a perfume.

Down at Jones Dock the refugees began to come ashore from the steamer. Women stood on the wharf blinded with tears when they saw their homes still there. Children raced ahead through the empty streets. Then down the gangway came a few awkward women with their faces hidden and their feet stumbling on their long skirts. As they crossed the wharf Oscar Saxon, the town's official teamster, eyed them sharply. He spat into the bay, scowled, and clumped over beside them. All at once he let go a volley of oaths. His foot swung and the toe of his boot landed hard. The women tried to run but they got tangled in their skirts. Oscar kicked and pounded them and the oaths kept pouring out. Finally the skirts dropped off and a half-dozen Menominee cowards, who had hidden all night with the women, took to their heels. Oscar's voice followed them down the street.

All through Menominee there was rejoicing over the spared town. But when news came from the shore below them, the faces were startled. The whole town of Peshtigo had gone up in the night, with seven hundred dead in her burning streets and drowned in her river. Then came word of a more fearful disaster. During the hours when Menominee was fighting for its life a great city had burned at the foot of Lake Michigan. Now six hundred city blocks lay in ruin and the ashes of Chicago were strewn over Lake Michigan for fifty miles.

At noon the captain of the Northern City prepared to cast off lines and make his scheduled run to Mackinac. The lines came aboard and the engines turned over. But the ship didn't budge from the dock. The captain scowled down from the bridge.

"The guldam ship is aground!" he said in a hollow voice.

The mate stared at him and they had a slow realization. The wind and heat of the night had lowered the water and hung them in the mud. If Menominee had caught fire the rescue ship would have burned like a haystack at her moorings.

For miles around Menominee the woods lay blackened. The peat bogs along Little Cedar River were burned so deeply that fire smouldered underground for many months. That winter smoke came through the snow.

Across Lake Michigan, on the shore of Sturgeon Bay, Captain James Davenport of the Lighthouse Service never forgot the somber days of 1871 when southwest winds blew the smoke of Chicago and of Wisconsin forest fires over all the upper lakes. He was then serving at Waugoshance and he was alone at the light for nine days because the dense smoke kept his crew in Cross Village where they had gone for supplies. On the fourth day of his one-man vigil the smoke cleared for a moment and he sighted a schooner wrecked on White Shoals. Then the clouds closed again. Before that acrid fog was gone there was a long list of disaster. On October tenth the tug Dispatch and five barges piled up on Pointe Aux Barques Reef. The barque Major Barbara went ashore near Big

Sable Point on Lake Michigan and the fine new steamer Coburn, loaded with grain for Buffalo, was wrecked in Saginaw
Bay.

Ten years later, in the summer of 1881, another pall of
smoke blew over the lakes. It was a hot dry summer over
Michigan. Day after day the sun blazed in a cloudless sky.
Night after night the stars burned in the hot summer dark.
Crops turned brown in the fields. Pastures seared. In the woods
the brush was wilting. There was not a drop of rainfall in the
"thumb" of Michigan, between Saginaw Bay and Lake Huron,
from June to September. Streams ran dry and wells were
empty. Swamps cracked open with heat.

On the last day of August fire started on the north edge
of Lapeer County. The dry wind fanned it. The whole country was ready to burst into flame. In three days that racing
fire seared four counties. Fish were boiled in the stagnant
rivers and birds were driven out on Lake Huron to drown.
Bears shambled out of the woods; they herded with cattle in
the fields and all were burned together. Along the Huron
shore at Forrester and Forestville settlers drove their horses
and cattle into the lake and waded out with them while the
smoke billowed over. For days afterward, as the wood ash
settled, Lake Huron was a sea of lye with the blinded schooners groping through it.

In that first week of September more than a hundred lives
were lost and a dozen villages were burned to ashes. Among
them was White Rock, Michigan's most notorious phantom
city.

During the fevered land speculation of the 1830's large
maps hung in Detroit hotels and barrooms, picturing White
Rock as a busy city overlooking a ship-filled harbor on Lake
Huron. Auctioneers sold property in block lots in this "future
metropolis of Michigan." When Bela Hubbard and Douglass
Houghton, state geologists, visited the place on their way to

northern Michigan, they found the naked rock, plastered with seagulls' droppings, jutting out of the harbor. But that was all. The "magnificent White Rock River" was not deep enough to float their canoe. In a bark shanty at the creek mouth lived one backwoodsman, with a shambling gait and furtive eyes. He wasn't used to visitors, but when they bade him share the kettle of tea on their driftwood fire he saw these were all right.

"White Rock?" he said. "Never heerd of it. Outside some Indians up the crick I'm the only settler here."

He sucked the tea out of his mustache and looked at them sideways. "If'n there's a town coming, I'll be moving on."

He was not the sort of citizen to appreciate the picture maps of the Detroit speculators.

In time a small settlement did grow up there, and was swept away by the fire of 1881. It was a dull place, unlike the phantom city, and it was rebuilt gradually as a village of farmers and fishermen.

One paltry benefit of forest fires was the quick growth of huckleberries that sprang up on the burned ground. They were big, fat, luscious berries, flourishing on wood ash. It wasn't necessary to pick them—just rake them off into a shirt or a blanket and send them down in bushel baskets to the markets at Port Huron and Detroit. So the once clamorous logging settlements turned to the humble trade of berry picking. As the business grew, villagers on the Huron shore set fires in the second growth scrub to enlarge their berry meadows. But it was easier to start a fire than to stop it. In 1911 the berry pickers burned the whole town of Au Sable and nearly obliterated the village of Oscoda. Only the waves of Lake Huron stopped those hungry flames.

Disaster on land meant danger on the lakes. Forest fires were as fearful to lake men as to people in the mill towns. Ships lost their bearings in that gray fog and in the viewless, choking night. Blinded vessels could run aground, and they could ram each other. But their greatest danger was from raft tows.

Rafting had grown with the lumber trade. Billions of feet of timber were rafted from Saginaw Bay to Detroit and Lake Erie. From the country north of Saginaw, the big Alger-Smith outfit rafted enormous volumes of logs, towing them with their own company barges to Toledo, Cleveland, Buffalo and the Tonawandas. Often they had four rafts, totaling eight million feet of lumber, on Lake Huron at one time. This company had $40,000 invested in rafting chains alone.

Rafting was economical for a lumber company but hazardous for navigation. A raft from Alpena to Chicago broke up in a blow on Thunder Bay, scattering four million feet of logs along the shore and making those waters perilous for many seasons. A heavy log, half-submerged, slowly growing water-soaked, could breach the bottom of the soundest wooden ship ever built. Even an intact raft, creeping behind its tug, low and dark on the water, could be a deadly menace to vessels driving through smoke and fog.

Eventually the Lake Carriers' Association opposed the towing of logs in the trade routes because of damage to vessels and the frequent carrying away of channel buoys and markers. After strenuous efforts they secured legislation restricting the size and the operations of log rafts. Now, as an added precaution, the Hydrographic Service sends out notices when a log raft is to go down the lakes. But there was no way of flashing messages of hazard in the smoke-shrouded channels of fifty years ago.

In later years of the trade, the towing of lumber barges grew common. A steamer carrying 600,000 feet of lumber would tow four barges, each with a similar load. To the lake man this was "the sow and her pigs." The one tow stretched out half a mile with the taut tow-line between the laden craft. In smoke or fog a vessel might sail directly into such a tow.

Ships had their upper works raked cleanly off when the look-out had no glimpse of any danger.

For two generations smoke was a unique and dreaded peril on the lakes. Within twenty years the Wisconsin pineries raged with the fires of Peshtigo, Oshkosh, Phillips, Marshfield, Iron River, Fifield, and Medford. Later, as logging moved north to Minnesota, the forest fires followed. Then it was the Hinckley and Cloquet and Moose Lake fires that darkened Duluth at noon and sent a pall of smoke over all of Lake Superior. In those seasons, boats moved at half speed in the harbors; out on Lake Superior the whalebacks passed in secret; and far away in the narrow rivers of the Soo, freighters lay all night with engines idle and whistles crying in that dark.

CHAPTER TEN

Wagon Wheels in the Rigging

THE WAYS TO THE WEST were by water. There were no railroads to St. Louis and Chicago until the 1850's, and the stage-coach was a cramped, slow vehicle over the uncertain roads of the sparsely settled country. Until the Civil War the highways to the West were the Great Lakes and the Ohio River. When the Erie Canal wedded Lake Erie to the Hudson there was an all-water route to the western prairies. Freight rates dropped from thirty-two dollars a ton for a hundred miles by wagon to a dollar a ton by canal boat and steamer. The lakes had an outlet to the seaboard and America had a living highway into the West. The immigrant boats steamed into blue Lake Erie with the founders of new commonwealths on their decks.

For fifty years the lakes steamers were devoted chiefly to passenger travel while the wind-driven vessels carried the bulk trade of freight. The early steamers were thronged with merchants, speculators, westward-moving Yankee settlers and the prophetic tide of immigrants. At first the steamboats went no farther than Detroit, but by 1835 they were running regularly to Milwaukee and Chicago. They carried multitudes of settlers to the pre-emption lands of Michigan, Illinois and Wisconsin.

Two small steamboats, the Frontenac and the Ontario, were built and operated on Lake Ontario immediately after the War of 1812. But the pioneer steamer to ply Lake Erie and the upper lakes was the short-lived Walk-in-the-Water. That historic craft, named for a friendly Wyandotte chief whose name meant "turtle," a creature which the Indians described as one that walks in the water, was a side-wheeler, 135 feet long with an eight-foot draught. She was launched in the Niagara River in the spring of 1818, and as her engine was not sufficient to overcome the current, fifteen yoke of oxen provided the "horned breeze" that towed her to Lake Erie. Under Captain Job Fish, a steamboat man from the Hudson River, she began her first voyage to Detroit on the twenty-third of August, 1818. She was three days on the way.

On her two masts the Walk-in-the-Water carried mainsail, foresail, and topmast staysail; in a fair wind that spread of canvas gave her more propulsion than her engine. Her stack, made of six jointed lengths of stove-pipe, reared up thirty feet above the paddle-boxes. Forty cords of hardwood on her deck supplied fuel for her clattering engine. She carried twenty-nine paying passengers. Her cabins were below deck, as it was thought that exposed cabins could not stand the storms of the lakes.

On the twenty-fourth of August the whole town of Cleveland gathered on a bluff to watch the first steamboat call at their entrance. Captain Fish stood in full uniform on the port paddle-box, with a megaphone carrying orders to his crew at the anchor windlass and in the boiler room. As the steam whistle had not yet been invented, the Walk-in-the-Water was announced by a salute from a four-pound cannon on her deck. Two years later that cannon worked loose in a gale and was washed overboard.

On the morning of August twenty-sixth the Walk-in-the-Water entered the Detroit River, and a French farmer ran to the house crying, "Jean! Jean! Look at the river! What are these Yankees sending us now but a sawmill!"

Some river settlers said that the sailless craft was drawn by sturgeons, and some believed it.

At Detroit the entire populace came down to the landing. Among that marveling crowd were Judge Augustus Woodward, "Uncle Ben" Woodworth, proprietor of the Steamboat Hotel, whose sign was freshly painted for the occasion, and a knot of Indians who took to their heels when the engineer let off a head of steam.

With completion of her first run confidence in the Walk-in-the-Water was established and she was given a contract to carry U.S. mail.

In 1820 the steamer extended her runs to Mackinac and far-off Green Bay. A New York paper compared those voyages to "the famous legendary expeditions in the Heroic Ages of Greece." She was a source of consternation to the Indians along the route. They called her "Scootie-nabbie-quon" and fled from her presence.

In the spring of 1820 the Walk-in-the-Water brought young Henry Schoolcraft to Detroit to join Governor Cass's expedition to the headwaters of the Mississippi. Perhaps it was the distrust of his ten Chippewa paddlers that led Cass to forgo a steamboat passage up to Mackinac. His party embarked in canoes from Detroit, paddling along the Huron shore toward De Tour and the distant shores of Lake Superior and the St. Louis River which led into the little known wilderness of Minnesota.

In the three seasons of her service the Walk-in-the-Water carried some notable travelers across the lakes. There were the Earl of Selkirk and his countess, the Reverend Jedediah Morse and his son Samuel F. B. Morse, a young portrait painter who in a dozen years was to turn his talents to the subject of electro-magnetism, and many United States Army officers on their way to western posts.

On the last day of October, 1821, the steamer cleared the port of Buffalo for her final trip of the season. Four hours out, she was struck by one of Lake Erie's sudden gales. Her seams opened and water poured into her hull. Her pumps labored to keep her afloat. Captain Jedediah Rogers threw over three anchors, two of them made fast to mooring lines. By midnight the two hawsers had parted and the ship was dragging toward the beach. She grounded on the shore of Point Abino. At daylight a line was carried ashore and secured to a tree trunk. With the aid of this life-line the passengers and crew were taken ashore in the vessel's small boat.

The Walk-in-the-Water was replaced promptly. Her successor, the side-wheeler Superior, was built at Black Rock in the following spring. She was launched sidewise, like all vessels built in the narrow rivers, and in the breathless moment when she started down the ways "Whistling Tom," Buffalo's notable mulatto roustabout, gave a shrill peal like a bugle note in his most artistic style. The Superior made a good launching.

Besides her main cabin the Superior was built with a long forward room, a steerage hold, fitted for families moving westward. Rows of bunks, cooking stoves, tables, open-shelved pantries and baggage bins made up those quarters. She was an authentic immigrant boat, carrying settlers at half the regular cabin fare.

She proved to be a sturdy ship, and a fast one for her time. Lake men derided the Hudson River steamers, claiming that they raced against the tide with lime kilns along the shore and that the lime kilns often held the lead. It was their boast that the Superior could do eight miles an hour if her fires were properly fed. She could consume a cord of wood in fifty minutes.

In the next few years new steamers were added, the Chippewa, the Henry Clay, the Pioneer, the Enterprise, and by 1830 there was a regular schedule of steamers smoking over Lake Erie. They were engaged in the fastest-growing business in America, the business of carrying immigrants to the West.

In the 1830's settlers arrived by thousands in Detroit. From the opening of navigation in April till the freezing of the harbors in December, there was a constant stream of newcomers journeying west. In a single day five thousand people took passage out of Buffalo. A Detroit newspaperman estimated that during the summer of 1836 a wagon left the city for the interior every five minutes between daylight and dark. Besides the wagon caravans there were people traveling by stage-coach, ox cart, on horseback and afoot. All were headed west, over the famous Detroit-Chicago turnpike, once an Indian trail, now U.S. 112, and over the Territorial Road through Kalamazoo.

But even more of the immigrant trade went on past De-

troit's busy waterfront, up Lake Huron and down Lake
Michigan. The western terminus of that stream of settlers was
the towns beside Lake Michigan and the farmsteads of the
Mississippi valley.

Steamboat commerce to Chicago was inaugurated in the
summer of 1832, when with the outbreak of Black Hawk's
War the United States Army chartered four vessels to transport troops and supplies from Buffalo to Fort Dearborn.
That proved to be a sorry inauguration, though a flood tide of
commerce quickly followed it.

Two of those four transports never reached their destination. When the Henry Clay came up Lake Erie to Detroit
with 370 soldiers, she brought a terrifying malady with them.
Behind her in Buffalo cholera had broken out and was sweeping the town. Before they reached Detroit a number of the
troops had been taken violently ill and when one of them died
the vessel was ordered away from the public wharf. Shunned
as a pest ship, with her sick list growing, the Henry Clay proceeded up the St. Clair River to Fort Gratiot, just above the
town of Port Huron. There the sick were carried ashore, and
the terrified men not yet stricken fled the ship. They scattered through fields and woods and some lay down in streets
and on the shore and died. A hundred and fifty of them made
their way back to Detroit where they were taken in by
Andrew Mack, proprietor of the Mansion House. In a short
time two hundred Detroit citizens were stricken with the
disease.

Another troopship, the Sheldon Thompson, sailed past Detroit but put in to Mackinac Island for fuel wood. While
the steamer fueled several stricken soldiers were taken ashore.
They died soon after the vessel had resumed her course. Two
fur traders who left Mackinac the next day fell ill before they
had traveled twenty miles. They struggled on, not knowing
the nature of their malady, until their bodies were fired with

fever and their shaking hands turned purple before their eyes. They died with the wilderness around them. But the disease did not spread in that latitude with its sparse settlement.

Meanwhile the Sheldon Thompson arrived outside the Chicago River (then undredged and fordable at its mouth). She anchored there with the doom spreading through her cabins. Sixteen of her troops were already dead and buried in Lake Michigan. During the next five days eighty-eight more bodies slipped into the water. When word reached a fleet of schooners anchored along shore they made sail frantically and scattered like gulls over the lake. Within a few weeks cholera broke out in St. Louis and New Orleans.

So the great epidemic of the 1830's passed through America's waterways. It had begun in central India, and was carried, by way of Teheran, to Moscow. In the spring of 1831 it took thousands of lives in Warsaw and that autumn it ravaged Hamburg. A trading vessel carried it to England in October. In June of 1832 a British ship arrived in the St. Lawrence with a list of 145 immigrants, of whom forty-two had died of cholera during the passage. In the next four months it spread from Buffalo up the Great Lakes and down the Mississippi. Disease traveled the trade routes of the New World.

During that summer the dread of plague lingered over the little town of Chicago. The Indians heard of the scourge and sought the immunity that came from the powerful "English milk" that gurgled out of oaken barrels. A Potawatomi chief appeared at the Agency house, observing in his own tongue that he was a good man, a very good man, and a loyal friend of the Long Knives. Could he not then have a dram of whisky? The agent replied that he never gave whisky to good men: good men never asked for whisky or liked to drink it. Before he had finished that brief homily the Indian spoke in English. "Me dam rascal."

WAGON WHEELS IN THE RIGGING

Plague and Black Hawk's rebellion discouraged western travel in 1832, but in the following seasons it grew greater and greater. The fever of land speculation filled the steamers' plush cabins with merchants, promoters, and land sharks, while their decks were heaped with the household goods of immigrants crowded in the steerage. In 1836 more than three thousand canal boats plied the Erie Canal. They left Albany every hour of the day and night, jammed with immigrants and their belongings. During the single month of May ninety steamboats arrived at Detroit, one of them, the United States, bringing seven hundred new settlers to the West. In that year steamboat owners earned seventy to eighty per cent of the cost of their vessels.

With thousands of passengers waiting for space new and larger ships were inevitable. In 1838 appeared the handsome Great Western, the first lakes steamer with an exposed upper cabin. Two years later came the Vandalia, the first lake ship to be driven by a screw propeller. In the next few years came the famous Empire and the City of Cleveland, which sounded the first steam whistle on the lakes. The Empire, launched in Cleveland in 1844, was for a few years the largest steamship in the world. She was 254 feet long and would have been longer, her builders boasted, had there been a straight place on the Cuyahoga for her launching.

Charles Dickens took passage from Sandusky eastbound in the steamer Constellation in 1842. He found her "handsomely fitted up," but her high-pressure engines gave him the feeling that he was lodging on the first floor of a powder mill. The ship's cargo space was loaded with flour, and the captain, stopping to converse with Dickens, sat astride a flour barrel. He pulled out a clasp knife and began to whittle as he talked. He pared down the edges till Dickens was sure nothing would remain but grist and shavings. But then he was called to the bridge.

THE VANISHED FLEETS

Less impressive and more numerous were the self-styled immigrant boats. By 1840 immigrant travel was so great that a line of eight vessels engaged in that traffic alone, with sailings from Buffalo every other day. Five years later there were three daily lines between Buffalo and the western cities.

These ships were jammed to. the guard rails with families and their goods. Wagon beds were crowded on deck and wagon wheels were lashed, like life-buoys, up and down the rigging. In each of those wagon beds was a family's past, and the tokens of its future: beds and cradles, farm implements and kitchen goods, barrels of provisions and chests of clothing. Over the crowded deck swarmed the new Americans in their wadmal and homespun garments. There was a medley of many voices and varied tongues. Women nursed their babies, looking across at the changing shores of America. Children climbed over the wagon beds and sat on the high seat driving imaginary horses into an imagined country. Men talked gravely together about the counties of Wisconsin and Illinois and discussed the plowing of soil that was a dream in their minds.

Some of them never had their dream. On a clear summer night in 1841 the steamer Erie, bound from Buffalo to Chicago, shook with a terrific explosion. Her boiler had gone out, blowing a hole in her side and spreading flames through her lower parts. The ship was crowded with immigrants. As smoke poured through the cabins and companionways, the bewildered people struggled to the upper decks. Some leaped into the lurid waters of Lake Erie, others collapsed with the heat and suffocation. One hundred and seventy of them were lost with all their savings. Fourteen years later a salvage party towed the Erie's charred hull (sunk in fifty feet of water) to shore and recovered a fortune in foreign coins: sovereigns and rubles, marks and kroner that crossed the Atlantic to buy Wisconsin land.

These were dramatic years for the lake states. Between

1830 and 1840 the population of Michigan grew from 31,000 to 212,000, and in the decade following Wisconsin's population grew from 30,000 to beyond 300,000. Past Mackinac Island there went a continual flow of commerce, and the harbor was always full of vessels fueling cordwood. Glad to stretch their legs outside the cramped space of the crowded decks, the immigrants jogged up and down the gangway getting fuel wood aboard; and through the village streets walked merchants and bankers, army officers and congressmen, domestic and foreign visitors, ready to stream back to the dock at the captain's warning bell. The Chippewas on the Mackinac shore stared at them without comprehension.

The line of steamers running up the lakes from Buffalo was well known in western Europe. People who knew no other words of English spoke of the immigrant boats by name and referred to Milwaukee or Chicago as the place of rendezvous. A season or two later the folk of a Dutch market town or a German village were meeting again, after months of separation, on the shores of Lake Michigan. They thronged the lake ports, along with land agents, speculators, merchants, horse and cattle traders. With that growing tide of life many Wisconsin towns doubled their population in a single year and whole counties were settled in half a decade.

To keep step with the new population a pioneer telegraph line was striding westward along the shore of Lake Erie and across the state of Michigan. Colonel Speed, the construction engineer, felt the significance of his task, and as each segment of the line was completed he keyed out sonorous messages from new stations to the world back East. In 1847 the line to Chicago was nearing completion, and another line grew north from Chicago along the lake. When it was completed Colonel Speed addressed a triumphant message to "the people of Littleport, Southport, Racine and Milwaukee." Telegraph news appeared in the papers under the heading "By Lightning."

One of the first reports that flashed over those western wires was a story of disaster. In the gray light of a November daybreak the propeller steamer Phoenix, with two hundred passengers nearing the end of a long journey, was lost on Lake Michigan. That news caused mourning in the market towns of Holland, four thousand miles away.

A quarter of the way up the eastern shore of Lake Michigan are the towns of Holland, Borculo, Zeeland, New Holland and Vriesland. That settlement, dating from the middle 1840's, was the result of a reform movement within the Dutch State Church. When civil authorities in Holland clamped down on the reformers a movement took shape and a migration began much like that of the English Puritans to New England two hundred years earlier. "The Society of Christians for the Holland Emigration to the United States" directed freedom-loving Hollanders to the midlands of America. In the autumn of 1846 the first party sailed from Rotterdam to New York, and early in the following year the emigrants took title to a thousand acres of government land on the east shore of Lake Michigan. At the same time other Dutch colonies began to grow in Wisconsin and Iowa.

It was to join their relatives and friends in these colonies that a band of Dutch settlers left Buffalo on November 11, 1847. Happy to begin the final leg of their long journey they boarded the steamer Phoenix, under Captain G. B. Sweet. Their voyage was to become a part of Great Lakes history and legend.

These Hollanders were not poverty-ridden peasants, lured across the Atlantic by the promise of cheap land. They were substantial people from the fertile provinces of Gelderland and Overijssel. Some of them were moderately wealthy. According to report, the Geerlings family carried more than 100,000 guilders in their heavy chests. It was the desire for religious freedom, not the hope of gain, that brought them to America. They had a hymn, based on a psalm of David, to celebrate their arrival after many weeks on the way. It thanked God for providing "a path over the angry billows" and praised Him "for bringing us safe to shore." But few of them ever set foot on land again.

The Phoenix, owned by the prosperous Cleveland firm of Pease and Allen, was a strong new ship, just completing her second season of operation. On this trip she carried two hundred passengers, most of them Dutch immigrants, along with a cargo of coffee, sugar, molasses and hardware. She ran through heavy seas to Fairport, Ohio, at the mouth of Grand River, and there her troubles began. A fall on deck left Captain Sweet with an injured knee which confined him to his cabin. For the rest of the voyage the ship was in charge of First Officer Watts, a veteran lake man from Cleveland.

Uneventfully the Phoenix called at Cleveland and Detroit and sailed on up Lake Huron. In charmed weather the Dutch colonists walked up and down the deck, making a . ne noise with their wooden *klompen* and speculating on their arrival on the shores of Michigan. Around them romped the tow-headed little Dirks and Jans and Hendriks, and the little Johannas and Gerritjes and Katrinas with their blue eyes and sunny hair. They were a happy lot of Hollanders, journeying under the bright autumn skies of the New World that held their future.

But beyond the Straits of Mackinac November's winds were waiting. A gale roared across from Bay de Noc, pounding the ship with long gray seas. All day and all night the decks were swept with stinging spray, and the fuel wood ran low under the bunker hatches. On the afternoon of November twentieth the Phoenix put in to Manitowoc to replenish her fuel and to wait out the storm. The Holland men left their close quarters and gave a hand with loading the cordwood. In a few hours the wind quieted and out beyond the river mouth the sea went down.

Shortly after midnight, on Sunday, November twenty-first, the lines were cast off and the engines began to turn. Out on the dark lake the Phoenix showed her running lights and down in her boiler room the firemen were cramming their furnaces. At four o'clock smoke billowed through the engine room and seeped along the passageways. Half-dressed passengers hurried out of their cabins as the fire alarm clanged through the ship. They stood together on the deck with clouds of smoke around them. Soon firelight washed their faces. When the pumps failed the Hollanders lined up in bucket brigades beside the crew. They poured sea water into the blazing engine room. The flames licked at them angrily.

Seeing that the fire was out of control, Chief Officer Watts headed his ship toward shore. The lights of Sheboygan came into sight on the starboard quarter. Just five miles off was the long, dark shore line of Wisconsin. In a fierce light the two small boats were lowered. When they pulled away, out of the lurid tent of the ship's burning, two hundred persons were left without hope of escape. As the flames spread through the ship's middle section they retreated to the bow and stern. Chests, hatch covers, wooden bulkheads were thrown overboard. Soon desperate forms were leaping into the water and floundering after makeshift rafts. Daylight showed the shore line clearly, and no rescue craft approaching. There was only a choice between the fiery death of the Phoenix and the numbing death of Lake Michigan. One man climbed to the crosstrees on the foremast and wedged himself in the rigging. He died of heat and suffocation and at last came down with the burning mast. It hissed furiously in the water. Families leaped hand in hand into the sea and perished together. Other families were terribly separated. Voices cried against the roar and crashing of the flames. A mother went into a smoking passageway to get a wrap for her child. She never came out again. Some prayed and some wept and some dropped quietly into the sea.

From Sheboygan harbor Captain Porter of the schooner

Liberty saw a ship burning like a torch in the gray November dawn. Lacking a fair wind he manned his lifeboat and soon his crew were pulling their arms out in an errand of rescue. As soon as she could get up steam the side-wheeler Delaware hurried out of the harbor. By daylight all Sheboygan had gathered on the shore and scores of small boats were putting out to the fiery Phoenix. The Delaware was the first to arrive. But she was too late. Already the gutted Phoenix was burning out and there were but three survivors to take away, clinging in the icy water to the ship's rudder chains. The Delaware picked up some floating bodies and took the smoking wreck in tow.

Those in the Phoenix two lifeboats had their own perils. One boat got away with but a single oar and was propelled on the starboard side with a broom. Both were overcrowded; they made poor headway and shipped water constantly. The Hollanders baled them out with wooden shoes. It was a numb and exhausted party that at last reached the bonfires kindled for them on the shore. The sun rising over the impassive, empty lake found them huddled there. Forty-three out of two hundred and fifty were saved.

The gaunt and blackened Phoenix was towed to the north pier at Sheboygan, where she sank in eight feet of water. Part of the hardware in her holds was salvaged, along with some fire-scarred coins that circulated that season in the town. The survivors were brought in wagons to Sheboygan, where they were given care and shelter by the townspeople. All up and down the Wisconsin shore sympathies poured out generously. In Milwaukee collections were taken in the churches and committees were appointed to aid the bereft Hollanders.

That somber Sunday afternoon the steamer Delaware, making her regular run to Manitowoc, passed scores of floating bodies. Captain Tuttle, thinking that other boats would come out to search those waters, did not stop. As snowstorms and winter winds struck Lake Michigan soon after, the bodies were never recovered.

For a season after the holocaust of the Phoenix, immigration from Holland was halted. But there was a destiny about the movement of settlers to the western country, and it went on despite disaster. New multitudes journeyed over the lakes in the grim years that closed the 1840's—grim for peoples of the Old World with the famine in Ireland and the unsuccessful revolution in Germany. In growing numbers they flocked to Wisconsin, which had no state debt and allowed aliens to vote after one year's residence. Milwaukee received as many as three thousand in a single week. All day long, wagon trains rattled off to the interior and new Americans in the homespun caps and bright peasant costumes of lands 4000 miles away traveled toward the sunset.

Around them lay a wide world, devoid of history, waiting for the men and events that would give it a nation's character. Senses were quickened and minds stirred by this transplanting; it was an experience like religion and like love. Leaving the confinements and restraints of a familiar life and adopting a strange country, months distant, with a new geography, new climate, new people and new thoughts—no one could keep a tight and settled mind through such a change as that. Curiosity kindled in their eyes, observation sharpened; there were fresh instincts for a new world, and there were minds, lifted out of old worn paths, ready to travel new roads or to travel where there were no roads at all.

One of that company arrived in America as a boy of eleven years, old enough to see the New World in the light of the re-membered one and young enough for a complete rebirth. On a spring day in 1849 John Muir, a thin Scotch boy with quick blue eyes and a thatch of sandy hair, was waiting on the wharf at Buffalo to board the big lake boat for Milwaukee. With him were his father, Daniel Muir, his brother David and his sister Sarah. His mother and four other children were left in Scotland till a house should be built for them somewhere in the vague spaces of America. For eight weeks this advance delegation of the Muir family had been on the way; they were six and a half weeks crossing the Atlantic. The gray ocean was printed in the boy's memory, a vast, solemn journey that had cut him off forever from the world of his childhood. He would not be a Scotch lad again.

In fine weather on that vessel the emigrants had gathered on deck, singing *The youthful sailor frank and bold*, and *Oh, why I left my hame, why did I cross the deep;* and on stormy days they sat around the long bare table in the steerage, calling the ship "the auld rockin' creel" and talking about America. Daniel Muir was a stern man, steeped in the Bible. Bad weather moved him to quote somber passages which made his fellow travelers avoid him. *The Lord sent out a great wind onto the sea, and there was a mighty tempest in the sea, so that the ship was like to be broken. . . . The wicked are like the troubled sea that cannot rest. There is no peace saith my God to the wicked. . . .* But when the wind died and the sea was quiet some of the sternness left his face and he was as eager as any to speculate about America.

He was bound, he thought, for Canada, where some of his Firth neighbors had settled in the new country beyond Lake Ontario. But these emigrants spoke of the rough country there.

"Miles of brush and woods, Mister Muir. Hundreds of miles, even. It takes years to bring a field under cultivation. All that country is rough, and bitter cold."

"No new country is easy," said Daniel Muir.

"We're told that Michigan and Wisconsin are more favorable. And the journey is easy there. By boat on the lakes from Buffalo."

Daniel Muir read his Bible by the poor light of a ship's lantern, but his thoughts got to wandering. Canada . . . Wisconsin . . . Michigan . . . He was not a man who gave up an idea easily.

At New York he herded his children into a boat up the Hudson and through the canal to Buffalo. There, still undecided, he saw the grain fleet. Schooners were crowded at the wharves, three, four, five abreast, with their hatches open and the prime wheat lying there for any wondering immigrant to stare at. He heard men talking about other fleets of vessels, hundreds of them, carrying grain up Lake Ontario to Kingston and Oswego, where the waterfront was walled by elevators heaped to the rafters with rich grain. But there was enough right under his nose to keep Daniel Muir staring. Tons and tons of wheat, thousands of tons, more than a Scotch farmer could see in all his life, in all the harvests of thin Scotch fields for many years. Men jumped into the holds and waded knee-deep in that wheat. They scooped it up with shovels, singing while they worked. They lost some of it in the water and spilled it on the dock, as though there were untold quantities where it came from.

Daniel Muir asked a schooner captain, standing feet apart above the open hatchway. He had to repeat his question, because his Scotch was as thick as sheep's wool.

"Where does that grain come from?" roared the captain. "It comes from Wisconsin. Loaded at the port of Milwaukee."

Daniel Muir kept staring.

"Yes, it's good wheat. Good plump kernels, and hard, too." He picked up a handful, cut a kernel with his thumbnail to show the meaty body, then tossed the rest into his mouth and began chewing. "Mighty good wheat," he said thickly. "But no better than they send out every season."

That decided it. Daniel Muir took passage to Milwaukee and carried his goods onto the steamboat. It was a back-breaking job—big, iron-bound boxes that weighed up to four hundred pounds. He was a thorough man, and he had brought a

lot of gear when he left Scotland. One of those boxes contained a complete set of beam scales with a series of counter-
weights, two of fifty-six pounds, one of twenty-eight, and on
down to a single pound. He was bound he would be able to
weigh a hog or a calf out there in the wilderness of America.
In another box he had a full set of carpenters' tools, including
a variety of iron wedges. Now at Buffalo he bought a big
iron stove, kettles and pots and pans, a scythe, a cumbersome
cradle for cutting grain, and some hundreds of pounds of
provisions. A man had to trust God for salvation, but he need
not go to a wild place like Wisconsin empty-handed. Having
got all this gear aboard, he guided his children up the gangplank. The long journey was nearing its end.

Day after day from the steamer's deck young John Muir
saw the fields of Ohio and Michigan go by. It was only a few
hours' journey across all of Scotland, from the Firth of Forth
to Clydemouth, but here the land went on and on, like the
ocean. At Mackinac he saw Indians, the furs of unknown
animals, and bark wigwams standing against the forest. America was endless and it had many faces. The Indians told a
story of a young wolf who set out to cross the land. He loped
over great tracts of field and forest and mountain; he went on
for many seasons and died of old age before he reached the
end. The yielding borders of a boy's mind opened wider on
that journey to Wisconsin.

In the noisy streets of Milwaukee, where the immigrants
thronged the land office and set out westward, Daniel Muir
found a farmer ready to return to Fort Winnebago in the
southern prairies of the state. He had brought a load of wheat
to the docks and was about to drive back in an empty wagon.
For thirty dollars he agreed to haul Daniel Muir, his children
and his goods a hundred miles west to the town of Kingston.
The prairies had not yet dried after the winter snows, and
under Daniel Muir's load the groaning wagon sank hub deep
in the mire. The horses lunged into their collars and the men

put their shoulders to the mud-caked wheels. John Muir, already feeling the responsibility of a new country, pushed beside them. The wagon moved on. Though the farmer declared he would never again contract to haul a settler's goods, they reached Kingston with the load intact. Soon Daniel Muir had located an attractive farm site in a sunny oak opening beside a small lake.

That summer John Muir walked hundreds of miles behind an ox team. In his father's plow fields, with wondering eyes and an ardor for discovery, he began to be American. All the borders of the farm were wild. There were open beechwoods where the great flights of passenger pigeons made their roost; there were valleys threaded by a dim Indian trail where after a long day's work a boy could lie still in the twilight, hearing the song of the hermit thrush and the vesper sparrow and watching the owls, slow-winged, under the August stars. There was the lake with its cool depths where a boy could learn to swim, and its weedy shallows where the frogs bellowed under the rushes and the red-winged blackbirds sang. When autumn brought the great bird migration those waters were the resting place of ducks and herons, swans and pelicans and cranes, wilderness birds of strange grace and wonderful plumage. To a boy with a quick eye and a trembling spirit the whole country was enthralling. For miles around his father's fields the land lay wild and beautiful, wood and swamp and plain unmarked by a shod hoof or a wagon wheel.

All his life John Muir was excited by landscape. He remembered Scotland as a set of pictures. There was the gray winter village, haunted like a shell by the sound of ocean on the broken coasts. On stormy days the salt spray flung up the rocks onto the school yard, even dashing the windows of the schoolroom where a boy sat behind his geography book, wondering about the far places of the world. From the school ground the sea stretched out, with the ships passing. A boy could study their rig, draw pictures of them in his Latin reader, and speculate on what ports they had sailed from and where they were going. In the summer there was freedom to wander the meadows and the moors, to climb the highest ridges and look over many miles of Scotland and the sea. The boys of that village had a game to play, lying on their backs and staring up at the sky where the larks were singing. The game was to follow the lark in its flight, to see who could follow it farthest, higher and higher and higher, till it was a speck in the blue. John Muir often won that competition. He had fine far vision.

Now in America his eyes were sharp for all the life of the wilderness. While he guided a plow across his father's fields his mind was ranging. At the end of the row, where he let the oxen breathe, he searched the oak boughs for a squirrel's quickness or a warbler's color. He was moved by the American landscape and he could not hear enough of its distant regions, forests and plains and mountains that no scientist had ever entered. A few years later he walked from Lake Michigan to the Gulf of Mexico, making the first careful study of the flora and the physiography of the great valley of the Mississippi. Then he turned to the West, to discover California's wildest valleys and to explore whole ranges from Mexico to Alaska. He sat around campfires in the high meadows of Yosemite with Teddy Roosevelt and met with Congressional commissions for the founding of the national forests. One man's efforts began the nation's first significant policy of conservation. The immigrant boats had brought a boy who left his mark on America.

In the middle years of the century the old lake passenger trade reached its climax. A series of splendid liners, the Western World, the Plymouth Rock, the Western Metropolis and others almost as magnificent set a new standard for luxury travel. These vessels were over three hundred feet long and had three hundred staterooms, with rosewood bedsteads, marble-topped washstands and embroidered lounging-chairs. They vied with each other for the most fashionable clientele. Captain Howe of the Chesapeake wintered regularly in New Orleans and attracted some of the leading families of the South to travel on his ship in the summer months. Down the lakes they voyaged with music and sports and dancing. Games of brag, with columns of gold coins on the tables, went on night and day, and there were midnight suppers of baked terrapin and roast young prairie chicken. In the ballroom colored waiters sang to their guitars:

Old Huron's long, old Huron's wide,
De engine keep de time,
Leabe de ladies on de side
And balance in a line—

and a marine engine marked the beat for a Virginia reel.

But lean years overtook the big liners. A sailing vessel had carried the first locomotive to Chicago in 1837. That was prophetic cargo. Fifteen years later the railroads reached from the seaboard to the Mississippi and the steamboat men had a rate-war on their hands. Then the financial panic of 1857 hit the big ships with more force than the storms of Lake Michigan or the winds of Thunder Bay. When the Civil War paralyzed the passenger trade many of the biggest liners were broken up. Their engines were salvaged to install in smaller vessels, and their gutted hulls were turned into drydocks that served the needs of humbler ships at Buffalo, Cleveland and Bay City.

One of the liners felt a panic grimmer than bankruptcy. On the night of August 20, 1852, the palatial Atlantic was running in dense fog six miles off Long Point in Lake Erie, westward bound. Head on, through the fog and night came the new propeller-driven Ogdensburg. The lookouts never glimpsed disaster. There was no cry of warning, only a sudden impact and the grinding of wooden timbers. The Ogdens-burg's bow drove into the liner's port side, just forward of the paddle-box. Quickly the Atlantic filled with water. Her five hundred passengers, including two hundred Norwegian im-migrants in the steerage, swarmed through the flooding passageways. Overboard they threw benches, chairs, tables —anything that would float. Then they leaped into the fog-shrouded waters. In the gray daylight the Ogdensburg saved 250 of them before the big liner, with seven pennants on her staffs, sank in thirty fathoms of water. But 250 other lives were lost. Many of those Norwegians from the steep farms of Stavanger and Christiansund never saw the broad prairies of the West.

At the panic of 1857 there were 106 side-wheel steamers on the lakes, 135 propeller-driven steamers, and slightly more than a thousand sailing vessels of all types. Most of them car-ried on through financial stress and the war to come, but the plush and rosewood liners could not be maintained. It was nearly twenty years before the next big passenger vessels took the water. Then they appeared in new design, with iron hulls, soon to give way to steel, and with propeller blades re-placing the old clumsy paddle-boxes.

Again, in this new age, there were famous ships. In the seven-ties a Buffalo man, Edwin Townsend Evans, a driving figure in the panorama of the lakes, built three palatial sister ships: India, China, and Japan. Today the India, a converted barge, deep laden with iron ore, tows humbly past Detroit where once every whistle saluted her as she swept through with her pen-nants flying. Later came the famous Christopher Columbus, the only whaleback passenger vessel ever built. She carried hundreds of thousands to that vast and splendid circus, the World's Fair of 1893, at its frontage on Lake Michigan. There were the two fine ships of Jim Hill, the empire builder—the North West and the Northland, with their white hulls and their three raked stacks; in the nineties they were the pride of inland waters. The twentieth century has brought new and larger vessels, the sleek North American and South American, the mammoth four-stacked Seeandbee that is too wide to pass the locks at the Soo, and the big fast liners Greater Buffalo and Greater Detroit.

But the shores have been bordered for ninety years by railroad lines, and for thirty years by motor highways, and the lanes of commerce are no longer limited to the navigator's course between Buffalo Light and Pelee Passage, or between Grays Reef Light and the Chicago River. The passenger ships are cruise ships now, or they save motorists a day's drive on the busy highways of the midlands. They no longer have steerage quarters below decks and wagon wheels lashed to the shrouds.

The lakes have had many trades, from baled peltry to cargoes of motor cars, but none so prophetic as that stream of immigrants. The Irish and the Germans, the Norwegians and the Swedes, the Cornishmen and the Finns, the Slovaks and the Italians, they opened up whole empires so that the timber, the ore and the grain could go down in ever growing volume. It is fitting that the lakes carried them to the West.

Sitting on deck, with the masts weaving slowly against the sky, they were thinking. All they had heard of America was in their minds while they watched those changing shores. There were the low green fields of Ohio with farmers striding behind their horses, the wooded islands, the populous river banks, the wide fields of Michigan, and the forests darkening in the north. All they had heard of America—the words of a letter read in a farmhouse in a steep Norwegian valley, the pages of a printed pamphlet circulated in a parish of Sweden, the voice of a schoolmaster in Denmark, a steamship folder passed from hand to hand in the market stalls of Prague, a priest's sober words in an Irish trading town.

There is much land that has never known a plow. It is good deep land and yields richly when it is farmed right. After the first seasons a man can be sure of a substantial income. He can buy machinery and put big fields under cultivation. You will hardly believe that all your farm in Nessdal is not so big as my smallest grain field. We are not now in wild country but nearer to town than you are and on a level road.

So, hour after hour, they stared at the shores of America, trying to see it all, trying to see what was beyond that shore line and what the future would bring. Some of them came from the flat fields under the dykes of Holland, some from the windswept plains of Russia, the hill towns of Norway, the cobbled streets of old cities on the Elbe and the Danube, the gray moors of Scotland and the green Irish valleys. The memory of old lands was in their thoughts. The lilting songs of Ireland and the sad songs of Russia went over Lake Huron when the nightfall came. But more urgent, more exciting, were the thoughts of new land, fair and fertile, their minds slowly believing in it as their journey went on, day after day, through a wide and waiting country.

Around them on the ship, and from the busy wharves in the rivers, they heard the American voices, workmen laughing together and answering the captain like equals. You might not understand the language, but there was something else. . . . *A man can more easily come to something here than in the Old Country. In this country everyone is called "you" no matter who he is, even the schoolmaster and the pastor. Even the president, also. One is not obliged to take off his cap to anyone. When a man is at a strange table they say "Help juselfs," and so also in other things.*

The wagon wheels lined against the bulkheads and lashed to the shrouds would take them many places. The old man with leaden rings in his ears, tearing tobacco apart and tamping it in his clay pipe, wondered whether American horses could learn to answer a man who spoke in a strange tongue. The mother with a baby in her arms and a child playing at her feet realized with wonder and a sudden pain that her children would speak a new language that could never be her own. Men with brown gnarled hands thought about land that they would work and own, men who had not owned a rod of land, or their fathers before them in many generations. The wrinkled old woman with a red comforter around her shoulders wondered what kind of burying ground people could have in a raw country.

The way by water was a good way to enter America. Night and day the land slipped by, distant and changing, certain but withheld. They could watch and wonder; their minds could grasp it slowly. By degrees it made real the promises that brought them across a wide ocean. *A man can make four Norwegian dollars a day, working on the canal with a shovel, or swinging an ax in the woods.* They remembered how in the other world a woman would go out sweeping or baking or digging potatoes in the fields for six cents a day, how the crofters did their statutory work for eight cents and a midday meal of porridge, how a man would cut wood and drag it over the snow for twelve cents a day, and be glad of that. *He can soon get enough money together to put himself in a small business or to buy animals and take up land.*

Many landscapes were behind those faces, but all were fading into a common picture. Beyond the blue waters, in the unseen country, was the place where they would mark the corners of their land. There would be hardship and uncertainty, sickness and toil, but there would also be freedom, equality, opportunity, participation. To them America meant something that existed nowhere else in the world.

So, eager and bewildered, ardent and homesick, singing their Old World songs on the crowded deck, counting their coins in secret, staring and staring at the shores of America with its teeming cities and its tracts of lonely land—they were journeying into new country and the future was in their eyes.

CHAPTER ELEVEN

Kingdom in Lake Michigan

WHEN HE QUIT salt water in 1873 Captain Charley Allers went to live on Beaver Island at the head of Lake Michigan. A few years ashore were enough for him; then he took to the lake in his famous schooner "Extenuate," with the name spelled X-10-U-8 on her stem and under her sloping fantail. He had borrowed the name from a saloon on 35th Street in Chicago.

Charley Allers and his X-10-U-8 were familiar in Lake Michigan ports for many years. He operated like a Yankee peddler, "lake-shoring" from port to port. He would buy a load of posts and sell them at Milwaukee, then load with flour to sell to the storekeepers on the Manitou Islands where he would take on a load of potatoes to sell to the highest bidder at Chicago; from there a load of dressed pork to Muskegon, then a load of fruit to hawk on the waterfront at Menominee, and down to Racine with tanbark under his hatches and a deckload of poles. He got around the lake pretty thoroughly. Perhaps it was his salt-water vocabulary that made people call him "the atheist of Beaver Island."

There are twelve of the Beaver Islands, of which Big Beaver, twelve miles by six, is the largest. Others are Garden Island, Hog, High, Gull, Squaw, Whisky, Trout and the classic pair, Paros and Patmos. The waters are traditionally good fishing; they are the home of the famous Mackinaw trout. Now a few hundred Irish fishermen, along with some Ottawa and Chippewa Indians, live on Big Beaver and conduct a prosperous fishing business. But the islands are famous not for fish nor for Charley Allers. They are famous for an episode of ninety years ago when James Jesse Strang, the only crowned king in all America, ruled over a colony of Mormons.

James Jesse Strang was born in 1813 among the hills and waters of western New York state. In his early years he suffered ill health which, though he outgrew that weakness, left him self-contained and surly. As a young man he had dreams of grandeur which seemed out of keeping with his slight stature, his slovenly dress and his blunt, stubborn, undistinguished face. The one remarkable thing in his appearance was a torch-red beard, and his single gift was a scathing power of oratory which withered his opponents in the debating societies around Chautauqua, New York.

Restless and energetic, he turned from one pursuit to another in those years. He read law and was admitted to the bar in 1836. He served five years as a village postmaster. For two years he owned and edited a small newspaper.

In 1843, when the Erie Canal was a highway teeming with settlers bound for the far shores of the Great Lakes, Strang moved to southern Wisconsin. He settled at Burlington, in Walworth County, near the home of his wife's family. There he found his brother-in-law, Moses Smith, an ardent Mormon. Before long Strang himself expressed some interest in the cult. But he was never a half-way man, he was either hot or cold, and to learn more about the Mormons he went in February of 1844, walking across a hundred miles of wintry prairie, to the Mormon center of Nauvoo, Illinois, on the banks of the Mississippi. There something happened to him. Though cold winds swept down the ice-filled Mississippi, Strang found his spirit burning fiercely. Something about the Mormon theology, the finality of its revelation and the discipline of its order, appealed to this restless, brooding man. In two weeks he was baptized by Joseph Smith himself, the founder of the movement, and sealed by the keys of the priesthood. Soon he was made an elder. Six months later, when Joseph Smith was killed by a mob at Carthage, Illinois, Strang announced a visitation from the angels of God who instructed him to become leader of the Mormons in their fallen leader's place. Further, he produced a letter, purportedly written by Joseph Smith, assigning Strang as his successor. When the Mormon Council, headed by Brigham Young, denied his claim and drove him out of Nauvoo, Strang led a contingent of his followers to Voree, near Burlington, Wisconsin, where they took up land. Strang claimed personal visions and revelations, including a series of copper plates whose inscriptions only he, in secret, could translate. These signs of God's approval filled his followers with missionary zeal. They made converts and their numbers grew.

At Voree, Strang established a tithing system, founded an official paper, planned a tabernacle and ordered a home for himself at the expense of the saints. But there was growing friction between his colony and the stubborn Gentiles around them, and Strang began to look for a better location. In the spring of 1847 he visited Beaver Island in the northern waters of Lake Michigan. It was a fertile island, twenty miles removed from the mainland, with abundant stone and timber and excellent fishing in the surrounding waters. This seemed the place—and in 1849 he began the removal of his colony to Big Beaver Island. They took up farming, fishing, and built a dock where they offered cordwood for sale to passing steamers.

Away from the distracting life of the frontier, with its currents of change and development, the Mormons proceeded to set up their social and religious order. They named their town St. James, in honor of Strang, their leader. An island creek they called the Jordan, a rough hill became Mt. Pisgah, a pond the Sea of Galilee. Beside the "Jordan" they built a mill which ground their grain and sawed their lumber.

On July 8, 1850, James Jesse Strang was crowned King of Beaver Island in a grotesque ceremony which involved numerous revelations that came to Strang in private. For his coronation he wore a red robe, discarded by a Shakesperean actor, and a metal crown. When the ceremony was done his subjects sang hosannas that carried far out over the blue water. In addition to his title of King, Strang was proclaimed Apostle, Prophet, Seer, Revelator and Translator.

Strang promptly exercised this varied office with decrees, based on fresh revelations, prohibiting the use of liquor, tea, coffee and tobacco, and instituting polygamy. The plan of polygamy King Strang had already adopted for himself, though secretly. A year before, he had induced one of his young schoolteachers, Elvira Field, to cut her long black hair and wear masculine dress and in that disguise to accompany him on his missionary campaigns. She traveled as his nephew, "Charles J. Douglas." Acting upon his proclamation in 1850 Strang installed four wives, two of them under eighteen years, in his whitewashed cottage on the hill above St. James harbor. His followers accepted the polygamous principle, but poverty and a dearth of unmarried women prevented most of them from its practice. Meanwhile Strang consolidated his kingdom. He built a tabernacle, established schools, debating clubs, a well-equipped printing shop called the Royal Press and a daily newspaper, *The Northern Islander*. From the Royal Press came *The Book of the Law of the Lord*, which served as a final authority on all social and theological matters. He set up a whipping post in a public place for the punishment of violators.

In Biblical imagery *The Book* gave precepts for the spiritual life of his subjects and also for such temporal affairs as diet, attire (women were to wear blouses and pantalets), construction of roads and houses, care of forests and draining of swamps. Whoever might question its divine origin had to admit that its author had a wide range of information.

Actually Strang was a student of broad interests and an accomplished naturalist. He contributed to the Smithsonian Institution a report on the Natural History of Beaver Island and wrote a sound, mundane book on "Ancient and Modern Michilimackinac." He found time to read in his well-stocked library and to carry on a varied correspondence, as well as to direct the growth of his movement and rule over the temporal and spiritual life of his kingdom.

The colony grew to two thousand, most of them primitive and ignorant people. Strang's hold on them is understandable:

he was shrewd, bold, widely informed, and he had a fanatic's gift of oratory. But there were stubborn fishermen on Whisky Point across the harbor of St. James and on the outlying islands who resented the presence of the Mormons and suspected their character. They told scandalous stories of what went on among the saints and occasionally they used force to prevent the Mormons from taking up new lands. Strang planned on military encounters with these Gentiles. He planted a cannon on his own hilltop to defend his harbor.

As the Mormons continued to gain in number and in territory their fame went out to the mainland and stories of their violence and cupidity were told by sailors in distant ports of the lakes. They were hated and feared all over the northern shores of Lake Michigan. Vessels rounding Grays Reef or Garden Island Shoal doubled their lookout and stared with mingled curiosity and distrust at the low-lying islands. There were stories of vessels boarded by Mormon "pirates," their crews murdered and their cargoes carried ashore.

Complaints were made to the United States government. In time officials became convinced that the charge of piracy was true, and further, that the islanders had robbed U.S. mails, cut government timber and harbored counterfeiters. So on a cloudless May day in 1851 the U.S.S. Michigan, the only gunboat on the lakes, appeared in St. James harbor and arrested Strang and twelve of his followers. At Detroit Strang, once a lawyer, pleaded his own case as one "persecuted for righteousness' sake." The little man with the fiery beard and the burning eyes had not lost the hypnotic power of his oratory. He was acquitted. With his followers he returned victoriously to Beaver Island, where his subjects received him with an ovation that carried far across the lake.

Perhaps that vindication enlarged Strang's ambition and made him dissatisfied with an island kingdom. Or perhaps he shrewdly planned to take over authority from those who had incited the government against him. At any rate he prepared a political campaign and in the fall of 1851 he carried the elections in Emmet (Mackinaw) County. Then within the fold of the Mormon Church were the new sheriff, prosecutor and other county officials. They proceeded to remove the county seat to St. James. Then in 1853 Strang had himself elected to the Michigan legislature. He went to Lansing and served with vigor and ability. So for two years he enjoyed a dual political life, ruling his people at home and representing them in a republican government at the capital.

But opposition was developing within the kingdom. Some of the women rebelled against wearing the bloomer costume he had ordained. The men grew restless under his stern treatment of tea drinkers and users of tobacco. They preferred charges which in June of 1856 brought the return of the U.S.S. Michigan to St. James harbor. The master of the gunboat sent ashore for Strang. But the king was not taken into custody again. As he stepped onto the pier two of his own subjects sprang from behind a woodpile and fired at him point-blank. Strang fell, mortally wounded. His assailants surrendered to the gunboat and were taken to Mackinac Island. There they were received with cheers and treated like heroes. They were never put on trial.

Strang, wounded beyond hope of recovery, was taken to Voree, Wisconsin, where in the company of two of his wives he died. He left them, Betsy McNutt and Phoebe Wright, each about to have a child. Two other posthumous children were born to his remaining wives, Elvira Field and Sarah Wright.

Meanwhile on Beaver Island the Mormons were feeling the wrath of the surrounding Gentiles. Legends surround the story of their dispersal, as they surround the six-year rule of King Strang. One story is that the body of a murdered woman drifting in a canoe to the mainland aroused the fury of the Gentiles. Probably no explanation is needed. For years the Strangites had been feared and hated: now the leader was dying and it was time to drive out his people. From neighboring islands and mainland came an armed mob, converging on the island in canoes, skiffs, scows and sailing craft. They burned Strang's tabernacle, sacked the "Royal Press," destroyed the king's extensive library and pillaged his house. The saints were driven off the islands and their homesteads seized.

With Strang's death came the end of his church. His love of power had prevented him from naming a successor, even though he knew he was dying. His followers scattered and made no attempt to revive the social or religious order in which they had lived on Beaver Island. Gradually Strang's name became forgotten, except on the shores of Lake Michigan and in the fo'c'sles of lakes vessels where the legends of King Strang and the Mormon pirates were to flourish for many years.

Today the Beaver Islands hump peacefully out of the blue-green waters of Lake Michigan. St. James, still bearing the prophet-ruler's name, is a quiet village of Irish fishermen and farmers. Across the harbor a tall stone lighthouse, flashing its fixed red light, rises on Whisky Point toward which Strang used to fire cannon balls at the Gentiles. The print shop (later converted into a hotel) from which came the sacred *Book of the Law of the Lord* still stands on the King's Highway, that runs through the town and across the island, and villagers point out, with considerable inaccuracy, the site of the kingdom's whipping post and the dock where Strang was assassinated. At several places on the island are ruins of Mormon homes and communities which have never been rebuilt. Visitors to St. James can stop at the King Strang Hotel, a relatively recent accommodation.

The island has a Roman Catholic church and convent, founded in 1863 by priests who accompanied the Irish immigrants. On the church grounds, at a high point overlooking the shore, is the Church Hill Weather Tower, which serves local fishermen and lake steamers. The tower is manned by a priest, who receives weather reports from the Coast Guard and transmits them by signals to the lake traffic. On stormy days the people of St. James watch those pennants anxiously; nearly every family has members in the fishing fleets.

King Strang was buried at Burlington, Wisconsin, two hundred and fifty miles away. Over the grave of the only crowned monarch in America is a plain marker bearing the inscription

JAMES J. STRANG

1813–56.

After Strang's death Captain Charley Allers, the atheist of the islands, was their best known citizen. His home port was the harbor of St. James, and he often sailed his X-10-U-8 along the storied shores. No one ever reported what he thought of the king who reigned there twenty years before his time. He could have supplied an interesting epitaph.

III

THIRD PART

A STAR TO STEER BY

CHAPTER TWELVE

The Fleet That Sailed on Land

A HUNDRED YEARS AGO the St. Mary's rapids ran loud over the rocks and the Chippewas shot their canoes through the eddies with cries that rang along the shore. There was fabulous fishing then: two Indian fishermen could scoop up a canoe load of whitefish in an hour. The town ran aimlessly along the portage trail. The population was five hundred—French, half-breeds and some Indians.

This was the town that William Cullen Bryant found when he visited the Soo in 1846. The author of "Thanatopsis" may have been reminded of the solemn Berkshire Hills of his boyhood as he strolled through that frontier settlement. All around lay forest and water and overhead arched the pale, clear northern sky. Nature dwarfed that little cluster of habitations.

There were two small hotels, Joshua Van Anden's "Van Anden House" and the St. Mary's Hotel kept by Moses Stevens. In the summer a few travelers, like William Cullen Bryant, curious and a little silenced by the primal nature of the North, mingled with the handful of fur traders and the officers from the uneventful post of Fort Brady. The winter was a long and silent siege when no strange face appeared. It held the waters tight and buried the land in incredible snow. Then the country was desolate, hostile, grimly splendid, locked in cold.

In that long season, social life consisted of dances at the homes of half-breeds who had unmarried daughters. The music was furnished by an old French fiddler known up and down the St. Mary's as "Excuse a la cord." He always broke a fiddle string at the height of the gay French tunes, and he was polite and apologetic while he mended the cord and dusted his bow with rosin. Soon he was sawing the tune again and the shod boots thumped on the floor. In the lamplight white teeth shone and eyes were lighted with the music. A man's rough hand around a girl's slim waist, and their feet keeping the time together.

A STAR TO STEER BY

Lon, lon laridon daine,
Lon, lon laridon dai!

The maple logs glowed in the iron stove. There were coffee and rum and hard-crusted French bread and the reek of black tobacco. Outside, the cold stars glittered over the snows, and the northern lights played their ghostly splendor above the Canadian hills.

On such a winter night a half-breed named La Branche was offered a bonus to make a trip on snowshoes from the Soo to Mackinac and return in thirty hours. It was a lifeless frozen country where men had perished. Their bodies, gnawed by wolves, were found months afterward. But La Branche swung along with his tireless snowshoe stride, leaving a broken path under the snow-hung cedars and across the mounded hills. At last that single path struck straight across the ice to Mackinac. There he ate a plate of fish and swallowed a pot of coffee. Then in the pale light of day he was on his way again. There was no sun that day. The cold intensified. Hour after hour he swung through lifeless country, marked only by the hurrying track of his own snowshoes. The branches creaked. From the ridges came the quaver of the wolves. La Branche swung his arms and chafed his hands inside his mittens. Under the waning sky he saw a familiar rise of land before him. He reached Coalpit Hill before dusk and looked down on the scattered town beside the frozen river. There he waited for two hours in order not to get back to the commissary before the expiration of his time; his bonus called for a trip in thirty hours and he wasn't going to risk it by arriving in twenty-eight. He danced all that night at a half-breed neighbor's house.

In that year, 1846, Sheldon McKnight and his old gray horse hauled every pound of freight that passed between Lake Huron and Lake Superior. He had a two-wheeled French cart, one of the famous Red River carts of the northwest fur traders, and in its bed he carried the peltry, the traps, the arms and ammunition, the whisky, pork, flour and tobacco that made up the Soo's first commerce.

There had been vessels on Lake Superior since the early 1800's. The North West Company and the Hudson's Bay Company had built small schooners, twenty to a hundred tons: the Discovery, Invincible, Otter, Mink, Recovery. They had lonely missions, sailing the vast expanses and the unmapped shores of that mysterious lake, making the rounds of the fur stations and a few scattered Indian villages. They had a perilous life. The Invincible was wrecked on Whitefish Point before 1823; Discovery and Otter were both lost in the attempt to run the St. Mary's rapids. Indian canoes could shoot the rapids, darting through the eddies with wild cries from the paddlers, but it was risky business for a sailing vessel. Captain Henry Wolsey Bayfield of the British Navy used the Mink to make the first rude survey of Lake Superior in 1823–5. Cautiously she rounded the capes and threaded the islands and entered all the coves from Whitefish Bay to the St. Louis River. Shortly after Captain Bayfield had completed his rough charts the little vessel went ashore in a gale and broke up on the Canadian shore above St. Mary's rapids. She was the property of the Hudson's Bay Company. The Recovery, belonging to the North West Company, lived a charmed life. During the War of 1812 she was hidden in one of the deep narrow bays of Isle Royale. Her spars were removed and her decks covered with evergreen boughs and brushwood. With ice frozen around her and snow drifting over, she looked as harmless as a blown-down tree. When peace returned to Lake Superior she was recommissioned, and for years she carried peltry and provisions between the Soo and the scattered posts. In 1829 she made a safe run over the rapids and into Lake Huron. That was a rare feat, and a remarkable one for a schooner of ninety tons. In the rushing current her masts swayed wildly. Her bow reeled and plunged. She trembled in the eddies. But a strong and nervy hand was on her wheel and sharp voices cried from her bow. She took the last swift chute with her spars leaning and coasted clear into the deep current below the falls. She was a sturdy ship, built of the spruce, pine and tamarack that line the shores of Lake Superior. She ended her days on the lower lakes.

From 1829–35 there were only the flat-bottomed bateaux and the heavy mackinaw boats on Lake Superior. The vast cold lake seemed too lonely and remote to support the navigation that was making busy waterways of the Detroit River and the Straits of Mackinac. But there was a commerce waiting. There were furs to carry, trading posts to provision, and a growing rumor of copper on the mysterious Isle Royale and the great humped cape of Keweenaw that thrusts into the heart of Lake Superior. In 1835 at the rude shipyard of the Soo, on the site of today's Sherman Park, the American Fur Trading Company built a schooner of 113 tons, the John Jacob Astor. She stuck midway on the skids when they launched her, but after three days of hard work she was floated free. In the middle of August she sailed into Lake Superior under Captain Stannard.

There were three Stannard brothers and they were famous navigators on Lake Superior in those years. Captains C. C., John J., and B. A. Stannard successively manned the Astor. They found that sailing Lake Superior was a different business from plying the trade routes of the lower lakes. Lake Superior had great distances and unpeopled shores, frequent fogs and bewildering mirages. The hills that rimmed the lake were veined with minerals and the compass needle might veer away from the north under the spell of local magnetisms. Often those mariners forgot their wayward compass and found a star to steer by. With that ancient dependence on the sky they skirted the dark capes and laid their course for the lonely harbors.

On the Astor's first trip Captain C. C. Stannard made a historic discovery. Almost on a line between Whitefish Point and the tip of Keweenaw, thirty miles from the nearest land, he saw a dark mass breaking the water-level. From a distance it appeared to be a capsized bateau. Captain Stannard sailed in close enough to see a rock shoal rising at its southern edge to a small rock island. Now Stannard Rock Light flashes its white repeated warning from a hundred-foot tower. The light is visible for eighteen miles.

Renewed interest in the Lake Superior country led to the hauling of the schooner Algonquin over the St. Mary's portage in 1839. The Algonquin, built in Cleveland by the Northern Lake Company in 1838, had been purchased by the Boston Mining Company, who were seeking to develop copper holdings on Isle Royale. The portaging of the fifty-ton schooner was done by Achille Cadotte who went to work as though he were moving a house. With a set of rollers, a horse and a capstan he hauled the Algonquin out of the water, cribbed her up in timbers and started her on her slow voyage over what is now Sault Ste. Marie's Water Street. The vessel moved five lengths a day, crawling along in snowstorms and bitter weather past the houses, shops and taverns of the little town. She took three and a half months to make that mile-long portage. But with the break-up of ice in April the Algonquin dipped her hull in the cold blue waters of Lake Superior and began her historic voyages. It was this vessel which rescued the Indian woman Angelique from starvation on Isle Royale, after she had braided her own hair to snare rabbits, and that carried John Hayes to his famous discovery of copper on Keweenaw's headland. She was a victim of Lake Superior before many years had passed, and now her hull lies fathoms deep in the cold water near Duluth, where she sank in 1856. But she showed other vessels, schooners and steamers alike, the way into Lake Superior before the canal was built. She was the first of the fleet that sailed on land.

In 1841 young Douglass Houghton, State Geologist of

Michigan, issued his report after a mineral survey of the shores of Lake Superior. The report was cautious and guarded, but it declared what had been rumor for centuries: there was copper on Lake Superior, copper in vast quantity. Soon the rush was on. Men flocked in. Two lonely Keweenaw posts, Copper Harbor and Eagle River, suddenly swarmed with life. Prospectors, merchants, and speculators clamored at the Soo for transportation to the mining country. A new era had begun on the greatest of the lakes.

The first shaft was sunk at Copper Harbor in 1844. The next year brought discovery of the rich vein of the Copper Cliff Mine on Eagle River. In the autumn of 1845 six schooners, Ocean, Fur Trader, Chippewa, Florence, Swallow, and Merchant, gathered at the Soo, along with two steamers, the Independence and the Julia Palmer. All were to make the mile-long portage and serve the clamoring trade of the copper country.

That winter the capstan was busy and the rollers grew battered as a fleet of vessels crawled overland beside the frost-rimed rapids. Mallets hammered in the cold air, the capstan creaked, the frost-white cables tautened. Men shouted orders, their voices jetting white in the bitter air. The horses leaned into their collars and tramped out dark circles in the hard-packed snow. There were no sails filling and no engines turning over, but the jib-booms of the schooners and the upright steamers' stems inched their way toward Lake Superior.

A boy who saw that fleet pass over the Soo's thoroughfare was to become famous on the lakes in later years. He was George Perry McKay, later Captain McKay, and his principal amusement in the fall of '45 was crawling over and under the steamer Independence, two hundred and eighty tons, as the big vessel made her way down Water Street. At that time he was eight years old. A lake man all his life, he had been born aboard the steamer Commodore Perry in Swan Creek (Toledo), where his parents were keeping ship during the winter. A few years later his father went to Lake Superior to command the Algonquin, and George McKay was put into the Reverend Mr. Bingham's school at the Soo. There he was listed as an Indian, because Mr. Bingham was paid by the head for teaching Indians. But George McKay soon left the schoolroom for his father's quarterdeck on Lake Superior. His first duty was to stand watches with his father, but before many years he was standing watches of his own. He lived to command some of the biggest vessels of a later era and to have an important part in the development of twentieth century shipping. One man's life spanned the whole story—from Achille Cadotte's capstan to the long freighters locking through with 15,000 tons of ore beneath their hatches. There were many eventful years in that lifetime—he was aboard the Independence when her boilers burst at the mouth of Whitefish Bay; later he was in other famous ships, mate of the Iron City, master of the General Taylor, the Mineral Rock, and the Pewabic until she was sunk by the Meteor in Thunder Bay, and many others. But no season was more memorable than the winter when a fleet passed through a village street, the rollers creaking and the sharp prows leaning in the air.

Before the canal was completed in 1855, fifteen vessels, aggregating three thousand tons, had been hauled over the portage. An old lake captain said it was a job that required considerable perseverance and some grease.

CHAPTER THIRTEEN

Death in the Copper Country

Douglass Houghton stood just five feet four inches in his explorer's boots, but he cast a shadow over all of Lake Superior. His strength was meager and his health was frail throughout the thirty-four years of his life. But he cruised five times the wild southern shore of Lake Superior in a birch canoe and he mapped the mineral resources of a region that was to have an epic history. A scholar more than an empire builder, he foresaw the empire that was coming. Despite exposure, illness, rheumatism, he led an arduous life and kept an ardent spirit. Years after he was gone men remembered his sea-blue eyes, his quick movements, his hilarious stories. His narrow shoulders were braced with an iron will.

He was twenty-one when he came to Detroit in 1830 as a teacher of science. He looked even younger than that, and the older residents called him "Bub." Ten years later he was their mayor and had declined the presidency of the University of Michigan.

Before that time, in his crowded brief career, he had been surgeon and botanist to Henry Schoolcraft's expedition to the headwaters of the Mississippi in 1832. Following that journey he persuaded the legislature of the young state to appropriate funds for a geological survey. In fact he was appointed State Geologist, and in 1837 began extensive surveys of both the upper and lower peninsulas of Michigan. Along the wooded shores of Whitefish Bay, past the steep and shifting dunes of Grand Sable Banks, under the vaulted caverns and the pictured rocks, along the deep bays and the wild promontories —he learned every mile of that wild Superior shore line. In all winds and weather he voyaged those lonely shores, making his camp on beaches and headlands, scouting the country and filling his specimen sacks to overflowing. What he found drew men to that land like a magnet.

So the first towns appeared on Lake Superior. They were copper towns, Eagle River and Copper Harbor, planted on the great cape of Keweenaw, and before long there were others,

Calumet, on the site of old Indian pits, and Hancock and Houghton, the twin cities above the Portage River. These names were to be known in the banking offices of New York and Boston, in the financial houses of London and Paris, and in circles of speculation around the world. In a single year the Calumet Mining Company stock rose from one dollar to seventy-five dollars a share. In fifty years the Keweenaw mines produced unnumbered fortunes.

But the first men paid the price. It was a big rough lonesome country. In the woods men waded through swamps and fought clouds of black flies and mosquitoes. Compasses were next to useless in that ore-veined land. Men wandered and were lost. The fierce autumn winds brought on a bitter season. 172 inches of snow have been recorded in that country. The average over many years was 114 inches. Men who escaped the perils did not also escape disappointment. Many worked their hearts out and moved on. In 1849 hundreds of Keweenaw miners threw down their tools and set off in the direction of a new bonanza—to the region of Sutter's Mill on a river bank in California. Still the stubborn ones stayed, and trade was growing on Lake Superior. Back at the Soo portage Sheldon McKnight retired his two-wheeled cart and with a partner, J. T. Whiting, he built a strap railroad and used horse-drawn cars between the landings. Business over the portage grew to 100,000 barrels a year.

The copper country was opened, but not without struggle and hardship. It took the lives of men. It took the life of the man who uncovered its treasure.

In late October, 1845, Douglass Houghton was making his way in a mackinaw boat along the rocky coast of Keweenaw. The season was growing late and he was nearing the end of his investigations. He looked forward to the comforts of Detroit, to his hosts of friends, to the companionship of men who could share the fruits of his mind, crowded as it was with science, exploration, projects, outlines for the future of a state whose riches he saw more clearly and soberly than any other. His thoughts that late October day were warm with anticipation.

Toward evening the wind freshened, bringing snow out of the northwest. The mackinaw boat, under its tanbark sail, pitched heavily. The snow drove in a white fury. His crew peered through the dusk to the safety of the shore. But Douglass Houghton could never have made his explorations if he had dodged bad weather. He headed out, around the last tongue of land below Eagle River.

A heavier sea rose up. It struck the craft solidly. While they struggled with the sail the wind rushed at them. The boat turned over. Then they were in the bitter water fighting to right their capsized boat. A wave flung over them, and another. While they clung to the boat's gunwales a sea rose angrily. It wrenched the craft from their hands and turned her over lengthwise. Two of that crew of five were washed ashore. They struggled through darkness and numbing cold toward the lights of Eagle River. The rest were lost.

There is a grim saying that Lake Superior never gives up its dead. But in the spring of 1846, while Little Silver River ran brimful of snow water and the moccasin flowers were bright in the woods, on the murmuring shores of Keweenaw was found the body of Douglass Houghton.

Charlie Mott was a trader who did business with the Indians at the old Chippewa capital of La Pointe, in the Apostle Islands. He got along well with the Indians, so well that he took a strapping Chippewa woman home to his lodge to be his wife. One day the schooner Algonquin rounded the long low point and reefed her sail under the red sandstone cliffs of Chequamegon Bay. Aboard were a party of Detroit speculators. They enlisted Charlie Mott and his wife, Angelique, to go with them to Isle Royale. From early times there had been stories of copper on the mysterious island. They approached its rugged shores with wonder and anticipation.

Isle Royale was a wilderness, forty-five miles long, three to ten miles wide, without a foot of road or trail anywhere. Its sheer cliffs stood up out of the lake and ran out in rock headlands hairy with pine. From remote high eyries, eagles soared over dark forests of spruce and balsam and shining groves of birch.

A prehistoric race of Indians had mined copper on the island. Shallow pits, shovels, hammers and axes remained from that vanished industry. And there were other wonders—ledges of agate and cornelian and the world's only beach of chlorastrolite, where all the stones are green.

To this fabled isle the copper hunters came. The interior was forbidding, with its dense growth of forest and its chaos of blow-downs in the thin soil that covers the volcanic rock. But they did not need to penetrate that fastness. On the shore they found mass copper.

The overjoyed speculators determined at once to file their claims, leaving Charlie Mott and his Angelique to guard their discovery. While the party journeyed to Detroit, Charlie and Angelique put in a supply of provisions at the Soo and returned to keep their vigil on the claim. So they were two people in the greatest, loneliest lake in the world, on an island that had never known permanent habitation. November brought heavy skies that shook out restless curtains of snow. December came, as Charlie checked the days off, one by one. Ice was coating the harbors. They searched the gray horizon for the schooner that should take them off. The waste of waters was empty. Not even a seagull moved over that winter sea.

Their provisions ran low. The snow came deeper. The cold dropped down, down, until the ground was hard as granite. With hunger gnawing them they ate the last measure of corn meal, and the wind howled louder in the forest.

DEATH IN THE COPPER COUNTRY

Charlie Mott stood hunger for a while. Then fever took possession of him. His eyes burned in his ravaged face. He began to sharpen a long-bladed knife. Angelique heard him, whetting, whetting, whetting that cold blade on stone, and muttering about killing a sheep. His eyes were on her, strangely, terribly. He was mad with hunger and his eyes followed her every movement. Angelique was the sheep that he would kill.

All day she watched him, and all night, not daring to sleep. Angelique was an Indian woman. Her race had known hunger many times. Perhaps she had armor against it. She remained calm, collected, silent. She watched the madman whetting his blade. The sound filled that four-walled shelter. When his eyes wandered once, she sprang. She twisted the knife from his hand.

The fever flamed and ebbed in Charlie Mott's blood. In the ebb he was weak and helpless. He came to himself. He looked quietly at the falling snow. He was gentle and empty as a child. She watched him shrink and shrivel. Then she was alone on that island, with a corpse.

Day after day Angelique fought the racking hunger in her own body. She stripped bark from the winter trees and chewed it to a paste that she could swallow. But the hunger bands were drawing tighter. Her strength was going. At last, outside her door her dull eyes sharpened. A rabbit track was printed in the snow. Her hands tensed with a desperate effort. She pulled a strand of hair from her head. Her fingers trembled while she wove those coarse threads into a snare. When she caught a rabbit she tore the skin apart and ate it raw.

The winter dragged on. Half of Angelique's dark hair was gone from her head and every day she made the rounds of snares she had set in the woods. She did not dare sit still; she might not summon strength to move again.

Winter is a long season in that country. In March the days

grew longer but snow still drove across the lake and ice still ringed the island. In April the ice went slowly. She contrived a fish hook and braided her hair for a line and caught a few mullets, which she ate raw. It was May when a gun sounded on the shore. She had not seen the schooner come in, with the men peering shoreward from her bow. The rifle rang again. She ran toward it in delirious hope. But her knees gave way and she fell on the beach.

The Algonquin, under Captain McKay, had come to take Charlie Mott and his wife off their imprisoning island. They could not remove Charlie Mott from his still bondage, but Angelique sailed away with never a look over her shoulder at the fading ridges of Isle Royale. In years to come she worked as a housemaid for an iron magnate in Marquette. When winter winds swept down and Lake Superior was dimmed by snow, there were shadows in her eyes.

CHAPTER FOURTEEN

Log of the Independence

On Keweenaw Peninsula the Lake Superior Copper Company and the Boston Mining Company had operations going. And on Lake Superior the vessels that had been hauled around the Soo were serving an urgent commerce. They were small ships hurrying on their rounds before there was a single lighthouse or a channel buoy in that greatest and cruelest lake in the world.

Of the fifteen vessels that sailed on land over the portage, all knew violence and danger and a dramatic end. The schooner Merchant left the Soo in July, 1847, with mixed cargo and a crowded list of passengers, and was never heard of again. The Manhattan, a steamer portaged over in 1850, was sunk in a collision. The steamer Monticello, brought over with the Manhattan, was beached to save her from shipwreck in a furious gale. The Julia Palmer, a veteran turtle-shaped side-wheeler, was caught in a snowstorm while bound back to the Soo from a late run to Copper Harbor. Her fuel gave out. They burned furniture and the wooden fittings. Then her engines were idle. For fourteen days she drifted out of sight of land. She sprang a leak and her passengers baled night and day with ice-rimmed buckets. Finally she drifted ashore on the Canadian side above Whitefish Bay. She was safe from that ordeal, but the strain of it weakened her joints and she was never seaworthy again. She made a few short runs in midsummer weather and then her hulk was left to rot in Marquette harbor.

But the most eventful logbook recorded the hard fortunes of the pioneer steamer Independence. She lasted seven seasons on Lake Superior, and considering her struggles that was a long life.

Brought up from Chicago and taken over the Soo late in the season of 1845, she began her career on Lake Superior with drama. She slid into the water above the rapids and was loaded up quickly to make a run before winter closed in. Captain Averill paced his deck while the hatches swallowed mixed cargo and the cabins filled with passengers. Among the passengers was a hollow-eyed young mother with a sick child in her arms. The child died before the vessel could cast off and sailing was delayed a day to allow for its burial. Then the lines were hauled aboard and with a blast of its whistle (the first steam whistle on Lake Superior and one of the first on any vessel) the Independence headed for the copper country.

She carried a crew of fourteen, comprising Greek, Scotch, Irish, English, and Yankee seamen. Along Whitefish Point the engineer playfully tooted his whistle, giving the Indians a bad fright. That whistle was regarded as a plaything to amuse the sailors and passengers more than for any navigating function it might serve.

In good time they put in at Copper Harbor, where three log barracks made up the garrison of Fort Wilkins and the scattered huts of prospectors completed the settlement. A few days later their whistle saluted Eagle Harbor with its new settlement of miners and "landlookers," and Eagle River with its Cliff Mine striking into the veined rock. Here Captain Averill discharged most of his cargo, but before he could put off fifty kegs of blasting powder the wind freshened from the northwest. Quickly it raised such a sea that he could not risk his vessel on that exposed shore. He weighed anchor and headed for La Pointe and the sheltered waters of Chequamegon Bay in the lee of the Apostles. When they were within sight of Madeline Island, beating into a head wind, the breeze quickened to a gale. Captain Averill reefed his sails and turned. He had no choice but to run for the lee of Keweenaw Point.

Lake Superior was blowing up in early winter fury. Seas broke over the Independence and washed her pitching decks.

In her main cabin people listened grimly to the smashing seas and the wind's high whistle. Then the stove broke loose from its foundation and went skidding across the cabin.

Sparks streamed out of the broken smoke pipe and burning embers strewed the deck. While they fought fire in that cabin all the faces were grim and set, but a few were haunted. A few of them had seen the fifty kegs of blasting powder stored beneath the hatches.

Around Keweenaw Point the storm blew furiously but the Independence floundered through. Captain Averill stood with his feet squared and his eyes narrowed as they swung around the cape. Cross seas tossed the vessel like a chip. Her engines labored loudly. Those two rotary engines could drive her at four miles an hour in calm weather with a full head of steam. Somehow they kept her going in that fury. She lurched through broken water into the shelter of Bete Grise Bay.

For four days she anchored there while the crew repaired her damage and the passengers went ashore in a yawl boat, with axes taken from her undischarged cargo, to cut fuel wood. In favorable weather she put back to Eagle River. Captain Averill breathed deeply as the fifty kegs of dynamite went ashore.

Down the Keweenaw shore they steamed to La Pointe and gave the Indians a scare with a blast of the steam whistle. A week later, with another bitter wind at her heels, the Independence swung into the Soo. There she laid up for the winter, along with the pioneer schooners whose hulls before long would be hung up on the rocks and ledges of that beautiful and savage lake.

The Independence lasted only a few more seasons before she was blown to bits by the explosion of her own boilers. In 1852, under Captain Redmond Rider, she went ashore on the beach of Ashland and was abandoned there. The next year Captain McKay, with his fourteen-year-old son at his side, spent the summer releasing her. He hired hundreds of Indians to tow her out to La Pointe where she was equipped to run to the Soo. He got sails on her schooner rig and limbered up her rotary engines. She made the Soo without incident. It was late in the season but there seemed time for a voyage that would help pay the cost of putting her back into commission. She loaded mixed freight for Ontonagon.

On a blue and windy day she left the Soo with a blithe blast of her whistle. She didn't get far. Still in the narrows, near the head of the present canal at International Bridge, her boilers gave way.

According to one story, Jonas Watson, her purser, was hurled a hundred and fifty feet into the air. But at the peak of his ascent he seized a flying bundle of hay and came down unharmed with it under him. Watson was a cool and practical purser. The story adds that he had the forethought to collect the ship's valuables just before he started upwards.

Of the Independence nothing but twisted timbers and shattered bulkheads were left. The hulk lay half out of water, whitened by the snows and warmed by the suns of many seasons. Fifty years later J. D. H. Everett of the Soo carried away one of those timbers. From it he made a variety of souvenirs—paper cutters, egg cups, gavels, and canes. They were the last remains of a famous and ill-fated vessel, the first steamer on Lake Superior.

CHAPTER FIFTEEN

The Iron Mountains

"GOLD IS PRECIOUS, but iron is priceless." When Andrew Carnegie made his sage comment, blast furnaces reddened the sky over the Ohio River and the Monongahela. But in 1843, when the Indian treaties opened Lake Superior's shores to exploration, it was visions of copper that drew men to the wilderness. Iron was discovered by accident, and its discovery produced no "iron fever." In the century to follow, however, it produced a new civilization.

William A. Burt was a government surveyor. He was a practical man, inventor of the solar compass and also of the "typographer" from which the typewriter evolved. He was a business-like surveyor with no notions of discovery in his head. In the year 1844 with his ten men, two of them Indians, he was intent on surveying Marquette County and getting out of that forsaken country before the winter set in. But on September 19, while running the east line of Township 47 North, Range 27 West, one mile south of Teal Lake, he had trouble with his compass needle. It quivered and veered. It hung uncertain and then swung off determinedly. At last Burt scattered his men in the brush to see what they could find.

What they found was iron outcrop. They broke off chunks of it, small chunks but heavy, so heavy that they did not add any of it to their already laden packs. They did not regard it as a discovery. Iron rock was a novelty and a nuisance to men trying to run their section lines. The nuisance made them remember it, and they spoke of it later to an old Chippewa chief named Majji Gesick (Moving Day), who lived at the mouth of Carp River. At the Soo that winter, when their field season was ended, they joked about their difficulties with the compass along that township line. One man remembered that joke. He was a half-breed named Louis Nolan.

The spring of 1845 brought hundreds of restless men to the Soo, all of them bound for the copper country. Among them was Philo Everett, with his four associates from Jackson, Michigan. They hired Nolan as a guide to take them to the copper country, but when Nolan told them about Burt's troubles with his compass in Marquette County they agreed to look at the iron outcrop on the way. Nolan led them to Teal Lake but he could not locate the iron. It was a rough country, of dense thickets and sudden cliffs and broken crowns of rock. Mosquitoes were a constant scourge. It was not a pleasant region to linger in. After a brief and fruitless search Everett impatiently struck camp and set out for the copper country, wading the tamarack swamps and tramping through dense stands of pine and birch and maple that are now Henry Ford's timber holding.

But fate had marked Philo Everett for an ironmaster. At L'Anse, the forgotten French station on the foggy shores of Keweenaw Bay, he met old Chief Majji Gesick, who knew the Marquette country and could locate the iron ore. So Philo Everett turned back.

There are various versions of the story. One is that the old chief would not approach the iron hill because it was bad medicine. But he drew a map in the pine needles on the ground and sent Everett direct to the location. Another version has Majji Gesick leading the party to the purple outcrop and grunting as he demonstrated the weight of a loose chunk of stone. Either way the result was the first iron mine on Lake Superior. In honor of his home town Everett named it the Jackson Mine. It began operations in the following year.

That first location was given an Indian name, Negaunee—or "Pioneer." Today at the western edge of the town of Negaunee a pyramid of iron-ore blocks marks the site. Ten miles west of it the Cleveland Mine was developed at Ishpeming, the "High Place," on the highest ground between Lake Michigan and Lake Superior. These were the beginnings of the Marquette Range, and in years to follow iron was discovered all along that height of land. It is not a lofty region. These are ancient, time-worn mountains, aeon-weathered hills —so old that they baffled the minds of geologists. They are the remains of the Laurentian range, the original land that rose out of primordial waters to form the North American continent. Beside these worn low hills the Rockies are infants and the Alps are young. The massed weight of ages has made the iron beds. More than a billion years have passed over the red and purple upthrusts and the flinty ledges where the deer moss creeps like a slow green shadow.

The first mines were open quarries. Now the woods and swamps are pitted with the old scars of mining, while the ore comes out of deep shafts, thousands of feet beneath that rugged ground. There are other monuments, the ruins of old charcoal ovens in the oak and maple groves and the remains of old forges by the rivers. For the first iron men did not conceive carrying bulk ore eight hundred miles down the lakes. They manufactured iron on Lake Superior.

It was a slow development. In 1848 six tons of iron was the daily output of the forges. Two six-horse teams hauled it over the twelve miles of rough road to the port of Marquette. In 1851 there were fewer than a hundred and fifty persons living in the iron country. Marquette was called Indian Town, and was no town at all. The first dock in that harbor was built of trees piled lengthwise in the water with gravel shoveled onto them. The night after the job was finished a gale blew across Lake Superior. In the morning no trace of the dock was left.

And it was an unprofitable business. In fact it was disastrous to make iron in the small forges on Lake Superior. Mining the ore, hauling finished iron to the lake shore, carriage down the lakes, with the costly business of portage at the Soo and the reloading into vessels for Lake Erie, made the cost of the bloom $200 a ton when the market rate was $80.

Within a few years the iron companies concluded that they could stay in business only by shipping ore to the lower lakes. Their conclusion was in tune with history. In half a century that became the largest single commerce in the world.

But it had small beginnings. The iron was hauled in sleds

over the twelve miles of swamped-out road to Marquette—a thousand tons was a winter's haul. Fortunately it was down grade, but the country was rough enough to give the teamsters trouble. Then H. B. Ely built a plank road. Wagons rumbled through swarms of mosquitoes and the red mounds of ore grew on the new dock at Marquette. In 1854 a thousand tons of ore was taken out by the steamers Sam Ward, Napoleon and Peninsula. It was wheeled aboard and dumped on deck, as iron ore was too heavy to hoist out of a ship's hold. At the Soo the ore was shoveled into barrows and wheeled ashore, where it was loaded into a portage cart. Sheldon McKnight's Chippewa Portage Company had expanded to a string of flat cars drawn by horses on a strap railroad. Further transport was provided by Spalding and Bacon, driving freight wagons with double teams on a plank road. But the labor of handling heavy ore was not diminished. At the far end of the portage it was shoveled into barrows and wheeled aboard a vessel for the lower lakes.

In those days a sailor on the ore vessels had the red dust worn into his hands. At Cleveland, eight hundred miles from the iron hills, he carried the tell-tale red stain on his dungarees. And on Lake Superior sailors sang a song about shovels and wheelbarrows, a queer song in a fo'c'sle with a sea wind blowing.

> *Oh, we're bound down from Marquette.*
> *My two hands are sore.*
> *I've been pushing a wheelbarrow,*
> *I'll do it no more.*

It was precious stuff that finally reached Cleveland. There it was found to be fine ore indeed, but no quantity of iron ore could be handled that way.

Across the St. Mary's River lay the barrier rapids, bottling up Lake Superior's iron. But already the drills were pounding and a pit was growing where the mules hauled their carts of stone and rubble. Business men at the Soo were opposed to the canal because it meant an end to the portage business. They didn't see that it would make their village one of the strategic points of the world. They didn't know that the digging going on in front of Water Street would make the steel age possible. But the canal was going through, and when it was done Lake Superior iron would flow unimpeded to the coal-rich valleys of Ohio and Pennsylvania.

CHAPTER SIXTEEN

Coming of the Scootie-nabbie-quon

IN THOSE DAYS Marquette was a lonely town. The first iron port on Lake Superior began as a settlement of log huts scattered up the hill where now a busy Front Street leads up to the spacious houses on Ridge Avenue. Every cabin faced the cold sweep of Iron Bay; that was the way to the world. Behind, the woods stretched wild and vast, threaded only by a few thin Indian trails and trampled here and there by exploring parties. It was a land of cedar and tamarack swamps, stands of pine and hardwood, all the way across the peninsula till Lake Michigan gleamed beyond the ridges.

To that settlement, called Indian Town, there came in 1849 a party of men in a mackinaw barge—after an eight-day trip up shore from the Soo. Their leader was Robert J. Graveraet who had the backing of some Massachusetts men in the city of Worcester. The lad of the party was a quick-eyed youngster who was to loom large in the development of the Marquette country. His name was Peter White.

At fifteen Peter White had shipped as deckhand on the schooner Bela Hubbard from Detroit to the Soo. The Hubbard, named for a geologist colleague of Douglass Houghton, called at Bay City on the way down, tying up beneath the lumber piles that bordered the Saginaw River. Young Peter, coming aboard the ship at night after a few hours ashore, had to climb over lumber stacked twenty feet high and jump down to the schooner's deck. He made the deck but broke his arm. Two days later, when the Hubbard arrived in Detroit, his arm was swelled to three times normal size. His shipmates told him the arm must be amputated, but Peter found a doctor who thought there was a chance to save it. While the youngster set his teeth the doctor poured whisky and scalding water on the swollen arm at intervals of fifteen minutes. In twenty-four hours the swelling went down. Then the doctor set the broken bone.

That was the arm that felled the first tree on Iron Bay where Graveraet was building a dock for iron shipments.

Other trees came down and the ground was cleared where the town should grow. The trees were hauled into the bay and gravel dumped onto them to make a dock. Horses and men were dead beat when the job was done. And that was the night when a sudden wind kicked up on Lake Superior. In the morning the bay was swept clean.

So there was a dock to build again, more solidly this time. Young Peter White was promoted to ox driver, a task he had never tried before. He learned to drive his team by taking them out of sight in the woods and letting them do the teaching. *Gee!* he shouted. *Haw!* and waited to see how they would respond. Soon he drove them back to the clearing and went confidently to work.

The new dock was built and Graveraet named the town Worcester; it was several years before it took the more appropriate name of Father Marquette who had labored among the Indians in that country. Graveraet then made a hurried trip to the busy immigrant port of Milwaukee and shipped back on the Fur Trader a load of German laborers to work the iron mines. Those Germans landed at Worcester shaking with fever and weak as worms. The grim word "cholera" went around the town. The Indians, in mortal dread of the white man's disease, vanished through the woods. But Peter White and a handful of others helped the distressed Germans into a log cabin and lugged up barrels of cold Lake Superior water to bathe their fevered bodies. It was ship's typhoid, and it quickly ran its course. In a few days the Germans were ready for the twelve-mile trek up to the mines.

One by one the Indians came out of the woods. Peter White made fast friends of them by learning their language. He had an ear for a strange tongue, and he picked up Chippewa, as he did French and German, by hearing it around him in that remote little town. In their own tongue he told the Indians wonderful stories. He told them that this village on Iron Bay would become a populous city, with three-story buildings and plank-paved streets. He told them that men would get rich from the dull red rock in the iron hills. He told them that over the empty lake would come Scootie-nabbie-quon, the smoke-puffing steamboat.

That steamboat was a great event in Marquette's early years. It linked a little northern town with the far-off busy world. Peter White was associated all his life with the Cleveland Mine and the Cleveland-Cliffs Company, and ultimately a giant ore boat carried his name up and down the lakes. He signed the bill of lading for the first shipment of ore—six barrels of it—from Marquette to Cleveland on July 7, 1852, and he was to live to see 42 million tons of iron ore shipped from Lake Superior in a single season. After the straggling town on the windswept bay became the busy and strategic port of Marquette he was elected mayor of the city without a dissenting vote, though he declined the office. Today his name is carved in stone on a handsome memorial library at the crest of Front Street. But back in 1850 it was a wonder to him, as much as to any Indian, that a steamboat should find them in that forgotten place.

From Marquette's hillside a man's eyes kept turning out to the wide water. Over that bright sea rim lay Sault Ste. Marie, gateway to the north, and the busy Straits of Mackinac and the friendly smoke of cities on the lower lakes. So in the fall of 1850, as provisions ran low in Marquette's one store, every face searched the horizon for the streamer of wood smoke, thinner than a cloud, that would be the steamer Napoleon on her rounds to the scattered ports.

In October the maples flamed in the valley and up the steep hillside the oak trees stood bronze among the pines. The air was crystal with autumn and the great lake was blue and cold under a cobalt sky. But no vessel appeared over the sea rim. November brought hurrying skies and squalls of snow. The lake pounded on the curving shore and the pine trees whitened around the cabins. Winter was closing in. The store was as bare as a cave. Its doors were no longer open. The horses were weak from want of feed. Now all eyes searched the tossing water. Even the Indians muttered as they waited for the Scootie-nabbie-quon. Business stopped. Every hour men scanned the horizon and turned away, not looking at each other. Starvation was a shadow in those sea-spent eyes.

The first day of December brought a northwest gale. The roar of waters ran along the coast and the pine trees moaned. Snow banked up against the cabins. Then it was decided to kill the horses and divide the coarse grain among the needy families. A few men discussed a long trip through the winter woods to Green Bay or the Soo.

Morning of the fifteenth was mild and hazy. The lake lapped quietly along the shore. Through the haze appeared another haze, blue and thin in the uncertain sky. With the oatmeal, cooked from the horses' oats, uneaten on their tables, people walked toward the shore. Their eyes stared out, unsure. But someone could wait no longer. A voice rang from the ridge.

"Propeller! Propeller!"

The frenzy spread like fire. "Propeller!" they answered from below, and then all Marquette was streaming down to the landing. They danced on the cold ground. They waved hats and coats and aprons. Their voices went out over the hazy waters.

A man whose span of horses had been shut up in a shanty to die found the tears streaming down his face. "Now if old Bill is not dead I can save him!" He hurried back to assure that horse.

The propeller steamer Napoleon coasted in to the dock. There were many hands to secure her mooring lines. Stores were carried ashore and fuel wood went aboard. Food and clothing and supplies were piled on the dock, and to get back to the Soo before the ice caught her the Napoleon chuffed up a column of wood smoke and diminished over the sea.

COMING OF THE SCOOTIE-NABBIE-QUON

That night there was feasting. Families gathered together and the tables were laden. In their stables the horses champed a double measure of grain and the hay was nested high in their mangers. The Indians dressed up in embroidered leggings and moccasins and tied their hair in colored ribbons braided with sewing thimbles. Nobody cared that the wind was shifting and the smell of snow was in the air. The Scootie-nabbie-quon had come

IV

FOURTH PART

THE LONG SHIPS PASSING

CHAPTER SEVENTEEN

Deep Voices at the Soo

THERE ARE PLACES where the currents and the commerce of the Great Lakes run together, and where the past and present mingle like streams of water. You think of Detroit, Mackinac and Sault Ste. Marie. Each one is a fulcrum on which America's destiny has turned. Especially that ancient town in the wilderness, beside the rushing water that the Jesuits called the Falls of St. Mary.

Picture Sault Ste. Marie on a summer evening. The long northern twilight lingers over the town; over the broad river below the rapids where the current runs in an amber light, over the green riverfront hillside that once was an army barracks and a trading compound, over the wooded park that skirts the canal. It is a quiet town, with the forest around it. You can see the spruce fringes beyond Fort Brady and the maple groves across the narrow channel on Sugar Island, and the dark range of the Laurentians above the Canadian Soo across the river. There are the stacks of the carbide works, smoking up a dusk of their own, a sawmill whining from the upper end of town and a train chuffing in on the Soo Line.

Then you hear a deep-throated whistle, not like a sawmill whistle, or a locomotive, or any factory in the world. Its echoes wander over the town and you can see black smoke drifting above the maple trees. The long dark hull grows in the river, a big freighter moving up into the Third Lock, while another comes down out of the Fourth. The upbound ship is light, a long band of red lead showing above the water, the deck inclined toward the storied superstructure at her bow, her engine room pulsing, a stream of water pouring from her side and the portholes glowing astern. The gates swing open. The deep whistle sounds again, shortly, and the ship moves into the great cold lake ringed in hills of iron; another 14,000 tons of ore move down the linked lakes to the smoking cities.

Darkness settles over the Soo and a chill wind freshens. People in this northern town don't put their overcoats away.

Around the big bend of the St. Mary's the riding lights are moving stars and the long ships come on. All night the whistles sound, deep and mellow and haunting. The locks open and close. The ships pass through. A hundred million tons of cargo in an eight-month season. And you realize that this border town is a place like Port Said and Cristobal. It is a strategic town with the currents of a continent's life passing through it and the smoke of an enormous commerce blowing over.

It has a rhythm, the rhythm of a northern city and a land that knows the tight grip of winter. The rhythm that the Indians knew for centuries, huddled in their lodges waiting for the ice to go and the whitefish to run in the rapids. Nature still makes the rules in that country. The snows fall, fall. The channels harden and farmers drive their teams across the ice. The roads drift full and fences are buried. The long piles of cordwood shrink around the farmhouses. The river is a white, curving road and at the Soo the locks are sheathed in ice. Then in April the air changes. The ice goes out. A whistle echoes up the winding river, over the islands and around the rocky shores. The church bells of Canada and America used to ring across the river when the first vessel came. It is still an event. The loosed tides of commerce flow through that living river. Coal comes up and ore goes down, the black and red cargoes under the hatches of that procession of ships, one every twenty minutes, that will not cease till the ice forms on Whitefish Bay in December.

No other canal in the world carries such a tonnage. But the vital waterway was not opened without political, financial and physical struggle.

There was a canal, with a nine-foot lock, on the Canadian side of the rapids a century and a half ago. It was built by the North West Fur Company in 1797. That canal, reconstructed, appears now, nearly obscured by the industrial plants of the

Canadian Soo, on its original site, and it is just about large enough to float a lifeboat from one of the big freighters that pass through the Third and Fourth locks every third of an hour. But that primitive lock served the laden bateaux of the fur traders until it was destroyed by American troops in the War of 1812.

For the next forty years the only route around the rapids was the portage road.

When Michigan was admitted into the Union in 1837 Governor Stevens T. Mason in an address to the legislature pointed out the need of a passage for shipping around the falls of the St. Mary's River. He spoke of it as a project for the federal government, but when the federal congress rejected the proposal he prepared the way for the state of Michigan to undertake the task. The fledgling state legislature then proceeded to contract for the construction of a canal with three lifts of six feet each, thirty-two feet wide, a hundred feet long, and ten feet deep. They estimated the cost at slightly more than $100,000.

In October 1838, one of the contractors went to the Soo to look over the ground. He wore a worried face as he surveyed the project, realizing that his firm had big losses ahead of them. As the story goes, he was dined and wined by the commanding officer of the garrison at Fort Brady. In the course of a convivial evening the contractor confessed his worries over the undertaking ahead of him, and added that they could not throw up the contract without forfeiting their bond. They stood to lose a tidy sum whether they built the canal or not.

Captain Johnson, who had no more imagination than was required to head a small and idle garrison, found this agreeable news. He didn't want the routine of Fort Brady disturbed— and the canal survey ran directly through the military reservation. Furthermore he had instructions from Washington to prohibit the contractors from cutting the mill race which served an abandoned sawmill on the military grounds. Quickly a solution occurred to Captain Johnson, who had a certain head for business if not a prophetic sense of history. The solution was simple: should the contractor begin his work where the line of the canal intersected the race-way, then the armed might of Fort Brady would be drawn up to prohibit his operations.

Next spring, on May 11, the contractor arrived on the Eliza Ward with fifty laborers and a load of tools and provisions. The strategy was acted out in solemn manner. The contractor set his men to work at the race-way and was promptly stopped by the thirty regulars of the garrison. The contractor, playing his part to the end, remonstrated, insisting that he had a contract to fulfill for the state of Michigan, and that the Congress had granted permission to build the canal through the military grounds. Captain Johnson went into his act, with a sharp word to his regulars. Their bayonets glinted in the bright May sun. So the baffled, happy contractor led his men down the river bank to McKnight's dock. They loaded picks and shovels, crowbars and hammers and wheelbarrows onto the schooner Eliza Ward. They sailed down the St. Mary's and went fishing.

It was thirteen years before a federal grant was made for the construction of the canal. During that time some noisy debates engaged the floors of Congress, and two of America's foremost statesmen dismissed the project in ringing language. Daniel Webster declared he would never vote one penny to bring the bleak, barren, rocky and uninhabitable shores of California one step nearer Boston; and Henry Clay made his famous wrong guess when he denounced the project of the St. Mary's Canal as "a work beyond the remotest settlement in the United States, if not in the moon."

Now the citizens of the Soo remember that derision with a peculiar American pride. "Beyond the moon" is a favorite phrase beside the great canal that carries a larger tonnage than the Panama, Suez and Kiel canals all together.

Webster and Clay were not easily over-ridden. The iron companies sent John Burt to Washington to lobby for the measure. Finally, in 1852, Congress passed an act granting the state of Michigan a right-of-way four hundred feet wide through the military reservation and appropriating 750,000 acres of public lands to pay for the canal's construction. The canal as newly surveyed by Captain Augustus Canfield of the U.S. Topographical Engineers was to be 12 feet deep, 100 feet wide at the water surface, and 5400 feet long. The locks comprised two lifts of 9 feet each, with a length of 350 feet, a width of 70 feet, and 11½ feet of water over the miter sills. Captain Canfield estimated the cost at slightly more than half a million dollars.

Captain Eber Ward, the largest owner of lake steamships at that time, protested vigorously over the size of the locks, not because they were too small but because they were "entirely too large" to be successfully financed. He feared that those locks would never be completed because the land that had been appropriated could not raise money enough to defray their cost. He estimated the value of the granted lands at twenty-five cents an acre, and at that figure the canal could never have been paid for. But the land company offered the holdings shrewdly and realized several times Captain Ward's estimate. The list of appropriated lands contained mineral property that was to come into great value—copper locations in Keweenaw County and iron property in the Marquette region later developed by the Cleveland-Cliffs Company. The location of the fabulous Calumet and Hecla copper mine was included in the grant, and though the true value of the location was not discovered until years later, the canal company realized $60,000 on its sale.

Charles T. Harvey, twenty-four years old, was at the Soo recuperating from an attack of typhoid fever. He was a salesman for the Vermont firm of E. T. Fairbanks and Company, manufacturers of scales, and he was in the Northwest to establish agencies for the Fairbanks products in that new country. While he recovered from typhoid he became victim to another fever, the fever of the Lake Superior country. He was young enough to see its tremendous potential riches, and as his health returned he had strength enough to drive the canal to completion. He forgot about scales and persuaded his company to enter a bigger business—to take over the granted lands and construct the canal. They made millions before the entire lands were disposed of, and young Charles Harvey, a Yankee salesman, became construction agent for the Soo Canal.

Harvey went to Detroit, engaged an excavation foreman, loaded the steamer Illinois with mules and horses, lumber, provisions, supplies, and four hundred men, and arrived at the Soo on the first day of June, 1853. In forty-eight hours he had the men housed in improvised barracks. On the fourth day of June his men, organized in work gangs, marched to the site where Harvey planted his spade in the ground and wheeled the first load of earth from the cut.

That was the beginning. Before the task was done young Charles Harvey had some new lines in his face. At that time there were only a dozen white families at the Soo. Indian camps dotted the shores and the islands. *Voyageurs* and fur traders gave color to the town, singing and swaggering down Water Street. But these men and these Indians had no taste for a pick and shovel. All of Harvey's labor crews had to come from hundreds of miles away; all the equipment, tools, and provisions had to be transported from the lower lakes.

But Charles Harvey was a man of prodigious energy. He lived at the Agency House near the bend of the St. Mary's, and he wore out three horses a day galloping over the canal works, between the workmen's quarters, the foremen's offices and the trampled portage road. He led his men and he kept their shovels swinging. The pounding of his horses' hoofs was a rhythm that drove them all.

That winter two thousand men were working in the frozen pit that would receive Lake Superior water. The temperature dropped below zero and stayed there for bitter weeks. Down in the pit the mules breathed jets of steam from their nostrils, the picks rang on the frozen ground, and the drills punched into the rock with a slow, cold din. A watchman was posted at the head of each wheelbarrow runway to rub snow on the gray faces that betrayed frostbite. For one stretch that winter it was 35 degrees below zero. In the mess barracks the meat froze solid. The cooks chopped it with an ax and rammed it into their ovens. They dug vegetables from frost cellars in the ground.

In the winter of 1854 typhoid and cholera struck the camp. Then a new pit was dug, out of sight in the woods. Burials were held quietly at night, to keep the knowledge of epidemic from the men. At the same time hundreds of workmen were lured by high wages to the copper and iron country, and scores went out to seek their own homesteads. To keep his gangs working Harvey sent company foremen to New York to board immigrant ships in the harbor. They signed on Irish and German workmen, herded them into trains for Detroit and delivered steamer loads of them to the growing excavation beside the rapids. The picks kept swinging.

There were other problems, besides engineering and labor and sanitation. The canal lines ran through a traditional Indian burial ground, above those rapids that the Chippewas had venerated as the home of many Manitous. Chief Shegud protested earnestly, then bitterly, but Charles Harvey could not move his lines. When the cut began to gnaw at that burial place he had reason to be fearful. Four thousand Indians came to the Soo every fall to receive their government payments. As the workmen threw up skeletons and bones Charles Harvey heard the muttering thump-thump-thump of the *wabeno* drums all along the shore where the Chippewas were camped. Rumors of Indian agitation grew and men recalled the bloody massacre at Old Fort Mackinac.

Then an old chief appeared on the excavation site with a long-barreled gun threatening in his hands. He had come from Lake Superior and he had an urgent mission. The old chief made his speech over and over, pointing his gun. He grew vehement, but he spoke in Chippewa, which Harvey could not understand. At last the Indian agent came and translated the old chief's speech.

"He says that he understands you are the government blacksmith, and he has brought his gun, which he wants to have put in good order."

One of the provisions of the treaty of 1843 was that the government would provide free repair service for Indian firearms.

Charles Harvey went immediately to work on that rifle. Soon the chief, grunting with satisfaction, returned to Lake Superior.

In twenty-two and a half months the job was done. The drills ceased to hammer. The last wheelbarrows came up the runways. The mules were hoisted out of the cut just before the gates were opened. Then Lake Superior flowed into the locks. The canal had cost just under a million dollars. Nearly that much was collected in tolls before the canal was transferred to the federal government and made free for public use.

On June 18, 1855, the St. Mary's Falls Ship Canal was opened. Captain Jack Wilson took the side-wheel steamer Illinois, with seven flags on her halyards, up through the locks for the first passage. The first vessel down was the steamer Baltimore. Ten others waited in line. Captain Wilson lost his life, along with 286 others, in the fog-shrouded waters of Lake Michigan when the topsail schooner Augusta, loaded with Muskegon pine, rammed his fine new steamer Lady

Elgin on a tragic September night in 1860. But he had a proud hour in his life, when the upper locks opened that summer day in 1855 and he steered the Illinois into Lake Superior.

Fifty years later, in June of 1905, Sault Ste. Marie celebrated the first half century of that vital waterway. By that time the locks that Captain Eber Ward had considered too large were replaced by the eight-hundred-foot Poe lock, in addition to the Weitzel lock, which had been opened to traffic in 1881. It was a part of the celebration to point out that those locks were inadequate to serve the growing commerce. Time brings dramatic changes on the lakes. Now the freighter Orlando M. Poe, loaded with iron ore from Lake Superior's ranges, cannot pass the lock bearing its builder's name. Its draft is too great.

Theodore Roosevelt was present for that fifty-year celebration. Bells rang from the American shore and the sound came back from the church steeples of Canada across the river. Whistles blared up and down the channel, echoing over the islands and the deep green woods. On the embankment of the canal, where Indians stared at silk-hatted Congressmen, history was recounted and the future was proclaimed. The town received gifts of commemoration: a Japanese Tori gate, a kiosk, an obelisk and many other markers. They still give the Soo a slightly incredible cosmopolitan air, with the Chippewas stalking through the streets and sawmills screaming at the upper end of town.

In 1914 and 1919 two more locks were added—the great Davis and Sabin locks. Each could take in one lockage, in tandem, two of the largest vessels in service. In a single day, on September 6, 1926, the canal carried 752,000 tons of freight—or the equivalent of 376 trainloads of forty cars each, which would mean one train passing every four minutes during the twenty-four-hour day.

By 1940 a bigger lock was in project on the site of the old

unused Weitzel lock. Engineers, shipbuilders and shipping men collaborated on plans for a new structure to fit in with the proposed St. Lawrence Seaway system. But its need and value were apparent in terms of the lakes trade alone.

A hundred years ago the Indians shouted as they ran the rapids. Today the steamers send their rich blend of bass and treble echoing over the ancient town that the Jesuits gave their most cherished name. No place in America has a more dramatic story.

CHAPTER EIGHTEEN

Boom Years on the Ranges

O N A C L E A R S U M M E R D A Y , August 14, 1855, the brig Columbia made sail in Marquette harbor and with a fair wind stood for the Soo, 160 miles away. Three days later she passed through the locks of the newly opened canal. On her deck, in little mounds like refuse, the Columbia carried 132 tons of red iron ore. It was the first bulk shipment of ore through the canal. In thirty years that was to be the predominant trade on the lakes.

By 1855 the Marquette range was vibrant. Cornishmen who had left the depleted tin and copper mines of Cornwall and Irishmen starved out of Erin by the potato famine worked the mines that were dotting the rough country along the height of land. Ishpeming became the capital of the range. In Indian its name meant "high ground," or heaven, but there were more who said it was a hell town in the early years. The mines went deeper and the ore came down to Marquette first on Ely's plank road and then on a strap railroad. Strings of jumper cars coasted down the twelve-mile grade, manned only by a brakeman who drew up his train on the docks. The shoe-brakes squealed on the iron wheels and sometimes the train kept going. More than a few jumper cars landed with a splash in Marquette harbor. Whole cargoes of iron ore have been dredged up from the bottom.

The mules, waiting to haul the empties back to Ishpeming, switched their tails at the deerflies and blinked their big eyes in the sun. They were soon to get away from both. The rest of their lives would be spent in the deep pits and the dim shafts of the mines. For in 1857 a steam railroad was completed up to Ishpeming. That summer the historic brig Columbia sailed into Marquette with a locomotive on her deck. It had a high, snorting stack, a stubby tender piled with cordwood and a fancy name: "Sebastopol."

By the end of the Civil War locomotive whistles were shrilling through the iron hills. An elevated wooden dock, built on heavy trestles, hunched over Marquette harbor, and ore rumbled down from its pockets to fill the holds of schooners. Sometimes a pocket of hard ore came too fast or too heavy. Holds were battered and framing sprung in many wooden bottoms.

Now the ore ships made a procession to the Soo, and up on the range the camps were growing, the shafts driving deeper and the shaft houses rising in the rocky valleys. The iron men went after iron. They found it leading in broken veins for fifty miles along those blunted hills. At Negaunee they moved a cemetery and near Ishpeming they drained a lake in order to sink new shafts down to the black magnetic rock.

Marquette grew. It overflowed the curving arms of its green hills. The sailing fleets gave way to lengthening steam freighters. For seventy years now they have come in steady procession. Above Front Street on the high striding trestle the toy trains pass. They pull up on the long overhead docks, all red with iron dust. At evening the water slowly darkens. On the point the wide white flashing begins and from the end of the breakwater comes a steady red winking to guide Scootienabbie-quon through the entrance.

To the Marquette range in early years came an increasing stream of miners from the worn-out mines of Cornwall. They worked the deposits in their old accustomed ways, and brought to Lake Superior a technique of mining and a mining idiom that became widespread in America. Even the familiar term "royalty" was their word, as the Cornish mines were leased from the crown of England and payments were made to the royalty which owned all the mineral resources of the realm.

Several hundred Cornish words became current in the Lake Superior ranges and around the iron ports. Some of the more common were:

LODE—a vein of ore
A BRAVE KEENLY LODE—a fine vein of ore
GRASS CAPTAIN—a surface boss

BOOM YEARS ON THE RANGES

TAILS or TAILINGS, also DEADS—waste
LEARY—empty
HORSE—a mass of country rock lying within a vein
SCRAM—to mine again
COLLAR—the mouth of a shaft
ALIVE—the production part of a lode
CHIMNEY—an ore chute
HUNGRY—poor ore
JIG—a vibrating machine
SKIP—the bucket in which ore is hoisted to the surface
WHIM—a capstan used in small operations
SUMP—place where water collects in a mine

One idiom they did not succeed in transplanting was the measurement of mine shafts in "fathoms." Feet were never supplanted by fathoms beyond the shore of Lake Superior.

The Cornish miner was independent, a good workman who resented too much supervision. An Austrian or an Italian might swing a pick faster with a boss standing over him, but a Cornishman stopped work on principle whenever the captain appeared.

The Cornish people brought to the range towns a love of sport and of social gathering. Their famous wrestling matches became seasonal events and their singing societies flourished in those old broken hills that had not heard a chorus of men's voices in a million years. They exchanged their traditional "Cousin Jack" stories, wry, blunt stories that are still current around Lake Superior.

In time they lost their dialect and some of their lore. But stubbornly they held on to their independence, their skill with a miner's gear, and their place in that hard country. Though the Swedes, the Finns and the Slavs came in, Cornish names still dot the iron towns and the iron ports.

By Tre, Ros, Car, Lan, Pol and Pen
You may know all Cornishmen.

THE LONG SHIPS PASSING

By 1880 iron had become a big commerce and Marquette was rivaled by a new iron port—Escanaba on Little Bay de Noc in upper Lake Michigan. There was a new iron range, the Menominee, and the miners of Negaunee, Ishpeming, and Michigamme were moving fifty miles south across the rugged country to new locations at Iron Mountain, Vulcan, Crystal Falls and Iron River. Great beds of soft purple hematite had been waiting for millions of years in those weathered hills.

Samuel J. Tilden of New York had run unsuccessfully for president against Rutherford B. Hayes, three times governor of Ohio, in 1876; but he ran the Chicago and North Western Railway successfully from the port of Escanaba up into the Menominee. Within a few years Escanaba was calling itself the Iron Port of the World. Then the sailors had a new version to sing:

Some sailors got shovels and others got spades,
And more got wheelbarrows—every man to his trade;
We worked like red devils, our fingers got sore,
And we cursed Escanaba and her damned iron ore.

The famous "iron" fleet arrived at Escanaba in the eighties— the Iron King, Iron Duke, Iron Cliff, Iron Age, big long vessels that could load 2000 tons of ore.

The iron prospectors were not through. West of the Menominee they uncovered a third range, the Gogebic. By 1890 it was shipping nearly three million tons of ore a season and was an equal of the older ranges. Its soft red hematite was admirably suited to the manufacture of Bessemer steel, and with the rapid growth of American railroads there was a soaring market for Bessemer steel rails. So the camps of Wakefield, Ironwood, and Hurley grew quickly into towns which felt compelled to pass laws against alley rioting, improper diversions, false fire alarms and smoking on the dynamite wagon.

BOOM YEARS ON THE RANGES

Over the hills to Ashland on Lake Superior went the trains of soft red ore and along with them came tales of the wild camps on the Gogebic. Ishpeming had been called a hellish place, Florence with its half-acre dance hall and barroom was the tough town of the Menominee, but no town on the other ranges had the notorious reputation of Wakefield and Hurley on the Gogebic.

Wakefield had its famous barrel house where whisky was sold by the bottle or the barrel, and a noted variety house opening from the rear of a big saloon next door to Bedell's respectable emporium. Wakefield was full of transient labor, miners drifting in and out of the vast open-pit mine at the edge of town, and the local amusement places were well patronized. One of the features of the variety house was a red-capped monkey that scampered among the guests while the vaudeville show was on. The monkey was trained to steal wallets and watches from the patrons' pockets. The animal had an extremely light-fingered touch, but once it failed him. On a bitter night in 1887 the monkey knocked over a lamp and burned Wakefield to the ground. The town's only fire department was a brigade of men who vainly threw snowballs on roofs in the path of the fire. The rebuilt Wakefield was a more sober town.

But Hurley continued to be the roaring camp of the range. It lay just across the Montreal River from Ironwood, in a region full of miners and lumberjacks, as "Ironwood" suggests. Actually that town was named for old Cap Wood, a mine captain, often nicknamed "Iron" Wood. Ironwood itself remained respectable, owing perhaps to the violent life of its neighbor town where Ironwood's population could go for their excesses.

A hurly-burly town, sprung up quickly with the mining and logging booms, Hurley had its duckboard sidewalks pitted with loggers' boots and over it everywhere the film of red dust that was the mark of an iron town. Its famous Silver

Street was lined almost solidly with saloons, dance halls and gambling rooms. Seven thousand citizens thronged its busy streets, along with other thousands of transient miners and lumberjacks. From Saginaw to Duluth it was said, "The four toughest places in the world are Cumberland, Hayward, Hurley, and Hell." And Hurley was second to none of them.

Meanwhile Ashland harbor was crowded with lumber schooners and iron barges. A fever of speculation raged in the windswept town and over the gaunt Gogebic country. Mining exchanges did a rush business at Ashland, Hurley and across the state of Wisconsin at Milwaukee. The rich Norrie Mine, the Newport, and the Iron King were producing wonderfully high-grade hematite. In the first years the ore was hauled overland to the docks, and the road between Ironwood and Ashland (now U.S. 2) became the most heavily traveled road in all the north. In those hectic seasons speculators flocked into the hills. Old settlers sold their property to wild-eyed newcomers who paid fantastic prices for future townsites and imaginary mine locations.

The bubble burst in 1887. Mining shares fell and real estate values collapsed. There was an exodus of the swindled and defeated. But iron was no bubble. It lay deep and rich in those ancient, hump-backed hills. They say it runs far out under Lake Superior to meet the deep lodes of the Mesabi.

Upper Michigan, the peninsula which the state considered worthless and accepted with bad grace, had proved to be enormously rich in minerals. But the greatest iron range was still waiting just a few feet beneath the sands, under the jackpine roots in St. Louis County, Minnesota, fifty miles northwest of the tip of Lake Superior. The Vermilion range, up in the wild Canadian border country, had created Minnesota's first mining excitement. It sent high-grade ore down to Lake Superior at Two Harbors. But the Vermilion and all the others were dwarfed when the Mesabi was uncovered.

BOOM YEARS ON THE RANGES

When the international boundary was drawn in 1783, the logic of geography would have run the line straight across Lake Superior, curving up around Point Keweenaw, to the mouth of the St. Louis River at the site of the present city of Duluth. But that is not the boundary. One explanation is that shrewd Ben Franklin, looking through old records of the French Fur Company in the government's archives at Paris, saw references to copper on Isle Royale, and so managed to shift the boundary north to the Pigeon River. That shift brought Isle Royale, and ultimately the Vermilion, Mesabi and Cuyuna iron ranges, into the territory of the United States. Not till a hundred and ten years after the Treaty of Paris did the full significance of the boundary appear. Long after Franklin's signature was blotted the country north of Lake Superior remained unknown.

Stephen Bonga, the Rainy Lake agent for the American Fur Company, knew the Mesabi country as early as the 1830's. A Negro-Chippewa half-breed, he had come up the Mississippi, across the Savannah River portage, and down the St. Louis River to Lake Superior. Then George Stuntz built his shanty on Lake Superior and dreamed of commerce, while the only transportation in that region was a dog team and sledge in the white waste of snow. In 1865 he went north and looked for gold on the 365 islands of Lake Vermilion. There he talked with the one white settler in the seven hundred miles between Lake Superior and Hudson Bay, a queer man named North Albert Posey who was teaching the Indians blacksmithing. But all that time the iron was waiting, as it had waited for a billion years.

Mesabi is the Chippewa word for Giant—and the Mesabi range proved to be the most prodigious basin of iron ore in the world. On November 11, 1892, the Mountain Iron Company shipped 2073 tons of Mesabi ore to Oglebay, Norton and Company in Cleveland. That was a historic day for Minnesota and for the lakes and for the age of steel. In four years the Mesabi had passed the other ranges in production. In ten years it was producing more than all the rest combined. Since then it has been a world's wonder, with the rich beds of ore in open pits, dug up with a steam shovel and loaded into hopper cars that carry it direct to the half-mile-long docks at Duluth and Superior.

The Oliver Mining Company, U.S. Steel's ore-producing agency, has dug pits in that range big enough to rival nature. When they found rich red ore under the streets of Hibbing they bought up the land and moved a city of 15,000 a full mile to the south. Houses were razed and better ones built on newly surveyed and graded streets. Churches were draped in log chain and hauled solemnly to their new locations. When public sentiment protested over abandoning a cemetery, the graves were "reverently scooped up by steam shovels" and a new cemetery was laid out.

Now on the site of the boom town of Hibbing the vast Mahoning Pit yawns into dull red strata and sends millions of tons of ore down to the lower lakes. There are hundreds of other mines on the Mesabi and they have marked the heart of the New World's steel industry in a single county which fifty years ago was a trackless waste. Much of it remains wilderness today, though that county possesses the greatest traffic railroad in the world, the Duluth, Mesabi and Northern.

In a great arc the iron ranges ring the shores of Lake Superior. Geologists say that the Mesabi formation dips toward the southeast and its veins of iron may meet the Gogebic under the deep floor of Lake Superior. So the sea that is ringed in iron is also rested upon iron sands. And the fleets out of Superior City and Duluth sail over a bed of iron beneath that great cold lake that is iron's route to the mills.

CHAPTER NINETEEN

Freshwater Ships

ONCE IT WAS an argosy of schooners, leaning in the wind, their sails billowed and their bobstays dipping, and the men light-footed on their rolling decks. They brought the ore down, a thousand tons at a time, to the narrow, twisting harbors of Ohio. Now the long flat freighters, with 14,000 tons beneath their hatches, round the dark cape of Keweenaw and snore through the rivers.

Between those fleets is a century of evolution. The schooners loaded iron by dint of back-breaking labor, and the labor waited again at the end of the run. The sailors on a modern freighter rarely feel the weight of iron ore. The heavy stuff comes aboard in chutes from the towering trestled docks, and three days later massive electric scoops rise whining out of the hold to disgorge it on the landings, seventeen tons to a single bite. Only in rare times, when a blow on Lake Superior puts a laden ship on her beam ends and shifts her cargo, do sailors know the feel of a shovel in iron ore. Then with the seas smashing over the long, low deck and a life-line strung taut above them, they open up hatches and descend into the yawning hold to trim the ore and square the ship again. Rarely is often enough.

Chase Osborn, once governor of Michigan and a leading conservationist of his day, said, "There is no ore in the world so beautiful as Lake Superior specular hematite." He found a colored and gleaming beach of it near his summer cottage on the St. Mary's where an old ore hooker had gone to pieces on the East Neebish rocks. But that specular hematite was never beautiful to a sweating man with a shovel in a pitching hold.

The lakes have never known a static trade. Every ten years has brought changes. As the schooners were succeeded by steam freighters, as the wooden hulls gave way to iron and the iron hulls to steel, so on the docks the horse-drawn block and tackle, lifting tubs of ore out of the hold and dumping it in wheelbarrows, gave way to a cable rig that hoisted ore out of the ship and conveyed it directly to the shore. There were still sweating and swearing sailors swinging shovels in a ship's hot hold, but it was a faster method than the old four-day job of discharging a vessel's cargo. This was followed by the "whirlie," a rotating derrick that controlled a bucket in the hold. Next came the self-filling bucket, which led to the electric scoop with its uncanny dexterity and its prodigious maw. These are the big iron grasshoppers that hunch over the Ohio harbors and devour thousands of tons of cargo in an hour.

By virtue of this machinery bulk cargo is handled at the lake ports with phenomenal speed. A salt-water man can't understand it; the lake man takes it for granted. So an average loading time is three to four hours for 10,000 tons of ore, and that same cargo is discharged in nine to ten hours. For a salt-water comparison take the record-breaking accomplishment of the steamship Tregarthen at Liverpool on March 19, 1937, when 4960 tons of iron ore were unloaded in twenty working hours. In the regular course of trade the steamer D. G. Kerr on July 15, 1919, loaded 12,689 tons of iron ore at Duluth in thirty minutes, and on August 27, 1940, the William A. Irvin discharged 13,856 tons of ore in two hours and fifty-five minutes from the moment of her arrival at Conneaut. The lake fleets approach these records every season. There is as much truth as humor in the story of the lake captain who went all summer without a haircut and couldn't get his shoes half-soled till the end of the season.

Three factors have determined the efficiency of the ore trade: the depth of harbor and river channels, the development of loading and unloading apparatus, and the size of the vessels themselves. All three underwent important changes in the closing years of the last century. The twelve-foot channel that the first Soo canal was adapted to, gave way in the eighties to the sixteen-foot channel. That improvement was hardly done before engineers were planning a twenty-foot channel. That in turn was deepened, and now the St. Lawrence Seaway project calls for a channel of greater depth from Duluth to the Gulf of St. Lawrence.

Freight carriers on the lakes have undergone an accompanying evolution. Changes came rapidly in the eighties when steamers all at once were replacing the sailing fleets. But before that the progress was going on. For half a century steamship companies evolved a steady succession of bigger, longer, stronger craft—a sequence of new designs and daring developments represented by such pioneer vessels as the Merchant of 1861, the R. J. Hackett of 1869, the V. H. Ketchum of 1874, the Onoko of 1882, the Victory of 1895, the Superior City of 1898 and the Augustus B. Wolvin of 1904.

The Merchant, built by the Evanses, father and son, of Buffalo, was the first commercial ship on the lakes to be built of iron. Old sailors shook their heads over her, declaring that it was against nature to put an iron ship in the water. She made a great splash when she went down the ways, but she floated. And she continued to float, with rich profits to her owners, until she foundered in the furious autumnal storm of 1878.

By that time the ore carrier was taking shape along the lines familiar to every lake harbor and every lake fairway today. The R. J. Hackett, built at Cleveland in 1869, was the pioneer bulk freighter of the present type, with engines aft and navigation quarters in a forecastle at the extreme bow, and a continuous hold extending unbroken from her forecastle to her boiler-room bulkheads. The Forest City, 213 feet long with a beam of 33 feet, was built as the Hackett's consort. For the next twenty years this system of ore transport, a steamer and her tow barge, was prevalent. The first sow had but one pig.

In 1874 the V. H. Ketchum was launched by James Davidson in his big yards at Bay City, where thousands had gathered on the lumber piles that lined the Saginaw to watch her take the water. She was a monster, a full twenty feet longer than anything then afloat. She had four masts, a leaning bowsprit, auxiliary sails and a startlingly high funnel. She was so big that skeptics called her "Davidson's Folly." That was an apt name, for a while. She was far in advance of harbor facilities and could not be used profitably in her early years. But when the channels and the docks caught up with her she earned fortunes.

The historic Onoko slid into the Cuyahoga at Cleveland in 1882. Over 300 feet long, with a single cavernous hold of 3000 tons capacity, this big ship established the permanent type of lake freighter. Her engines were aft, her bridge forward, and her long cargo deck was broken only by a deckhouse for the crew. She was a famous vessel for thirty years before she was finally lost in a storm on Lake Superior in 1915.

In the nineties, after the enormous Mesabi came into production, the ore trade grew so fast that General Poe, watching the never ending line of ships that passed beneath his office at the Soo, said: "The wildest expectations of one year seem absolutely tame the next." In those years the red pits were yawning where the muskeg swamps had been, ore trains were tooting through the Minnesota forests, and the skies glared all night long above the Ohio and the Monongahela.

The trade was demanding larger and larger ships. The Victory appeared in 1895, built by W. I. Babcock in Chicago. That historic vessel, whose launching set a new standard in strength and carrying capacity, had many years on the lakes under the name Victorious and the flag of the Upper Lakes and St. Lawrence Transportation Company. But it was dwarfed by newer ships. In 1897 Rockefeller, whose hands were deep in Minnesota iron, in a single order called for twelve carriers larger than any ever floated on the lakes. The big freighter, designed for enormous burden and the speedy handling of cargo, had come. As the ships grew the cost of transporting ore dropped—from three dollars a ton in 1855 to sixty cents a ton a half century later. Every decade the shipyards sent vaster vessels down their sideward ways. With their launching a wash of water hurried through the rivers and onto the broad lake lanes. Five hundred feet was a proud dimension, for a while. Then it was six hundred. Now a class of new carriers building at Lorain and River Rouge for the Pittsburgh Steamship Company measures six hundred forty feet from stem to stern.

One aspect of the trade has not changed. Winter still brings back emptiness to the lakeways and silence to the rivers, as it did when the fur posts were lonely stations in a wild land. Spring brought its rush of traders and trappers, its bright and noisy brigades, and sent its canoe caravans singing over the sweet-water seas. Now April brings the season's first ship. At every port on the lakes that is an event.

In Toronto in 1850 harbormaster Hugh Richardson offered a silk hat to the master who brought into Toronto harbor the first cargo of the season. That began a custom followed to this day in the lake ports of Canada. At Toronto, Midland, Owen Sound, the Canadian Soo, Port Arthur and Fort William, the season's first vessel is given a hilarious welcome. Whistles blow, horns blare, there are singing and speech-making. The ceremony's climax comes when the local harbormaster fits a tile onto the head of the feted captain and presents the chief engineer with a gold-headed cane. When the affair is over the symbolic tile is put away for next year and the captain is taken to the port's best clothing store to pick out a hat of his own choosing. No Texas cattleman is prouder of his Stetson.

In American ports the celebration of first arrival is just as noisy, though the prizes are more various. On an April day the village of Mackinac gleams white under its wooded cliffs, and all the villagers line their waterside to cheer the first steamer working through the straits. It may carry a cargo of coal for Escanaba or Menominee. There, before the big dippers drop into the hatches, a delegation from the Chamber of Commerce comes aboard and the mayor presents the vessel's captain with a big box of fresh-caught smelt. At Duluth the master of the first ship is presented with a desk set or a framed picture, or some other dubious prize. But there is nothing dubious about the whistles blowing, the horns roaring and the voices raised to welcome the first arrival at every port from Chicago to the dark northern shores. For all its vastness and efficiency the lakes trade is an excitement in men's eyes when the first smoke grows over the empty sea and the great voice, after months of stillness, cries across the water.

CHAPTER TWENTY

A Fleet Was Frozen In

THE ST. MARY'S RIVER was a wilderness waterway when the Jesuits gave it their most lovely name. Today, though its deep-dredged up- and down-bound channels carry an endless commerce, that waterway is still framed in wilderness. A few Finnish farmers tend their cattle on Sugar and Neebish Islands, and there are summer fishing camps on St. Joseph Island and around De Tour. The Indians live in tar-paper shacks, dark huts among the white boles of birch trees, and they watch without wonder the greatest procession of shipping in the world. The best timber has been cut. Now there is dense second-growth where the tall pines stood. But the land is still wild and nearly empty.

The Indians have changed a little. They are lazier, by all accounts. And their traditional arts have been forgotten while they have looked on the white man's ways. In the 1930's a WPA school on Sugar Island taught them the lost craft of basket making. Around them life has changed from the generations of the past that gathered spring and autumn to spear the sporting whitefish and to boil the sap from the maple trees on Sugar Island. And yet it has not changed in essence. It is still the life of an elemental country. Here is the land of their legends, the starlit lakes and the soughing forests, the bright skies and the shining waters. It is touched but little by the passing commerce of the age of steel.

The St. Mary's is really not a river but an intricate and beautiful strait. It broadens and narrows for forty-two miles from De Tour to the Soo. Every bend and bay has memories of hazard and disaster. The swift current below the rapids led to the earliest restrictions of commerce on all the lakes. The government required reduced speed in the channels and stationed a patrol to check the speed of passing vessels. An old joke on the St. Mary's is the story of a steamer and tow barge that were checked by the patrol. The steamer was within the law but her tow was exceeding the limit. The currents in those winding channels almost take the joke out of that story.

THE LONG SHIPS PASSING

Those channels are busy enough when the procession moves steadily around the big bends and through the narrows. But on a foggy night, or in the smoke of forest fires, the ships creep in with whistles sounding. In a few hours a fleet of twenty vessels will assemble in the basin below the locks. They let their anchors go; the clank of massive chain roars out among those deep-voiced whistles. In the gray dawn more ships crawl alongside. They cry out over the river and the echoes come back from the unseen Canadian hills.

A century ago the St. Mary's channel, unimproved, with all its hazards of swift current, sunken rocks, cross channels and shoals, was tricky sailing. Few captains knew the tortuous channel well enough to take their own vessels through. Pilots were employed between the Soo and the great turn into Lake Huron at De Tour. Nicolas Riel of De Tour and Owen Rains and William Greenough of Sailors Encampment were noted pilots in the years before the canal was built. They steered the nervous schooners and the first fuming steamers from Frying Pan Island past the fields of rushes along the St. Joseph shore, over the wide reach of Muddy Lake (crystal clear and blue as the sky, but the least wind churns up its black bottom) through the Neebish narrows and into the fairway of Lake George that was the old way around Sugar Island. Those pilots knew every hidden rock and shoal between De Tour and the Soo.

The first steamer to navigate the St. Mary's was the historic Superior, the second steamship on the lakes, which came up the river in 1822, bringing Henry Rowe Schoolcraft to his post as Indian Agent along with a company of soldiers who were to erect Fort Brady. But the Superior did not reach the Soo. She drew eight feet of water and could not pass "the flats," a limestone bar at the foot of Lake George. At that point her company disembarked, completing their journey to the Soo in three bateaux. Not till 1827 did a steamer, the Henry Clay (whose namesake said that the Soo was more remote than the moon), succeed in reaching Sault Ste. Marie.

Even after the canal was opened and the river channel deepened to fourteen feet, the St. Mary's remained a tricky stretch of sailing. There were still rocky points and sunken ledges and many another peril to navigation. It was a Yankee storekeeper who first did something about it.

Philetus Church, a York state man who kept a store at the head of Sugar Island, sometimes had trouble getting his new season's merchandise up the river for the spring trade. In April of 1863, he hired his captain, David Tate, who brought up Church's stores each season, to stake out the channel to De Tour. The scheme worked so well that he had it done annually. On his last trip before the freeze in December, Captain Tate pulled up his stakes, and in the wanton sun and wind of April he set them out again. So the schooner-men between Michilimackinac and the Soo had a marked course to follow. It was one of these traders who tired of writing the long word Michilimackinac and decided to abbreviate it. He settled on the first syllable and called his island Mich. When this was confused with the state of Michigan he had to abandon his abbreviation. But his example led to the use of the last three syllables, and the Great Turtle of the Chippewas became Mackinac.

Philetus Church was an enterprising man who even succeeded in putting the Indians to work. He persuaded the Garden River tribe to gather raspberries from the St. Mary's islands and he became the first commercial manufacturer of raspberry jam. In the woods beside his store he kept the big kettles bubbling over a slow fire of maple logs. The Indians stood around with watering mouths. They ate the thick sweet stuff like porridge. But Philetus Church consigned most of his product to the lower lakes. In the fifties he exported ten tons annually.

In those years the growing fleet of ore schooners followed the old channel through Big Lake George along the Canadian shore and around the arrowhead shape of Sugar Island. They had only the natural ranges to steer by, Partridge Point, Farmer's Ridges and Topsail Island, until they rounded the last sharp bend into sight of the Soo.

Through the wide sweep of water that the British had named for King George there were two channels around a middle ground. The first improvement there was carried on by Canada. Huge rocks were swept up in the hazardous East Neebish channel. Finding the American shore a convenient dumping ground, the Canadians bought a small tract at the lower end of Sugar Island, holding it in the name of Queen Victoria. Aside from Britain's embassies, that spit of lonely land was the good queen's only American property.

In those days the most populous place on the river was Sailors Encampment, a forest-fringed meadow above the current that swept past Neebish Island. It became an encampment by necessity, when an early party of boatmen coming down from Lake Superior were caught in a December freeze. They pulled their craft ashore and built a big lean-to to shelter them till the skim of ice should loosen. But the ice did not go out. Winter had come in earnest. After two days of numbing cold and stinging snow they realized their camp would be a long one. The living water was locked tight, the murmur of the current was stilled, and the gray skies let fall a deeper snow. That camp was their habitation for the long siege of winter. They built up their fire and sang their songs and waited for the soft winds of April to set them free.

For many years their camp site was the stopping place for vessels up-bound through the St. Mary's. Schooners could beat up Munuscong Lake to the narrows, but from there they depended on a favorable wind. While they waited, the crews left their cramped dark fo'c'sles and made a sailors' camp ashore. There were deepwater songs around a forest campfire, and seamen slept like hunters under the soughing pines.

From the middle fifties, with the opening of the canal, the

smoke of steamers drifted over the islands and Sailors Encampment became a fuel stop for craft that need not wait for an auspicious wind. "Wooding up" tugs and steamers became a lively business for the scattered settlers, and the thud of axes rang in the great stands of hard wood on the islands. The larger steamers fueled three hundred cords at a time, enough for a round trip to the ore ports, and the woodmen collected $1.50 a cord. Some of them hired Indians to work in the woods, but whenever the sun came out the Indians went to sleep. It was mostly white man's cordwood that fired those early boilers.

Even the steamers spent the night at Sailors Encampment because the St. Mary's channels were dangerous for night navigation. They amused each other and the settlers ashore by tooting their new steam whistles. A favorite vessel, because of the melodious blasts, like a calliope, she could send over those twilit shores, was the Mineral Rock. Her chime whistle was the talk of the upper lakes. Another famous caller was the Cuyago with her high-pressure exhaust that was audible for miles. From the moment she passed De Tour the islanders knew she was coming.

With nightfall, the crews of a dozen ships, steam and sail, might gather aboard one of the vessels or in the log hut of a hospitable half-breed along the shore. Dances were boisterous; heavy feet jigged to hilarious music. There were food and drink and a midnight round of story-telling. Often the stories touched the old traditions of St. Mary's. Stories of shipwreck among the reefs and bays of the thirty-five Les Cheneaux Islands, with the ghost of the Griffin still beating into a head wind and the ill-starred Nancy lying with a broken back on a rock ledge nine fathoms down. Tales of the Spanish pirates hiding out in the mysterious island of Espanore, and of the Mormon privateers from Beaver Island stealing off to harry the peaceful shipping of the straits. But the most stubborn tale of all was the story rooted in the grim winter of this country. Two British soldiers, Privates Keary and Myaugh, deserted their post at Fort St. Joseph in the dead of winter, setting out on foot for Mackinac, forty-five miles away. Three days later Sergeant Drennan found deserter Myaugh opposite Goose Island. He found him like a length of log on the ground, frozen dead. Nine miles farther they came on Keary, sunk down in the snow, insensible but with a pulse still struggling. They brought him back to Fort St. Joseph with his hands and feet frozen dreadfully. Private Keary lived but he never walked his post again. When spring came round both his legs were amputated and his hands were clubs with all the fingers gone.

As they went back aboard their vessels the sailors looked up at the starlit summer sky and around at the murmuring forest. It had its other moods, this country.

The Vessel Owners' Association installed the first range lights on the river. Bernard's Light, Roulleau's Light and the rest of them took their names from the half-breed tenders who lived nearby. Soon the Canadian and U.S. governments began surveys and channel improvements and in 1892 official ranges were placed at all the dangerous angles. Meanwhile General Orlando M. Poe from his office overlooking the busy canal was charting a new channel which would save eleven miles and take the hazard out of night navigation. Committees of congressmen and senators came up in the guest quarters of big freighters, and officials of the Lake Carriers' Association explained the project to them. At last, on June 7, 1894, the Middle Neebish Channel was opened. Gone were the years when the vessels lay all night off the friendly Neebish shore. Steamers swept past the meadow where those campfires had flickered against the forest. Sailors Encampment became a summer fishing ground for vacationers from down below.

But that new channel still kept some problems for a navigator. Its sharp turns, obscured by high land, became a menace to growing traffic, and the strong current required down-bound vessels to maintain speeds of eight to twelve miles an hour to keep steerage way. Even so it was difficult to control large loaded vessels at the turns.

In the first week of September, 1899, the steamer Douglass Houghton, down-bound, swung across the channel at Sailors Encampment. There she was rammed and sunk by the John Fritz. The Fritz then went aground and blocked the channel for a week, tying up 350 vessels with a loss to navigation of $600,000. In a Thanksgiving Day snowstorm that same year a three-way collision occurred in the channel. The steamer Sir William Siemens towing the barge Alexander Holly parted her wheel chains and drove aground, crosswise of the channel, at the head of Little Rapids Cut. The deeply loaded Holly rammed a hole in her escort and struck on the opposite bank. The North Star, following the two vessels, swung wildly to avoid ramming them and piled up just above the Siemens.

To reduce these dangers a new channel was excavated on the west side of Neebish Island, so that up- and down-bound vessels could travel separate courses. Of that thirteen-mile channel, two and a half miles were driven through solid rock. To the Algonquins "Neebish" meant "boiling water," and where the rapids once foamed over the rocks the deep, clear channel was blasted out. Now the long freighters steam past where the island farmers remember crossing on a log between the stones.

On May 16, 1908, the West Neebish Channel was opened to navigation. The first passage was made by the steamer George F. Baker, which left the Soo by night so as to reach the new channel's entrance at daybreak. Captain W. W. Smith took her through the cut, with its cliffs of limestone giving back the blasts from her whistle. Standing in her bow were General Superintendent L. C. Sabin of the St. Mary's Falls Ship Canal, Captain Charles Saterlee of the river's Revenue Cutter, and President William Livingstone of the Lake Carriers' Association. A splendid daybreak bathed the shores.

The value of the new channel was promptly dramatized when the steamer Edwin N. Ohl ran aground in the Middle Neebish and blocked the up-bound channel. Up-bound traffic was diverted to the new channel and a cessation of shipping was averted.

The "boiling water" had become a deep canal but the land remained primitive and the weather was still untamed. Weather in that country means winter. In places along the roads the limestone outcrop has been piled up in snowbreaks. Those lasting snow fences are a reminder of what winter can bring to the St. Mary's. In 1826 Thomas McKenney reported seventeen feet of snow at the Soo, and Schoolcraft wrote, "The whole village seems like so many beavers in a snowbank, who cut away the snow and make paths, every morning, from one lodge to another." At De Tour in the nineties a saloon-keeper kept his barreled beer in a lean-to, behind his tavern. By January, according to the story, the beer was frozen so hard that it was chopped off in chunks and patrons carried it home under their arms.

From early years winter has held drama and hardship for the crews of freighters making the first or the final runs of the season. Steamers have come through the Soo locks sheathed in ice from stem to stern. The W. E. Fitzgerald carried 1200 tons of ice after passing through "fog frost" and a furious gale on Lake Superior at the end of the season in 1926. Another vessel in that severe first week of December froze fast in the dock while taking a cargo of wheat. She waited there for spring to release her.

Winter can begin early on Lake Superior, and it often lasts late. All through May of 1917 the Lake Superior harbors were choked with ice. On May 23rd a heavy snowstorm blanketed the Soo and the St. Mary's shores. On June 6th a gale packed the ice so thick in Duluth harbor that seventeen vessels were locked tight. When the harbor broke up, menacing ice fields remained in the lake and bergs extending seventy feet under water were encountered in Whitefish Bay on the 15th of June. The end of that season was as severe as the beginning. By New Year's Day of 1918 the ice at Duluth extended in a solid sheet for thirty miles. In the Straits of Mackinac ice was reported thirty feet thick before the winter was done.

Another dramatic season was 1926. It began with late spring snowstorms and bitter winds that swept the entire length of the lakes. A thousand miles away from the ice-bound harbor of Duluth in the second week of May, 78 steamers were fast in the ice of Lake Erie, fourteen miles above Buffalo. Ice remained in Buffalo harbor until May 15th. That was the season's beginning. The Great Freeze in the St. Mary's River was its end.

One of the features of the lakes trade is the final dash of the grain fleet with a last cargo before the expiration of insurance rates at the end of November. On November 30, 1926, in the twin Canadian grain ports of Fort William and Port Arthur, there was a heavy snowstorm. This involved delay in loading the waiting vessels, because the Canadian Board of Grain Commissioners had prohibited the loading of grain during rain or snow. At four in the afternoon the snow stopped falling. Just eight hours were left to get a large fleet out before the expiration of insurance rates at midnight. In those eight hours twenty-two bulk freighters took on five and a half million bushels of wheat and cleared from under the dim, snow-hooded mass of Thunder Cape. They fled across the bleak waste of Lake Superior, with ice coating their cabins and sailors gripping the tight-strung life-line as they crossed the icy deck. They passed through the Soo in a temperature of twelve degrees below zero, and found an enormous fleet locked in ice in the down-bound channel. The steamer Coulee was wedged in at Rock Cut, partially swung across the channel. She was the key to the blockade.

Panic threatened in the Chicago Grain Market, and in Cleveland and Pittsburgh the iron masters were alarmed. 247 vessels were fast in the ice. Their thermometers dropped to thirty-five degrees below zero, and the biggest ice-crushing car ferry on the lakes, the St. Marie, threshed up from Lake Michigan to break the channel open.

Farmers drove bobsleds out to the ships and did a good business with meat and provisions. Sailors walked ashore in search of tobacco, swinging their arms and lowering their faces in the wind. By day the smoke of that marooned fleet drifted across the frozen land. At night there seemed a great city on the ice, with miles of smoking stacks and acres of lights under the winter sky.

After ten days, winter relented briefly. The St. Marie broke through. With whistles roaring, 247 ships pushed through the ice fields toward open water.

After the freeze of 1926 it was predicted that half a century might elapse before such a weather condition could recur. And the next season brought an identical blockade. A last-minute fleet of twenty-six grain carriers left Fort William and encountered a gale off Thunder Cape. For twenty-four hours they waited in the shelter of the Welcome Islands. But the dropping temperature reminded them that there could be trouble in the St. Mary's channels. So they labored toward the Soo. In the run across Lake Superior the master of the Val-cartier recorded his ship thermometer at forty below.

There was trouble waiting for them in the river. The Steel Trust steamer James B. Eads jammed in the ice in the dike of West Neebish Channel. For five days tugs struggled to release her. But the ice was growing thicker, hour by hour. At last the tugs churned home and the Eads was left ice-bound for the winter. Behind her a fleet of twenty-two steamers, loaded with six million bushels of grain, went into winter quarters at the Soo. They finished their voyage the next April.

CHAPTER TWENTY-ONE

Fathoms Deep But Not Forgotten

On the 18th of August, 1861, Mrs. E. Bowen, who lived on the west side of Cleveland's busy Cuyahoga River, was walking along the dock near the west pier. Her curiosity was aroused by a corked bottle floating at the water's edge. It contained a message: *On board schooner Amelia, August 12, off Grand River, schooner lost foremast, also mainsail, leaking badly, cargo iron. Must go down. All hands must be lost. C. S. Brace, capt.*

There had been a gale on August 12, lashing the shallow waters of Lake Erie and sending ships under reefed sails to the lee of the islands or to sheltered river mouths. But the Amelia had not found shelter. All day and half the night the gale raged. The dismasted schooner wallowed in those hungry seas and went down with her crew clinging to the rigging. There was nothing left of her to greet the dawn that came up quietly, with a green light over the subsiding seas. Only a corked bottle drifting toward Cleveland, Ohio. And a woman in America's midlands, six hundred miles from tidewater, would read a message of shipwreck and disaster.

That was merely a gale. There were many gales, along with other hazards. The rocky shores, unlighted for many years, the upthrust islands, the blindness of fog and forest fires, the bitter winds of November that can sheathe a ship in freshwater ice, and the occasional hurricanes that roar down the seaways—many salt-water men have learned new perils on the lakes. Vessels that sailed the ocean have gone down to freshwater graves. The schooner Green Bay, after voyages to England and South America, came home to Lake Michigan and was lost with all hands and a cargo of iron ore. Two of the victims of the Big Storm of 1913, the Wexford and the Leafield, were British tramp steamers. They had weathered storms in all parts of the world, but the lakes sent them under. The lakes commerce opened with disaster, when the Griffin sailed past Washington Island and was never seen again. That began a long tradition.

The first fierce storm of detailed record was the hurricane that raged through four days of November in 1869. A gale blew up on Lake Superior; it whistled past the Soo and rose to frenzy on Lake Huron; undiminished it roared over Lake Erie, lashing those shallow waters into chaos; it went screaming over Lake Ontario and out to the Atlantic. From Thunder Cape to the St. Lawrence, shore lines were strewn with masts and spars, hulls and sails, and the battered ruins of lifeboats. In the shipping registers at Buffalo, Cleveland, Detroit, Chicago, men struck out the names of vessels that would never make port again. Those four days took a dreadful toll—seven steamships, one tug, eight barques, four brigs, fifty-six schooners, eighteen scows, three barges—a total of ninety-seven vessels lost or wrecked beyond reclaim. No one knew how many lives that wind extinguished.

Such a storm occurred once in a generation. But year after year the lakes took a steady and less spectacular toll. In 1860, a mild season, 377 wrecks were listed, with a loss of 594 lives. In 1871 a Manitowoc captain listed 1167 disasters—founderings, collisions, groundings, loss of deck loads, explosions, burnings. Between 1878 and 1898 the records compiled by the U.S. Commissioner of Navigation showed 5999 vessels wrecked on the lakes, with 1093 of them totally lost.

Some of the casualties were as mysterious as the Griffin—ships that sailed into the wide waters and vanished without a trace. Lake Superior has its secrets, and so has Lake Michigan. The steamer Telegraph, bound past Beaver Island in the great loneliness of northern Lake Michigan, never arrived at any destination. According to a tradition, King Strang and his Mormon pirates sank the vessel off Pyramid Point. But no sign of her turned up at Beaver Island or any other shore. On a stormy winter night the big strong passenger steamer Chicora left St. Joseph, Michigan, for Chicago. She sailed out into Lake Michigan, and to oblivion. Far out in the windy dark her lights blazed like the Pleiades; slowly they dropped over the sea rim, on the track for Chicago. But she never arrived, and no sign of her was ever found. Somewhere in those same waters disappeared the tragic steamer Alpena, last seen thirty miles from Chicago, with fifty-seven persons in her cabins.

An old Lake Huron mystery is the "two lost tows" that parted, on a stormy night, from their steamer escort. In the stress of storm the captain did not know until dawn that his barges had been cast adrift. Then he turned back to pick them up. He steamed in circles over the lake, but they did not appear. Other vessels joined the search until all Lake Huron was scoured. The two lost tows, with their crews aboard, had vanished.

The great cold lake of the north has been the scene of many disasters. Perhaps the strangest was the disappearance of the Bannockburn, a big strong freighter, twenty-four hours out from Duluth. She had passed Keweenaw Point and was steering straight for Whitefish Bay in a rising gale of wind. Her three masts swayed in the sky and the smoke poured out of her tall funnel. But she never rounded Whitefish Point. Eighteen months later an oar was uncovered from a mat of driftwood on the wilderness shore of upper Michigan. Around the handle was wrapped a ragged piece of canvas and beneath the canvas appeared the letters BANNOCKBURN carved roughly in the wood. No other trace of the freighter, or her crew of twenty-two men, ever came to light.

There were other wrecks, of known location. Fathoms deep they lie in the cold, pure water, uncorrupted and sound, and treasure hunters have brooded on the riches that pave the floor of the great traffic lanes. Especially along the immigrant route the wrecks lie thick, with rumored fortunes in them —like the side-wheeler Erie lost four hours out of Buffalo with more than a hundred thousand dollars in foreign currency and the New World hopes of all its west-bound immigrants.

One of the memorable losses on Lake Michigan was that of the steamer Westmoreland. Somewhere in the wide northern waters she sank with $100,000 in gold in her safe. The crew saved themselves and lived to tell the story of seventeen lumberjacks who locked themselves in their cabin at the first signs of storm. They had grown familiar with the perils of falling timber and the treacherous skidroad, but they had no stomach for a storm at sea. Around a barrel of whisky in that lurching cabin they drank away their fears, and their senses. So the waters of Lake Michigan closed over them. The Chippewas in the woods had learned to put bottles of whisky (skitty-wah-boo) on the graves of the dead, to warm them on their journey to the great hunting. The old sea dog, Captain Turner of the Mayflower, known over the lakes as a crusading teetotaler, often called up the ghost of those seventeen lumberjacks around their whisky barrel in the dark, cold depths of Lake Michigan.

Fortunes in copper and iron ingots, in whisky, in machinery, in shingles, coal and limestone, in tobacco, corn and wheat rest beneath the traffic lanes. In Lake Erie, off the mouth of the Detroit River, lies the steamer Clarion with a cargo of locomotives that never pulled a string of boxcars across the new rail ribbons of the prairies. Near her, on the soft Lake Erie bottom, lies the schooner Lexington loaded to her hatch covers with barreled whisky. Another cargo of whisky is in the steamer Templeton just off South Manitou Island in Lake Michigan. A cargo of oak and walnut timbers, worth a fortune at the present rate, went down in the schooner New Brunswick off Point Pelee in Lake Erie's western shallows. A legend still persists of a mysterious vessel that sank off Poverty Island, near Escanaba, with four and a half million dollars in her safe.

Other cargoes, less durable, have strewed the bottom of the lakes. Late in November, 1853, the schooner Sparrow, with a herd of cattle on its decks, was caught in a storm in Saginaw Bay. The cattle milled in their enclosure, frightened by the pitching ship and the whipping of the tattered sails. At last, to lighten the vessel and reduce the confusion on her decks, the crew cut the rails and drove the cattle overboard. They floundered in the heaving water and sank.

Captain Davenport of the Waugoshance Light (Wobble-shanks to the lake crews) once saw three schooners crash in a gale of snow. All went down together. During another storm in those waters a cargo of lard was dumped into Lake Michigan to lighten a ship grounded on Waugoshance Reef. For months the residents on shore gathered lard from their beaches. Still another grounded ship jettisoned a cargo of apples, and apples were plentiful along that shore all winter.

The schooner Rouse Simmons cleared from Manistique in a rising gale on November 25, 1913. It was just thirteen days after the "Big Storm" that had taken many ships and lives, and the shores from Duluth to Buffalo were still scarred with the pounding they had taken. The Rouse Simmons was loaded with Christmas trees for the Chicago market. She carried the spicy tang of spruce and balsam over the lake. Then snow began to fly and her Christmas trees were etched in white. On November 26, the Coast Guard patrol at Sturgeon Bay, scanning the lake during a lull in the driving snow, saw a schooner with a deckload of evergreen trees and distress signals flying. The guardsmen could not launch a boat in that water, but they telephoned the Coast Guard Station at Kewaunee, Wisconsin. The Kewaunee crew in their bigger surf boat searched through the wind and snow. Once they glimpsed the schooner. Her sails were blown to tatters, her deck was swept clean and her hull was sheathed in ice. Then she vanished in the snow.

That was the last ever seen of the Rouse Simmons, but the next April, fishermen on the Wisconsin shore complained that all their nets were fouled with Christmas trees.

On an August evening in 1865, while the amber light lay over Lake Huron, a boy walked over the lonely shore of Thunder Bay Island. Behind him seagulls were circling, and beyond the mainland the sun was a dying splendor over the great pine flats of northern Michigan. But his eyes were fixed across the water, a mile off shore, where two proud steamers, the Pewabic and the Meteor, were about to pass. The setting sun warmed their painted superstructures and made golden coins of all their portholes. The Pewabic was one of the finest ships of her time, on fresh water or salt, and the Meteor was a big strong vessel with a haze of wood smoke streaming over her counter. It was a sight for a boy standing in the sunset on an island shore. He could hear their engines throbbing, and see the people moving on their decks.

The boy was John D. Persons. Later he became Captain Persons of the big liners. He lived on the lakes all his life, but he never forgot that tranquil summer evening when two great ships came together with a sound like thunder. In that golden light the Meteor's wheelsman, supposedly executing a mistaken order, rammed his sharp prow square into the side of the Pewabic.

It nearly cut the Pewabic in two. She plunged twenty fathoms to the bottom of Lake Huron before the crew could reach their stations. With her she carried 125 lives, 300 tons of copper ingots, and a supposed $40,000 of currency in the purser's safe.

John Persons, standing astonished on that sea beach, saw the water close over the proud Pewabic. He knew the exact spot where she went down. A few years later he located the wreck and a salvage company began operations. But the Pewabic lay too deep. They could not reach her. Yet the knowledge of that sunken treasure burned in men's minds, and one vain attempt was followed by another. In fifty years ten divers were killed by the terrific pressure of that depth.

Into the twentieth century the Pewabic lay untouched, far beneath all currents and the great storms' agitation. Then in 1917 B. F. Leavitt, inventor of an armored diving suit, anchored his barge where the sea had closed over the stricken ship fifty-two years before. His diver found the vessel's rigging and structure still intact. In that armored suit, trailing his surface lines behind him, moving with that grotesque, slow underwater step, he walked the decks and entered the cabins of a vanished steamer. He found skeletons, patient and still in their cabins, with their trunks open and the garments of the 1860's hanging on the bulkheads. He found cheeses and bottled beer and quarters of beef in the steward's pantry. And an unfinished game of cards on a folding table.

From staterooms and saloons he brought up souvenirs that brought high prices on the Huron shore. Clothing, rings, watches, an ancient revolver, gold coins, box-toed shoes and slippers, paper money, bottled beverages, spectacles, toilet articles, walking sticks. That pure cold water had preserved all but the human lives entrusted to it.

There were three autumnal storms in 1905. The last one was the worst, though the others were bad enough. The final storm wrecked the Mataafa, of the Pittsburgh Steamer Company, in one of the sensational disasters in the history of the lakes.

On the morning of November 28, the steamers Ellwood, R. W. England, Edenborn and Mataafa set out on their last trip down from Duluth. They cleared the channel piers with the traditional farewell salute, three long and two short, and felt the breeze freshen out on the lake. The Mataafa was towing the barge Nasmuth, loaded with ore. The vessels were still in sight of the steep streets of Duluth when a violent northeast gale struck them. Quickly they turned back to the shelter of the harbor. Crowds gathered at the entrance piers to watch the race between four steamers and their old adversary the northeast wind.

The Edenborn and the England came driving on, with the wind on their after quarter, and their cargo decks awash. They gained the narrow entrance and made the harbor safely. The Ellwood was close behind them. As she breached the entrance a sea rose under her. It flung her steel hull against a pier. Bells clanged in the wheelhouse on her bow and in her throbbing engine room. She shuddered and freed herself. Her screw threshed the angry water. With black smoke streaming on the wind she staggered through to the inner harbor. There, before her pumps were all going, she foundered and sank. But her crew were saved.

Out in the furious seaway, a dark shape through the blowing spray, appeared the Mataafa with her tow. As she struggled toward the entrance she cast the Nasmuth adrift; it was hopeless to try to bring her through those narrow piers. The barge dropped two anchors, but the storm dragged her toward the rocks. Finally the anchors caught and held. With seas crashing over her like a tide rock, the Nasmuth survived.

Meanwhile the Mataafa was driving toward the canal piers. She made a fair entry, with half her length inside the canal, when a backwater checked her headway. For a moment she struggled there. Then a sea caught her stern. It hurled her against the north pier. Her whole frame quivered, and ice rained down from her rigging. Her engines pounded vainly. Her bow swung around, heading out to sea. But the storm flung her stern against the pierhead, tearing off her rudder. Unmanageable then, she went broadside onto the rocky beach. There her battered hull broke in two.

Part of her crew were forward and part were aft, with wild water over the broken deck between them. Rescue squads stared helpless from the shore. No boat could live in those pounding seas. Life-lines fell short. One man in the Mataafa tried to pass over the broken deck. Four times the hungry water swept him overboard, and four times he caught the railing cables and pulled himself back. Then while the thronged spectators shouted into the wind, he went back to the after cabin and froze with his mates.

From shore a life-saving crew shot rockets, and got a line aboard. But the small line froze and broke before they could haul out the heavy hawser. The doomed crew tried to float hawsers ashore on hatch covers and chests of drawers, but the seas smashed them on the rocks.

So forty thousand people gathered on piers and along the storm-swept beaches and on the heights of Duluth, watching the Mataafa's crew freeze to death. All night, while a snowstorm raged, they kept bonfires blazing to cheer the helpless men. In the morning the wind went down and the sea subsided. It was bitter cold. Part of the crew, in the forward cabin, were taken off alive. Aft, there were nine still men. Their eyes were staring and their faces were gray with frost.

In that storm thirty vessels were wrecked on Lake Superior. The steamer Western Star was thrown so far up on a shallow beach that people walked on dry land all around her. When the storm was over Duluth was buried in six feet of snow.

For years that tragedy on the doorstep of Duluth was commemorated with the "Mataafa" cigar, bearing a picture of the lost freighter on its band.

There was once a gospel ship, the steamer Good Tidings, on the lakes. She carried a cross on her foremast and her fo'c'sle was brightened by a trim of gold leaf. She cruised on a circuit of evangelism, putting in to many harbors. Her skipper, Captain Bundy, was a sky pilot as well as a navigator, who pictured the perils of wind and water and laid out the true course to salvation. In those days a seaman's calling was risky enough to insure him of an interested audience.

Captain Edward Carus of Manitowoc, the veteran shipmaster and marine historian, once served as mate under a captain of equal religious zeal. Three times daily in the officers' mess he recited a lengthy and eloquent prayer. It was a prayer of mixed metaphors and great fervor, and before a season was done every man at that table had it by heart. Years afterward Carus remembered that captain roaring his supplication while soup steamed on the table and coffee cooled in the

247

cups. "O Lord, lift up our feet from the rough road of life and help us to safely cross the gangplank of temptation into the ship of salvation. Let the hand of prudence guide our helm, the winds of love fill our sails, and the Good Book be our compass. And Almighty God, whose patience with humanity is everlasting, keep all hidden rocks of adversity off our course; let our bow cut clean the fresh waters of righteousness; steer us clear of Satan's derelicts; and may the bright rays of hope never die out of the lighthouses along the shore that we may make the run of life without disaster. And, O Lord, if it be thy pleasure, let the tides bear unto us in letters of gold the true meaning of thy Ten Commandments, that we may be mariners worthy of thy blessing. Let not our eyes be darkened by fogs of evil; keep ringing loud for our guidance the bell-buoys of faith. And when at last we have sailed into and anchored in the very port of death, may the good skipper of the universe say: Well done, thou good and faithful mariner, come and sign the log and receive eternal happiness as your salvage reward."

That prayer, with its knowledge of the sea's peril and its hope of refuge, came from an era of unmarked reefs and unreported weather. Now there are weather forecasts from government stations. Storm warnings precede the fury on the lakes. Modern ships carry direction finders, radio telephones and gyroscopic compasses. But no man knows when the Big Sea Water will rage, or stormwinds sweep down Lake Huron and make a frenzy of the shallow levels of Lake Erie.

CHAPTER TWENTY-TWO

The Big Storm

THE GOVERNMENT weather forecast for the upper lakes as published in Cleveland on November 8, 1913, was: *Snow or rain and colder, Saturday, with west to southwest winds. Sunday, unsettled.*

There was nothing to worry about in that forecast, but Milton Smith, assistant engineer of the steamer Charles F. Price, had an uneasy feeling. It was only three weeks till the end of the season, when the Price would tie up for the winter and the crew would receive their bonus along with the regular payday. But there was that gnawing in Milton Smith's mind. Despite the protests of John Groundwater, his chief engineer, he paid off the Price, packed his bag and walked ashore. Twenty-seven hours later the Charles F. Price went down with all hands. In the next three days forty vessels were wrecked and 235 lives were lost on the lakes.

On Saturday morning, November 8, an early winter storm struck Lake Superior. Vessels remained in port or kept under shelter of land until its violence was spent. Early Sunday morning the wind died to a breeze and the sea heaved slowly. Ships that had waited in the St. Mary's put out onto Lake Huron. Schedules had to be fulfilled even if the wind kicked up again. The crews battened down, stretched their life-lines from the forespar to the boiler-room bulkheads and watched the slate-colored sea.

Far out on the plains of Manitoba a new wind was growing. At the weather stations of De Tour and Mackinac, at Cheboygan and Bay City and Harbor Beach, storm signals were flying, the red flags flat against the hurrying sky.

At noon the wind freshened and changed direction. It swung abruptly from northwest to north, with increasing pressure, and then quickly to northeast. From that quarter it struck. All at once it was a hurricane, blowing at eighty miles an hour. Vessels on Lake Huron headed for shelter of the east shore, but the wind changed direction and beat them off their courses. Seas poured over cargo decks and pounded at the upper works. The wind brought a fury of snow, and waves ran higher. The most violent storm in history had struck the lakes.

It was a storm of cyclonic character. The wind swung from one quarter to another and the seas were a battering confusion. Masters who survived the storm said they had never experienced such violence, waves running one way and the wind another, with the ship assaulted between them. It lasted all afternoon and all night with never slacking fury. Winds of that velocity had never held for longer than five hours, but this storm maintained for sixteen hours a velocity above sixty miles per hour. Waves rose to unprecedented heights. Many masters stated that waves thirty-five feet high, following in quick succession, often three in a sequence, hurled and battered their vessels. In that ordeal eight staunch ships totally disappeared from Lake Huron and two from Lake Superior. There were no survivors to tell of the punishment that those ships took before they foundered. In addition, two barges sank in Lake Michigan, and a lightship was lost in Lake Erie. Twenty-six other steamers were driven ashore and mangled by the terrific seas.

That storm lashed every mile of shore from Duluth to Chicago and Buffalo. Beaches on Lake Huron were destroyed for scores of miles, gutted for hundreds of feet above the normal shore line. At Chicago whole sections of the newly made shore at Jackson Park were washed away. The Chicago Park Commission had spent eight years in construction of that land; it was destroyed in as many hours. In one of the Chicago water cribs, windows twenty feet above lake level were shattered and heavy furniture was licked out like driftwood. Miles of sea walls, terraces and piling washed away from Chicago's waterfront. At Milwaukee a massive breakwater, part of the new harbor project, was battered to rubble. At Cleveland twenty-one inches of snow blanketed the city and communications were cut off for two days. In Buffalo harbor entrance the lightship was torn from its moorings and no trace of it ever found. Another lightship at the entrance to Port Huron was torn loose and thrown upon the Canadian shore.

But the full fury and destruction were borne by the vessels in open water on the long traffic lanes.

The steamer L. C. Waldo, loaded with iron ore at Two Harbors, was midway across Lake Superior when the wind struck. Green-gray seas swamped her deck and the driving spray froze over all her upper works. The windows of the pilothouse iced over. That did not much matter in the blinding snow. Then darkness came, and the wind screamed higher. At midnight Captain Duddleson, a native of the Soo, was bent over his chart in the pilothouse, laying a compass course for Manitou Island, off the point of Keweenaw. His hope was to gain the island's shelter from that blasting wind. Thunderous seas smashed at the wallowing vessel. Each time the ship staggered, and drove on. But a dark sea, masthead-high, was gathering. It struck with the solid weight of a hundred tons of water. The captain and his wheelsman clung to a stanchion as the bulkheads gave way. Sea water poured over them. There was a wrenching roar. The ship lurched and straightened. But her pilothouse was gone, wiped off like a crate of cabbages from her deck. Worse than that, her compass was demolished and her steering gear was damaged so that she could not maintain a course against the wind.

Captain Duddleson sent his wheelsman aft, over the pitching ice-sheathed deck, to get a compass from the lifeboats. For four hours they steered the Waldo by hand compass in the flickering light of a hurricane lantern. With the wind dead aft, seas broke over her stern till only the ship's stack was visible pouring black smoke into the storm of snow.

With broken steering gear and a hand compass Captain Duddleson almost made his desperate passage between Gull Rock and the point of Keweenaw. He held his course to within half a mile of his reckoning. But that half mile was fatal. Just before daylight the Waldo fetched up on a reef running out from Gull Rock.

Now the seas battered her with an insane fury. Under those terrible blows the after deckhouse began to crumple. The crew went forward, clinging to the life-line while the waves broke over them. For two days and nights they crouched in the battered forward house. They burned the wooden furnishings in a bathtub to keep from freezing and ate the last of their provisions. On the third day the wind abated and the seas heaved with their spent anger. Help came from the Coast Guard crews of Portage and Eagle Harbor.

Other ships fought the same fight, with no survivors to recount their struggle. The James Carruthers was a big new freighter, just commissioned a month before. On her third voyage, loaded with grain, she stood out from Fort William, between Pie Island and the humped form of the Sleeping Giant. Then a wind came up and hurried her across Lake Superior. She waited a few hours in the St. Mary's River till the weather was reported breaking. Out into Lake Huron she sailed on that dreadful Sunday. She was never seen again. Some twisted wreckage and the bodies of a few of her men were found on the ravaged Huron shore.

To Captain Paddington and seventeen men in the steamer Turret Chief came one of the most harrowing ordeals in all lakes history. The Turret Chief, an iron ship of 4000 tons, bound light for Fort William, was driven off her course and disabled by the Saturday gale. After drifting fifty miles she was cast up on the rugged coast of Keweenaw Peninsula, six miles north of Copper Harbor. The seas drove her high on the rocks and left her wedged there with the wave crests lashing at her. The crew, dead beat after hours of struggle, had fallen asleep in their bunkrooms just before the ship piled up. They tumbled out to find themselves hard aground and the old wooden hull groaning in every joint. She would break up

at any minute. Without time to gather food or clothing they
threw lines over the side and went down like spiders. They
picked their way over the storm-swept rocks. On the wooded
shore they beat life into their numbed bodies and built a
shelter of boughs and driftwood. Here, without food or fire,
with a blizzard raging around them, they huddled from Saturday night till Monday morning. They grew grim with hunger
and gray with cold. Eighteen men were crouched in that
bleak shelter. They avoided each other's eyes, but the knowledge of death was in all their faces. Then a man stared incred-
ulous over that desolate shore. A shaking hand pointed. A file
of Indians came tramping through the snow. Two hours later
Captain Paddington and his men were drinking coffee around
a barrel stove in Copper Harbor.

Meanwhile, the steamer William Nottingham, bound down
from Fort William with a cargo of grain, fought for her life
on Lake Superior. After forty-eight hours of those punishing
seas she was still afloat. But her bunkers were empty. The
coal-passers raked out the last corner banks of fuel and the
firemen threw it into their dying furnaces. The steam had
dropped in the gauges and the Nottingham was swinging in
those long seas. Without her engines she would be hurled on
the rocks of Coppermine Point. Desperate, her master ordered
his crew to open the hatches. While the seas washed in they
shoveled grain up on deck and down the bunker hatch. In
the boiler room the shovels clanged again as wheat went into
the fire doors. The flames smoldered and hesitated. The drafts
whined and the firemen raked with their slice bars. At last the
heated wheat took fire; there was a low roar under the boilers
and the drafts whined higher. The gauges lifted a little. Soon
the Nottingham swung round till the wind was on her quarter. Stubbornly she labored into Whitefish Bay. It looked as
though she would make the Soo in safety. But she struck a
shoal four miles east of the steamship lane. There the seas

threatened to break her to pieces. Three of her men perished while trying to launch a lifeboat. A few hours later the Coast Guard took the rest of them to shore.

Two big freighters floundering through the ravenous seas of Lake Huron were lost just thirteen miles from the shelter of the St. Clair River. They were the Regina and the Charles F. Price. After the storm was over the Price was found with her 10,000-ton hull floating bottom side up a few miles off the Huron shore. It was days before anyone could identify her.

Milton Smith, who on November 8 had an uneasy feeling, had stayed ashore in Cleveland when the Price cast off her lines. Five days later he arrived in Port Huron to identify his former shipmates. The first body he recognized was that of John Groundwater, the Price's chief engineer.

"Are you sure?" demanded the coroner.

Smith was certain. He knew John Groundwater well, even after Lake Huron had put its somber mark upon him.

"John Groundwater, chief engineer of the Charles F. Price," the coroner repeated.

Smith nodded.

"Well," said the coroner. "This man had one of the Regina's life preservers wrapped around his body."

There was only one explanation. The Regina and the Price, laboring to keep afloat, had collided in the storm's fury and foundered together. Men from both crews struggled in the water. Life belts were thrown down and they floundered into them with their last numb movements. Bodies of the men in the two crews were cast up together on the shore, some even clasped in each other's arms. Herbert Jones, of Superior City, the Price's steward, was found with his apron frozen stiff around him, as though he were about to prepare a meal.

There was nothing more to do for those chaps, after the bodies were identified. So Milton Smith went back to Cleveland. He still had an uneasy feeling.

CHAPTER TWENTY-THREE

Freshwater Men

For MANY YEARS Martin Knudson kept the light on Pilot Island at the Porte des Morts passage from Lake Michigan into Green Bay. With a strong current and a broken coast that was an infamous entrance. In one week of 1872 eight schooners went ashore on the naked ledges. It was a literal Death's Door for many years.

After the reef of Pilot Island had taken scores of lives a fog horn was installed at the edge of the shoal. At first it deafened Martin Knudson's own ears, but in time he got used to it, even fond of it. He boasted that it could be heard for forty miles and regarded it with a kind of personal pride. Certainly it was a powerful horn. Farmers complained that its vibration put out kerosene lamps ten miles away. They said it killed young chickens in the egg and curdled milk in a few minutes. All the landsmen around Death's Door hated that moaning voice. But every steamer that swung through the passage, in fair or foul weather, gave Martin Knudson a blast of greeting, deep and long like his own fog horn.

One of the things a salt-water man observes on the lakes is that friendly salute. It roars out between ships passing; it greets the lock-tender at the Soo and the light-keeper at many a lonely point; a retired captain in his cottage on the St. Mary's is saluted at all hours, day or night, by the passing vessels of his line. For many years there has been a fraternal spirit on the lakes. It appears in the Shipmasters' Association, in the Lake Carriers' Association, even in the assembly halls for seamen in the large lake ports. It is reflected in the long history of amity and cooperation between rival companies, between officers and their crews. The lakes are big, but there are frequent meetings: ships pass within speaking distance and tie up alongside in the docks. And it is a single trade, all carrying the same cargoes, or nearly all, and sharing the same tradition. Though there are twenty separate lines of bulk freighters there is a unity among them. A green deckhand in a single voyage learns the colors of their stacks and the insignia at their mastheads. A veteran master knows all the ships of the fleet. He can name a vessel from a distance through his glasses, and he can tell the history, the reputation and the secret failings of every one.

For a century that common trade has given men a character in common: endurance, enterprise, imagination, patience. No other country has a seaway within its borders, and no other thousand miles of continent are linked so closely as the lakes basin. It has given inland men a wide sense of geography and a habit of thinking in large terms.

All through the expanding years the lakes had a lure for restless and far-seeing men. Men of many backgrounds met in the engine rooms and the fo'c'sles of the freighters—lads from the Soo and the towns along the St. Clair River, young mill hands from the lumber cities and farm youths from the grain ports. Among them appeared Irish and German immigrants, Scotch and British seamen direct from the Atlantic, and a growing number of Scandinavian settlers who found in the heart of America a mariner's calling. Most of these were anonymous men, who did their work and left no lasting name. But there are some whose names belong to the story of the lakes.

As a thirteen-year-old boy standing on the banks of the Hudson, Isaac Newton watched the historic Clermont make her first run. A light kindled in his eyes as the little steamer, puffing wood smoke out of its stove-pipe stack, disappeared around the bend. That light never died, and in later years he designed the largest and fastest boats on the river. But in time the wider waters lured him. He went to the lakes and designed the Western World and Plymouth Rock, the finest steamers on fresh water in the fifties.

In that decade a family emigrated to Canada from the lonely island of Islay off the southwest coast of Scotland. They settled in the Scotch community of Collingwood at the southern end of Georgian Bay. There the boy Alexander McDougall looked out at the blue horizon of Lake Huron. Apprenticed to a blacksmith, he worked half-heartedly at his trade. The other half of his heart was given to those wide waters. At sixteen he ran away to sea, shipping as a deckhand to Chicago. The throbbing lake steamers were more to his liking than a smith's steady forge. At eighteen he was a second mate; at twenty-five he was master of the Thomas A. Scott, one of the finest ships of the seventies. During those years in the wheelhouse and pacing the narrow bridge his mind was always busy, thinking about ships, lake ships that would carry a greater commerce than anyone could foresee. When he was twenty-six years old he helped to design the famous ships of the Anchor Line, the China, India, and Japan. That experience spurred him to develop his own design for freight carriers. In 1889 his first "whaleback" appeared—a ship with every non-essential stripped away, a ship that was nothing but a power-driven cargo hold with a pilothouse stuck on her bow and engines allowed a grudging place in her stern. The seas washed over her rounded sides, her snub nose poked through the crests. She rooted and wallowed on her course. "McDougall's dream" the other designers called his ships. The sailors called them "pigs."

Some fifty of these vessels came from Alexander McDougall's yards in Superior and Duluth. They snorted down the lakes, burying their snouts in the windy seas of Lake Superior and rolling in the cross-seas off Saginaw. For thirty years they were famous, though they never were purely typical of the Great Lakes trade. Two of them were still running in 1940; one had been converted into an automobile carrier, the other lunged down the lakes with red iron ore in her belly. No whalebacks have been built since the turn of the century.

Other men came to the lakes. James Davidson, George Ashley Tomlinson, Thomas Wilson, William P. Snyder, Augustus B. Wolvin, Harry Coulby and Henry G. Dalton are some of the memorable names.

THE LONG SHIPS PASSING

James Davidson, born of Scotch immigrants in Buffalo, was orphaned while still a boy. But even a boy could find his place in Buffalo's busy harbor. He built a rowboat and took up his stand at the foot of Main Street. Across the river stood a big fleet of grain schooners, crowded beneath the blank walls of the terminal elevators. Late at night, when the sailors were returning from the waterfront taverns, a boy's voice piped, with a trace of thick Scotch accent, and a boy's thin arms pulled at the oars as he ferried his passengers to their ships. Soon he was himself a sailor, learning a schooner's rig and the feel of a rolling deck. He was cabin boy, then seaman, and as his shoulders broadened his mind broadened also. He spent a term in young manhood on salt water—in the famous Black Ball packets to England, Russia and the storied ports of India. But he was a lake man, and salt water did not hold him. Back on the lakes he became master of sound ships. He saved money and bought into them, the Seagull, the Balina Mills, and the Louis Wells which could load 27,000 bushels of wheat and was famous in her time. Those were expanding years and James Davidson expanded with them. The Scotch boy who had built his own rowboat had come a long way, but he was still a builder. In 1871 he established his shipyard at Bay City on the Saginaw, close to the finest lumber that the continent possessed. There he built the James Davidson, the biggest wooden steamer on the lakes. Before his building was done he had launched more than a hundred ships and had left his name written large in the lakes story. The present steel steamer James Davidson is the flagship of the Tomlinson fleet.

George Ashley Tomlinson was a man of great energy and many interests. By turns he was a cowboy in Wyoming, a newspaper reporter in Detroit, a fancy rider with Buffalo Bill's Wild West Show, a special writer for the *New York Sun*. Back a second time as a newspaper man in Detroit, he married the daughter of James Davidson, shipping magnate of Bay City. Curious, restless, a pioneer by nature, he heard

James Davidson's stories of the lakes and soon the lakes had put their mark on him. He became one of the influential operators and built some of the biggest ships in the trade.

On Sugar Island in the St. Mary's River young Tom Wilson cut the wild hay and drove the cattle in from pasture. He was a boy who hated a farm. Island blood was in his veins—his father had come to the St. Mary's wilderness from the wind-swept Orkneys north of Scotland—and he had an eye for the water margin of that hayfield and the ships passing in the stream. When the mate of a sailing vessel saw the boy's broad shoulders and spoke of being short-handed on his ship, young Tom Wilson dropped his hayfork and jumped aboard. In a few years he was Captain Wilson, and before his voyages were over he had founded the Wilson Transit Company. Today the wakes of the big Wilson freighters wash the shores where young Tom Wilson watched the ships go by.

Across the Atlantic an English boy, Harry Coulby of Claypool in Nottinghamshire, heard of the Great Lakes, and determined to come to America to see them for himself. He came at the age of seventeen, and he walked from New York to Cleveland, six hundred miles. He not only saw the lakes but for forty years he played a part in their history. When he was buried, back in the village of Claypool, his name was on the big steel stem and under the sloping fantail of one of the largest freighters in the trade.

There is an old rhyme about the notorious serpentining of Cleveland's river.

> *You sail both north and south*
> *To reach the harbor mouth.*

And there is also some steering east and west before a ship gains the entrance. From the high level bridge you look down on a writhing river, straddled by railroad bridges and walled with warehouses, ore docks and elevators. That busy basin was the old Irishtown, where Irish workmen in their red woolen shirts bandied Irish jokes with men leaning on the chain rails of slowly passing ships. Down in those flats Henry Dalton spent a lively boyhood. He played on the riverfront, walked the ties of the railroad bridges, swam under the fantails of schooners and barges. As a lad he went to work on the ore docks. The lakes trade was his schooling, the endless cargoes, the noisy workmen, the tooting of tugboats and the blaring of big ships creeping round the turns. At twenty he began his career with the big iron-mining and shipping concern of Pickands, Mather. Eventually he was in charge of all their vessels. Henry Dalton grew up in a clamorous place, but he was a reticent man. When he was president of the Interlake Steamship Company they called him "the silent iron king."

But not all of the freshwater men became iron kings. Captain Jerry (Sockless) Simpson went to sea on the lakes as a boy of fourteen. He began as cook, but in time he was captain of some of the biggest ships of the 1870's. He had a career on the lakes before he went to Kansas to become a cattle farmer. Even after he took up Populism and politics, he remembered the way he had handled a ship's crew. Political storms were easy for a man who had weathered twenty-three seasons on the lakes. So he walked with a sailor's rolling step into the halls of Congress. He was a tall man, homespun, with a homely humor and a half-sad voice. The people in Kansas likened him to Lincoln and made a folk-hero of him. He kept the narrowed, far-seeing eyes of a navigator all his life.

Years ago, when the Poe lock was opened in 1896, a lad arrived at the Soo with an old-fashioned camera slung from his shoulder. He wanted to get pictures of the big boats going through. He stayed at that trade for the rest of his life, becoming official photographer for the lake marine. But he didn't snap all his pictures from the stone jetty of the canal. He went out through fog and storm and ice jams to get wreck pictures and collision scenes, required for admiralty trials. He was on the scene of every disaster and his camera recorded the drama of many seasons' commerce.

All around their shores the lakes have attracted collectors of their legends and historians of their trade. One of the most ardent and authentic of them was Eugene Herman, who from his cluttered office overlooking Cleveland's shipping basin published his monthly *Great Lakes News*. Gene Herman was a freshwater man from the start. Eighty years ago he sold newspapers on the Milwaukee docks. Even then he had a memory that didn't let things go; he knew every ship and every captain that entered the port. With his newsbag over his shoulder he shouted up headlines from the pierhead, and he was as ready to give a hand with a hawser as to sell his papers. Often he filled in as porter on ships that were short-handed. Whenever he didn't come home his mother knew he had gone out on a vessel. So he remembered the hum of the vanished sawmills at Cheboygan, when the mountain of sawdust was still growing above the river, and the tugboats towing ragged bergs of straits ice down to the icehouses on the lower Huron shore. Those memories went into the pages of his paper, but in the midst of a vanished scene he heard a whistle and saw a ship entering the turns of the Cuyahoga. He left his rickety old typewriter and ran down to the river to renew acquaintance with a mate or a steward or an engineer, and to glean an item for the *News*. He might begin a news story with rhyme, as when Miss Babette Block christened the big ship named for her father—

Cheerful Miss Block
Just took in stock
And looked the ship all over—

or with a reminiscence of the Milwaukee newsboy of 1892, or with the unabashed sentiment of an old-timer. His mind was a panorama of lakes history and his walls and cabinets were crowded with pictures and clippings that covered a lifetime. Sitting at his littered desk, with his rumpled frosty hair, his surprisingly youthful and expressive hands, his blue eyes suddenly lighting as he said, "That was fifty years ago," he was a fervent freshwater man. His paper was the product of an excitement that lasted half a century.

CHAPTER TWENTY-FOUR

From Duluth to Salt Water

FOR OVER A CENTURY the lake ports have been seaports, with access and trade to the ocean. In the 1940's there were four routes to tidewater: the Illinois Waterway, connecting the Chicago River to the Illinois, the Mississippi and the Gulf of Mexico, with a nine-foot channel; the New York State Barge Canal, joining Lake Erie to the Hudson and the Atlantic, with a twelve-foot channel: the Oswego branch of the Barge Canal, linking Lake Ontario with the Hudson; and the St. Lawrence canals, providing a fourteen-foot channel around the rapids of the St. Lawrence River. A considerable volume of shipping has used these waterways to carry cargo between the lakes and domestic and foreign seaports.

Deepwater trade from the lakes had its beginnings when the brigantine Pacific sailed out of Cleveland in 1844 with a cargo of wheat for Liverpool. In 1849, at the height of the gold rush, the barque Eureka cleared Cleveland for San Francisco, carrying fifty-nine passengers and a manifest of merchandise. The next year saw the first lakes steamer reach salt water. The propeller steamship Ontario churned out of Cleveland and took the long loop around Cape Horn for San Francisco.

The 1850's brought a growing trade between fresh and salt water. In 1854 John Thorson, a native of Stavanger, Norway, sailed his brig Scott from Lake Michigan to Norway and return. So in the hill-locked harbor of Stavanger there rode a trim craft with "St. Joseph, Michigan" painted under her fantail. Two years later the farmers on Lake Michigan sent their first grain direct to Europe. The steamer Dean Richmond loaded 14,000 bushels of wheat at Chicago and Milwaukee in mid-July, arriving in Liverpool on September 29. In 1857 the Madeira Pet loaded hides in Chicago and staves in Detroit, and delivered them in Liverpool. She came back that winter with a cargo of ironware and crockery. She reached the St. Lawrence too late in the season to pass the canals, and so returned to Detroit in the spring of 1858.

In 1858 eleven lakes vessels crossed the Atlantic, and in 1859 there were perhaps twice as many; one account lists forty-one vessels that cleared the lakes in that year for London and Liverpool, but the records are not consistent. At least, 1859 was a banner season for early trade to deep water.

The reason for this growth in foreign trade is found in the condition that was tying up sound new lakes vessels in the fifties. Railroad lines had spanned the lakes basin, and railroad competition cut into the domestic water-borne commerce, thus encouraging direct shipping to foreign ports. But the deep-water commerce dwindled more rapidly than it had begun. The Civil War put a sharp end to it, and after the war the dramatic growth of bulk traffic in iron ore, coupled with the growth in grain shipments, required all available tonnage for domestic trade. With the impetus of these new demands, lakes vessels grew beyond the dimensions of the St. Lawrence canals, and so there could be no resumption of foreign traffic on any considerable scale.

But at the end of the century, interest in Great Lakes-to-ocean shipping was revived. In 1895 began joint U.S.-Canadian discussions over an improved seaway from the lakes to the Gulf of the St. Lawrence. The idea took hold of midland farmers, merchants and manufacturers; they began to picture their lake harbors as seaports open to a vast and unimpeded traffic from the world's seaways. In 1901 Chicago was fired with a desire to ship grain direct to European markets. Five small steamers, built to the specifications of the St. Lawrence canals, loaded cargoes for northern Europe. But the ships were too small to make a clearly profitable venture, and no permanent traffic developed. The midwestern shippers began to urge an improved seaway that would accommodate efficient carriers.

In 1918 the International Deepwater Commission met at Ashland and heard a plea for decentralization of the foreign commerce of the United States. Wheat farmers told of the advantage of direct shipment to foreign markets, pointing out that half the cost of shipping grain from Duluth to Liverpool was incurred between Buffalo and the holds of ocean freighters in New York harbor. They argued that with the saving of handling, transfer and inspection costs, seaway-borne cargoes could reach Europe at rates but little higher than shipping costs from lake ports to Atlantic harbors in this country. Iron shippers said that with a new seaway iron ore could be shipped direct to Bethlehem, Philadelphia, and Sparrows Point, on a water level. Wisconsin paper manufacturers argued the need of a seaway to facilitate import of foreign pulp and pulpwood. The entire conference pictured the ships of many nations in the harbors of Michigan, Illinois and Minnesota and saw a vastly vitalized trade resulting.

The next year the Great Lakes-Tidewater Association was founded at Washington. It began as an association of seven Great Lakes states. Soon other middle-western and western states came in. They joined with the International Deepwater Commission in projecting a new deep lock at the St. Mary's Canal, dredging in the St. Mary's, St. Clair and Detroit Rivers, new and enlarged locks at the Welland Canal and new canals around the rapids of the St. Lawrence. These improvements would bring the Atlantic 1500 miles inland and permit farmers and manufacturers of the midwest to ship direct to the world's markets.

Even without those new channels foreign trade was developing. In the years following the first World War freighters from England, Sweden, Norway, Holland, Denmark, and Germany became familiar in the harbors of the lakes. When the new Welland Canal opened in 1930 with its spectacular locks carrying thirty feet of water on the sills, the greatest lakes vessels could enter Lake Ontario; but there remained the fourteen-foot channels of the St. Lawrence canals. Through that shallow draft a trade grew, coastal and South American, in sugar, sulphur, phosphate, soda, ore, steel, and an increasing trade went to European ports. In 1933 more than a hundred vessels from overseas brought to the lakes cod liver oil, canned fish and merchandise, and loaded return cargoes of machinery and motor cars for northern Europe. Before World War II a steady foreign trade was established, despite the limited channels.

During the dark 1930's the Seaway became a New Deal objective, the brightest of them all. Most of the proposal's critics had forgotten that Presidents Harding, Coolidge and Hoover all supported the project, and got nowhere with it. President Roosevelt had longer time to support it with his office, and he believed in it more ardently; it combined his two favorite measures, the development of water power and the prospect of increased maritime trade. Through the 1930's the project had intense support and equally intense opposition. The arguments on both sides were complicated and convincing.

Geographically the Seaway is the kind of undertaking that American people like. It is big, it is dramatic, it promised to release tremendous energies. Its supporters believed it would transform the Great Lakes into a Mediterranean Sea of the Western Hemisphere and bring new stages of development to a vast lake-bordered country. It would become the greatest marketing device ever created and would affect the lives of fifty million people. They claimed that its profit to farmers alone in a single year would equal the entire cost of the waterway, and that the hydroelectric power it would produce would pay for the whole project. In a more idealistic mood they boasted of it as the greatest achievement ever planned by two nations jointly for the good of their peoples.

There were more detailed and specific arguments to support the undertaking. Two huge dams in the International Rapids below Montreal would produce a large block of energy, which could be distributed in an area already in need of increased power. Shipways on the lakes could be utilized for building vitally needed naval and merchant fleets; already the United States Navy was building submarines at Lake Michigan shipyards. Transportation costs would be cut so deeply as to create vast new markets and stimulate business all over the country. One sanguine source estimated that savings to shippers on various commodities would approach a hundred million dollars a year. Other estimates put it below ten million.

Opponents of the Seaway argued that it would ruin the trade of Boston and cut heavily into the commerce of New York harbor. They feared that Buffalo, losing its rail-lake trans-shipping business, would face commercial paralysis; and in faraway New Orleans there was a conviction that the port's business would suffer. The eastern railroads, fearing a loss of coal, oil and motor-car traffic, saw the project as a dagger aimed at their continued profitable existence; the argument reminded veteran legislators of the railroads' lugubrious assurance many years ago that grass would grow on all the transcontinental lines as soon as the Panama Canal was opened. The shipping companies of the lakes opposed the Seaway on the grounds that, with the high wages and superior living conditions in their vessels, they could not compete with the foreign shipping that would crowd the traffic lanes of the lakes. Further it was argued that the Seaway, being closed by ice for five months of the year, could not function economically. All its opponents saw the proposal as a gigantic pork-barrel measure, threatening to drain the American treasury and to ruin many existing business interests.

Supporters of the Seaway insisted that the entire cost of the project to the United States would be about $285,000,000—"less than the cost of three battleships." Although shipping companies had opposed the measure, partly on the ground that the St. Lawrence River would present hazards to navigation, the late Robert Dollar wrote to the Senate Foreign Relations Committee in 1933: "Ships will certainly go to the Lakes for cargo; in fact, ships will go anywhere and everywhere to get cargoes. We have big ocean-going steamers running 1,000 miles up the Yangtze River, where the current is very swift and navigation quite difficult, far more difficult than it would be going to Lake Superior from Montreal. When the canal is finished there is no more reason for doubting that ships will go from the ocean to the Great Lakes than there is that ships will go to any port on the Atlantic seaboard."

The proponents argued that New York, though losing some of the foreign trade that passes through its harbor, would profit from increased coastal and intercoastal traffic. They saw grain, meat, dairy products and automobiles moving by ship into New York harbor, while iron and steel products, refined copper and zinc, brass, sugar and other commodities would move from New York by way of the St. Lawrence to the lakes. They added that Boston, Philadelphia, Baltimore and other ocean ports would have substantial gains in shipping traffic direct from the Middle West.

It was that kind of argument, one side contradicting the other, with no common agreement of the Seaway's effects on domestic and foreign trade. It was as much a division of opinion as of regional interests. One authority saw Boston's docks crumbling in disuse while rubber, wool and woodpulp went to the lakes harbors through the Seaway. The other saw a new boom for Boston, as New England shoes, machinery, fish and leather products went from Boston harbor to the lakes by water transport. The same contradictory arguments revolved about Buffalo. The opponents foresaw the end of Buffalo's commercial importance. The proponents asserted that though the port would lose some of its grain receipts it would retain all its flour-milling business and would gain so much new activity in steel, chemicals, aluminum and metal alloys that a generally increased prosperity would come to the city.

For two decades these controversies continued. The Seaway's potential or prospective victims cried out in an anticipation of injury, and its proponents exuberantly

274

described the new era it would bring to the industrial and commercial life of the Midwest. Then, in the 1950's the argument was ended, not by persuasion but by crisis in the North American steel industry.

During World War II half a billion tons of Lake Superior ore went into the Midwest blast furnaces, and in the yawning mine pits steam shovels were biting bottom. While direct-shipping ore ran out, mining companies concentrated lean ores and began extracting the iron content of taconite rock. These measures did not satisfy the hungry mills, and the steel industry looked for foreign ores. Rich iron ranges were explored in Venezuela, Chile, Peru, Brazil and Liberia. But dependence on such sources would compel the industry to move from its Midwestern base—the Ohio valley and the lower lakes—to coastal districts receiving imported ore. For a time it seemed the Midwest steel industry was doomed.

Then came reports of iron in Labrador, huge ore bodies just beneath the frozen muskeg in a lifeless land north of the Gulf of the St. Lawrence. Drilling crews packed into the Labrador bush. Engineers projected railroads, hydroelectric plants, mines and townsites in the interior, and deepwater loading docks at Shelter Bay and Seven Islands on the broad tidal mouth of the St. Lawrence River. Meanwhile powerful new voices were urging immediate construction of a seaway that would assure the future of the Midwest mills. It was estimated that iron ore from the Quebec-Labrador border would become 30 percent of the future Seaway traffic. First promoted by Canada, then by the grain-producing plains states, then by the lake ports, the Seaway finally had the crucial support of the steel industry.

After forty years of controversy came four strenuous years of construction. On a summer morning in 1954 the first dynamite blast rumbled beside the St. Lawrence rapids. Work began on a channel 192 miles long and 27 feet deep, including 45 miles of canal and seven high-lift locks. On April 25, 1959,

THE LONG SHIPS PASSING

the Dutch freighter Prins Wilhelm George Frederick dressed in all her pennants, steamed past Montreal and into the canal. She was the first vessel to navigate the Seaway.

In its first season twenty million tons of commerce used the new waterway. A third of the tonnage was iron ore from Labrador. Another third was grain from the great plains of the United States and Canada. The rest was coal, petroleum products, pulpwood and general cargo. The tonnage was carried in ships from seventeen countries. Since 1970 Seaway commerce has exceeded fifty million tons a year.

Thousands of miles from the St. Lawrence and the Great Lakes, shipbuilders designed vessels for the Seaway trade. From the big yards of Oslo came three 700- by 75-foot freighters. In 1968 the first of them, M/V Rowli, brought 21,000 tons of steel from Antwerp to Cleveland, unloading that cargo within sight of the Cuyahoga mills. In Cleveland the Rowli, working both ends of the trade, took on 20,000 tons of steel coils for delivery in Spain. Since then the international competition has increased—food products, chemicals and machinery crossing the Atlantic both ways. In June, 1974, for example, the spanking new British motorship Ajax, a sky-blue funnel above her snow-white six-deck superstructure, left $500,000 worth of Swedish automobiles on the Cleveland docks and took on a deckload of farm tractors. Officers of the Ajax were ruddy Scotsmen; the crew were Africans from Sierra Leone. Nearby on the Cleveland lakefront the Black Sea Line's Danetsky Khimik was loading farm machinery consigned to Constanza, Romania. In Toledo during the 1960's nearly 300,000 Volkswagons were unloaded from Seaway ships; lined up bumper to bumper they would reach from the Maumee River to the Hudson. Direct overseas trade now comprises two-fifths of Seaway commerce. One-fourth of its tonnage is Labrador iron ore consigned to the lower Lakes.

Although American and Canadian freighters have shared

276

the Great Lakes channels for a century, there are few American-flag vessels in the Seaway commerce. A typical Seaway voyage begins with a Canadian carrier downbound on a June morning in the Welland Canal. She lies deep in the water, burdened with 22,000 tons of grain from Thunder Bay on Lake Superior. Lake Erie is less than thirty miles from Lake Ontario, but is 326 feet higher. Through a pleasant countryside spaced with leafy towns the canal steps down by eight locks to the lower level. After twelve hours of watch and wait, stop and go, the ship moves through the Niagara portal into the wide, blue waters of Lake Ontario. The towers of Toronto, thirty miles northward, are like a mirage on the horizon.

After 150 miles, the lake narrows at Cape Vincent into the St. Lawrence, strewn with its Thousand Islands. At Iroquois the Seaway channel lies over the site of a town that twenty years ago was picked up and moved to higher ground. Here begins a 225-foot descent, by seven locks, to the near-sea level elevation of Montreal harbor, a hundred miles northeastward.

Approaching the Eisenhower Lock the freighter moves through a morning stillness, water mirroring the sunrise, and birdsong in the reedy shores. At this lock a tradition has developed; lake vessels put off a bag of grain that the lock tenders scatter. It is shared by bluejays, quail, blackbirds and a flock of Canada geese that nest in the foxgrass and cattails within sight of a massive powerhouse and a huge aluminum plant. This stretch of the St. Lawrence is a wildlife refuge.

Beside the seven Seaway locks—two of them American, five Canadian—are green lawns, bright flower beds, grouped benches and picnic tables, and many-windowed official buildings under the flags of the two nations. A different touch, haphazard and arresting, has been added by anonymous seamen. Soon after the Seaway opened, the sailors of many nations began to record their arrival. Put ashore to handle mooring lines, waiting on the long approach piers, they painted the names of their vessels on the pavement. The two governments sent cleanup squads to erase that graffiti and threatened vessel operators with fines for defacing public property. The names reappeared, in bolder letters and brighter colors—white, black, red, green, blue, yellow—in a greater variety of tongues and places. Regulation could not quell the instinct of world-wandering men to leave a name in passing. Now each approach is a carpet of color and geography—some names painted in darkness, some in daylight; some done quickly and carelessly, others (there are long waits at the locks) with meticulous care. Eisenhower, Snell, Beauharnois, St. Catherine, St. Lambert—each is a polyglot atlas and anthology that the lockmasters ignore. Kipling would have made a ballad of them.

Some of the records are just a name, others add a date, a few include a houseflag or fleet insignia. From many hundreds certain names stand out: Festivity, Panama, 14–6–73; Koltrona; La Chacra 20–8–71; Atlantic Eagle; M/S Exilona; Birim River; British Tramp Nicota de Labringa 22–7–71; M/V City of S. Albans; Blue Dolphin, Pireaus; Gloxinia; Penhir; M/S Matthias Bari; Archangelsk, Leningrad; M/S Bonoy, Philippines; M/V Delphic Sky; Marita Leonhart; Santom–V–Nurmahal; Pico Blanco; M/S Akita Maru; M/V Avenir Lucas, Chile, 1974; Visna Yash, S L J Lines: Scotspark 7–7–69; M/V Madhyapradesh; Gerd Denmark; M/V Jalakala; Queen of Ampelos; and in letters faded by sun and snow a plaintive Condoléance, Dernier Voyage 11–5–70. Along with the English alphabet are exotic registers in Greek, Russian, Bengali, Arabic and Japanese.

Massive energy is generated by the Seaway dams. Around the Eisenhower Lock a pastoral countryside is overlaced with power lines leading to huge industrial plants. The approach to the Snell Lock is framed by seven steel skeleton towers stretching a hundred strands over the canal; black-and-white cattle graze beneath a ceaseless silent transmission of a million horsepower.

For a hundred miles the pastoral and industrial commingle. Evergreen branches are lashed to automated channel buoys, to accent them in dim or hazy weather. Ships' whistles are answered by the twittering of skimmers, swifts and swallows. Beyond a horizon of metals plants lie Isle St. Regis and Ile Jaune, comprising Indian Reserve 15. Weathered barns and sheds show through the scattered trees. On the riverbank are garden patches, an old car dump, and a rusty tractor in a half-plowed field.

Below Cornwall the river widens into Lake St. Francis, a tranquil reach of thirty miles in the long late afternoon light. With an exchange of whistles our Canadian freighter passes the tanker Edgewater from Monrovia. Ahead is a red-hulled laker with a yellow-banded funnel. She rides high, her white forward house catching the sun. There is no smoke from the raked stack, but two towboats, bow and stern, are churning white water. An old Columbia Transportation Company vessel, she is being towed to Quebec City where ocean tugs will haul her on a last long voyage to breaking yards in the Mediterranean.

The stern tug obscures the vessel's name, but soon one can count her thirty-two hatches and spell out the rusted name at her bow—James Davidson. Built in 1920, a giant in her time, the Davidson has steamed three million miles on the Lakes and steered into scores of harbors between Buffalo and Chicago and Duluth. In 1930 a Margaret Bourke-White photograph in *Fortune* magazine showed the Davidson locking upbound, light, through the Soo, a dynamic portrayal of Great Lakes shipping. Now, hauled by two tugboats of the Marine Salvage Company of Port Colburne, the Davidson is dead as a derelict. Her engine room ventilators are hooded with sooty canvas; cabin doors, fore and aft, swing open; the wheelhouse windows are boarded blind. With her the name of a great man in Great Lakes annals goes to the scrapyard of an Italian steel mill.

As the old laker drops behind, the Canadian freighter passes Aizu Maru of Yokohama and Zawercie of Gdynia, her deck lined with container cargo from Poland. Other ocean ships appear, bringing fruit from South Africa, olives from Spain, wines from France, cameras and radios from Japan, whisky from Scotland, glassware from Denmark and Sweden. In the lake ports they will load machine tools, petrochemicals, soybean meal for European livestock and dried milk for school lunches in Japan.

Under the skyline of Montreal the St. Lambert Lock lowers the long freighter almost to sea level. Ten hours' sailing, past farms, forests, villages and the busy harbor of Three Rivers, brings the Norman roofs and spires of Quebec City. The lower town remains unchanged beside the river, and the Plains of Abraham still lean against the sky. But glass and steel towers almost eclipse the old church and university spires. The gray, enduring city has changed more in the last two decades than in the previous century. In hazy Quebec harbor, foreign ships line the cargo terminals. There is a distant glimpse of Montmorency Falls, a white gash in the steep green forest, soon hidden by the shores of Ile d'Orleans where each old village is gathered around a stone church with a silvered spire. Below the island the river widens, the long dark mountain slopes rising from tidal water.

At the mouth of the Saguenay, that fjordlike river 80 miles long and 900 feet deep, lights gleam and glitter in the northern twilight. The deliberate slow flashing to starboard warns of White Shoal. On the port side comes the double flash, at six-second intervals, of Prince Shoal Light, 83 feet above the water, visible for 14 miles. In thick weather its foghorn moans like a great beast. Long manned by lonely keepers, these lights are now automatic; sailors say the foghorn is sometimes triggered by the smoke of an old coal-burning cargo tramp. Now the lights flash from a steel mast above a pedestaled platform; twice a year the service crew land there by helicopter. Off the mouth of La Petite River, just above Baie St. Paul, suction dredges gush silt water into a pair of old mud-stained tankers. Tugs haul them to disposal sites for discharge. The St. Lawrence channel is being deepened and widened to take larger cargo vessels.

Grain from the heart of North America goes to many St. Lawrence ports for transshipment overseas. The easternmost grain terminal is at Port Cartier on Shelter Bay at the mouth of Rivière aux Rochers. Hacked out of granite and muskeg, Port Cartier is both wilderness and a vast, complex technology. Its roads, glinting with silica, connect ten-story granaries, a huge pulp and paper plant, acres of stockpiled iron ore and deepwater loading docks. Moss and lichen carpet the glacial rock. Labrador-tea (*ledum groenlandicum*) raises a clustered pale blossom out of the spaghnum bog. In tidal inlets strewn with huge boulders the water-willow lifts its single purple flower. Dwarf cornel with four white bracts around a bunch of scarlet berries spatters the gray-green muskeg. Amid these sparse fruits of the northern wilderness rise enormous elevators filled with the harvests of Manitoba and Saskatchewan.

The June daybreak comes to Shelter Bay at 3:30. In growing light the long dark shores emerge. Although there is no wind, scattered whitecaps break the slate-gray sea; black whales and white dolphins sport in Shelter Bay. At the ship's rail crewmen jig for codfish. Seals swim past and a wedge of geese fly low over the water.

The sun's first rays find two lake freighters lying at the grain dock. In the broad anchorage two Bombay ships ride high and empty: Jagat Pamini and Antipargos, each with a forest of king posts and cargo booms and an abrupt stern cabin surmounted by a blue-and-yellow funnel. Toward noon the Canadian freighter moves into a berth alongside the 60,000-ton Bettina of Oslo and across from the Victore of London. Beneath the huge granaries, twin legs of the unloader dip into the golden cargo. Rivers of oats, wheat and barley flow upward on an endless chain to conveyors that pour into lofty storage bins.

Away from the dust and rumble of the long dock a plaintive birdsong is answered and repeated in the roadside bush. Mosquitoes swarm up from bog water and the black flies stick like nettles. (Never forget the repellant.) Technology came to this place in the 1960's, as it did to Lake Superior shores a century earlier. But here it came full-blown and swiftly. Beyond the ore dock and railroad yards future plants are staked out in the tangled bush. A drilling rig, half hidden in stunted spruce and cedar, has been probing the sites of new construction. History is hurrying to this primeval place.

Prodded by tugboats the empty Canadian freighter slips out of her berth and heads seaward. Fifty miles north is the city of Sept-Iles, "metropolis of the North Coast." To Sept-Iles a railroad brings ten mile-long trains a day of iron concentrate from mines on the Labrador plateau. The ore trains have neither engineers nor brakemen. An electric eye in the lead diesel halts the cars when caribou are crossing.

Two hundred miles north of Sept-Iles and 2,000 feet higher begins the Labrador Trough, which extends 400 miles northward to Ungava Bay. One of the earth's great mineral deposits, its exploitation has just begun with mining of an orebody four miles long, over a mile across, and deeper than anyone knows. Here are the new twin towns of Wabush and Labrador City, with churches, schools, theaters, restaurants, bowling alleys, public libraries and shopping plazas. The mining and milling are done by monstrous machines controlled at a console of buttons, switches and winking colored lights. In never-resting machines the iron-rich rock is crushed, ground, filtered, cleaned and concentrated. As a black sparkling dust it is conveyed to loading bins that automatically fill the railway cars that carry it to Sept-Iles. Nowhere in the world is there greater production with fewer men. Power for this huge labor comes from Twin Falls on the Unknown

River, on lines strung over an almost impassable land.

Sept-Iles began as a trading post three hundred years ago. By 1910 it had thirty-four white families and some 600 Montagnais Indians. From their fishing village, explorers trekked into the endless bush and brought back rude maps of mineral riches on the Quebec-Labrador border. To reach those riches the Quebec, North Shore and Labrador Railway was built in the early 1950's. In 1975, with 30,000 people and an area of 210 square miles, Sept-Iles has 8 banks, 14 hotels, 7 churches, 3 weekly newspapers, a baseball stadium, 21 schools and a Junior College. At the eastern edge of Seven Islands Bay is the plant and loading dock of the Iron Ore Company of Canada, which began shipping ore in 1954. At Pointe Noire on the western edge, thirty miles around the horseshoe harbor, is the pellet plant and loading dock of Wabush Mines, which began shipment in 1965. What the Mesabi towns of Hibbing and Eveleth were to Duluth seventy years ago, the towns of Wabush and Labrador City are to Sept-Iles. An endless tonnage of ore comes down to the big deep harbor.

At Pointe Noire in long, many-leveled, windowless buildings the concentrated ore from Wabush Mines is ground to powder and then agglomerated into marble-size pellets. The plant works day and night, the year round. Its huge grinding mills and balling drums are never silent, the fiery indurating grates never grow cold. From those traveling grates the hard round iron pellets move through a stacker to stockpile and loading dock. Still warm from the baking, they pour from the long conveyor into the holds of ships bound for Ontario, Illinois, Ohio, Italy, Germany and Japan.

Five days from Sept-Iles the Canadian freighter is berthed under the Hulett unloaders in Ashtabula harbor. When the hatches are open, the mounded black cargo shows patches of pale green vegetation; stray seeds of wheat and barley had lodged in seams and ledges of the hull. Grain that never grew in Labrador has sprouted on that rich warm cargo from the tundra.

CHAPTER TWENTY-FIVE

Iron Is Master

DURING HIS LATER YEARS Thomas Edison took wilderness vacations with Henry Ford and Harvey Firestone, making camp beyond the reach of electricity and motor cars. In 1924 they visited Ford's iron and lumber properties in upper Michigan, under the Huron Mountains. If the talk occasionally turned to business, that did not bother Edison; deaf from boyhood, he couldn't hear it anyway. He liked the clear blue skies, the far blue water, the slowly fading sunsets, and the aurora shimmering in the northern heavens. A poor sleeper, he sometimes strolled at midnight with his thoughts for company.

Edison had some memories of the Lake Superior country. At the western end of the Marquette range the Baron-Humboldt mine had thinned out in the 1880's, leaving the town of Humboldt half empty. In 1888 Edison came out from New Jersey and built a crusher and magnetic separator to upgrade the ore. The process looked promising, but before the mill achieved full operation it was destroyed by fire. Back in the East, Edison tried again. On a Long Island fishing trip he found immense beds of heavy black sand on the beach near Hampton Bays. Wherever he held a magnet, particles swarmed to it like tiny ants. To concentrate that magnetic sand he began construction of an experimental plant on the empty beach. Before the building was done, a storm washed the black sand into the sea. His third attempt, a plant in Rhode Island, produced marketable ore. Then in New Jersey he built a full-scale plant—just as the rich Mesabi ores overwhelmed the market. At this point Edison converted his machinery to the manufacture of cement, and in his laboratory he resumed work on the fluoroscope and the kinetograph, which made the world's first motion pictures. In iron ore projects he was ahead of his time, but the processing of lean ores was inevitable. Even the vast Mesabi pits would not yield rich ore forever.

Modern civilization rests upon steel—from the surgeon's

scalpel to the dynamo, the skyscraper and the suspension bridge. Equally dependent upon steel is modern warfare—guns, tanks, ships, planes, ammunition. Bombs away! means steel roaring through the sky and steel raining on the earth. During World War I the Lake Superior mines yielded record tonnages of iron ore. Between 1920 and 1941 annual shipments down the lakes averaged forty-five million tons. In 1942, with the United States at war in Europe, Africa and Asia, the Lake Superior loadings soared past ninety million tons. The shafts probed deeper into the Michigan ranges and in Minnesota steam shovels enlarged the yawning pits. To the United States War Production Board came a warning that the reserves of high-grade ore were disappearing.

With direct-shipping ores—ready for the blast furnaces—nearing exhaustion, a new generation of men took up Edison's task of beneficiating inferior ores. "Beneficiation" was an umbrella name for several processes: crushing and washing and drying, removing such wastes as silica, fusing by heat a sintered ore of adequate iron content. These were temporary measures. Even the lean ores would soon be gone.

Meanwhile a new generation of explorers were hacking through the woods and swamps, hauling three-legged diamond drills over corduroy roads and fire-scarred barrens. No more mule- and man-power, these crews had bulldozers, trucks and gasoline engines. They were sampling the entire iron-bearing formation that loops around western Lake Superior. In it like raisins in a breadloaf were the pockets of rich ore that had already been dug out and shipped away. Now it was the mother rock, the hundreds of miles of mineral strata, they were exploring. In Michigan the mother rock was jasper, a tawny iron-bearing quartz. In Minnesota it was a granite-gray taconite.

Back in 1892 men thronged the Hotel Spalding in Duluth, crowding around prospectors just in from the Mesabi. The most excited city in America, Duluth buzzed with rumors of iron outcrop and great beds of rich red hematite. Among the lumberjacks and bush-whackers, their boots stained red and purple from the test pits, was a slow-speaking man with a neat book of field notes. He was state geologist N. H. Winchell, who had covered more ground than any timber cruiser. In his systematic survey he had found a vast body of pre-Cambrian rock with 20 to 35 percent iron content. There was nothing exciting in that, or in his low-keyed report: "The rock is widely spread over the whole length of the Mesabi, and being different from anything found elsewhere and peculiar to the horizon of the Taconic, has been called *Taconyte* by the writer." Only a scholar would have known that name. In the geologic timetable the taconic age bridges the Ordovician and the Cambrian, and certain taconic strata are iron-bearing formations. Hence the Taconic Mountains of western Connecticut and Massachusetts, from whose iron furnaces came cannons for the American Revolution.

Following Winchell's explorations later geologists found that Mesabi taconite lies in a great band, 110 miles long and up to 2 miles across, and from 500 to 700 feet deep. During the age-long folding and upheaval, percolating waters leached away the silica, enriching iron content at certain points along the range. Those rich pockets became the open pit mines of the twentieth century, excavations that yielded two and a half billion tons of iron ore. But the end came in the 1950's, shovels scraping bottom and trucks hauling up the last of the soft rich hematite.

What remained was the taconite, billions of tons the geologists said. But it was harder than granite and the iron locked in it was in particles that only a microscope could see. If that adamant rock could be brought up, crushed, pulverized; if the granules of iron oxide could be extracted and then put together for smelting, Lake Superior mining had an almost endless future.

So began a long sequence of experiments. In 1915 a group

including Horace Winchell, son of the geologist who named the taconic strata, set up a pilot plant on the lake shore at Duluth. After five years they moved their operation up onto the range. Twelve miles north of the old Mesabi station they built a mill and a shack settlement in the woods. A bookish man like his father, Winchell wanted to name the raw town Argo, for the myth of Jason and the Golden Fleece. But it was given a more mundane name, Babbitt, for a mining company lawyer in New York. Through two years Babbitt was a scene of frustration—broken shafts in the crushing plant, shattered couplings in the grinding mill, men plagued by dust in the rolling mill, and the sintering machine breaking down after each repair. The plant closed down in 1922, and the men went back to Duluth. Taconite, they said, was a heartbreaker.

In England a seventeenth-century clergyman, Joseph Glanvill, wrote learned works on both Witchcraft and the Advancement of Knowledge. "Iron seemeth a simple metal," he wrote in 1668, "but in its nature are many mysteries." He never heard of taconite but he might have been describing it. Hard enough to cut glass—the old diamond drill broke like a matchstick in that strata—it yields particles of iron finer than talcum powder. It demanded a new method of mining, but what method? The answer came with fusion piercing, kerosene burned with oxygen in a blowpipe rotating against the rock face. With terriffic heat the drill burns in, and a jet of water following the flame splits off heated fragments, opening the strata to charges of blasting powder. The blast leaves chunks of taconite. Some of the chunks are ready for the crusher, others require breaking down by the "skull cracker," dropped by a movable crane. All of it has to be ground finer than gunpowder before the iron can be extracted.

At Frank Hibbing's lumber camp in 1892 the loggers found iron ore while digging a well for drinking water. In the next half century five of the Mesabi's largest mines, each one big enough to swallow an Astrodome, yawned within the Hibbing village limits. A single location, the fabulous Mahoning pit, yielded 121 million tons of ore during World War II. With the hematite about exhausted in the 1950's, Hibbing men looked to taconite. After repeated trial and error, hope and disappointment, came the development of efficient magnetic separators. Extracting the minute particles of iron was half the problem; the other half was putting them together for consumption in the blast furnace. Again trial and error, failure and hope. In fiery ovens the laboratory men tried fusing the material into clinkers, nodulizing it into lumps, baking it into pea-size pebbles. When the pebbles were enlarged to pellets, they had the answer. Pellets did not stick, freeze or shatter. They were free-dumping in all weather and all seasons. They were porous enough for ready reduction in the blast furnace. Out of the pilot assembly came high-grade pellets, 64 percent iron, hard and round like a hazelnut but ten times as heavy.

For full-scale production further tests led to better equipment—from steel cloth to nylon cloth in the filters, from a cylindrical to a rectangular furnace for the baking process. At last experiment gave way to steady production.

At the crushing plant the rock went in, jagged, hard, heavy. After four stages of crushing, it was reduced to pebble size. With water added it moved on to the rod and ball mills that ground it to a black mud from which magnetic separators drew off the iron particles. Pumped into the pellet plant, where water was filtered out and an adhesive added, the concentrate was rolled into pellets in huge revolving drums. Dried and hardened in the baking furnace, the pellets passed on to a conveyor belt that dropped them into railroad cars. During aeons past, while the earth heaved, cracked and folded, and ground water leached away the silica, nature turned taconite, at certain locations, into iron ore. In a few hours modern technology does the work that it takes nature over millions of years to do. The taconite plants create an industrial resource from primordial rock.

The Minnesota arrowhead, the wedge of land north of Lake Superior that comes to a point where the Canadian border meets the lake, is a silent, somber country. Big as the state of Connecticut, it is crossed by a Y-shaped highway, one leg ending at Two Harbors, the other at the mouth of the Baptism River. A few forest roads thread the bush; they mostly begin and end at nowhere. But that lonely country has three busy railroads carrying a huge tonnage of iron ore. The Duluth, Mesabi and Iron Range road dates back to 1894 when it began hauling Vermilion range ore over the unguessed riches of the Mesabi. The other two railroads are recent. Built since World War II the Reserve Mining Company railway runs from Babbitt sixty miles south to Silver Bay; the Erie Mining Company road runs seventy-four miles east from a big processing plant just above Hoyt Lakes to Taconite Harbor.

In a lorn landscape swept by fire sixty years ago and now grown up in spruce, birch and poplar, industry has made an island in the wilderness six miles north of the new town of Hoyt Lakes. Under a long northern ridge that marks the height of the Mesabi range, stretch huge blank-walled steel buildings. A curving road climbs up, past the grind of trucks and the rumble of railroad cars, to a windy crest. East and west lie the taconite quarries, with jet-piercing drills flying plumes of steam. A powder blast echoes and massive shovels load the rock into side-dumping railroad cars. The crushing and concentrating plants swallow 4,000 tons an hour, a 100,000 tons a day, more than 30 million tons a year—which yields 10 million tons of pellets.

From storage bins the pellets pour into railroad cars. Beyond the plant the long ore trains travel through a green silence. Hawks, herons and killdeer fly up from the marshes; the track of deer, bear and moose is printed around pink clumps of fireweed. This has been a land without habitation since time began, but at Milepost 10 the Erie line crosses under the Reserve railroad, which moves crushed taconite to a plant at Silver Bay. When two trains pass, the wail of their whistles hangs over the wilderness. Beyond the Greenwood River the Erie line traverses the "big muskeg" where ten miles of bog was replaced with stable track bed. The railroad crosses and recrosses twisting streams, the Partridge, Stony, Manitou and Two Island rivers. At Milepost 62 the train bores into a tunnel through the rock escarpment that frames the lake shore. It comes out to a dramatic sweep of down-sloping forest and the far, bright horizon of Lake Superior. Tracks end on the high white cliffs of Taconite Harbor. At Tac Harbor—as the lakemen say—a hundred-car train is emptied in an hour, dumping the pellets into bins above a row of conveyor belts. While a freighter pumps out its ballast water, pellets pour into the hold, 10,000 tons an hour. Asked how many pellets in a ton, an Interlake mate once weighed a pound of pellets and counted 192. That gave him 384,000 to a ton, and something like 5 billion in a cargo.

In November, 1973, at Hibbing, Minnesota, came the end of a legend on the Mesabi. After eighty years that yielded 130 million tons of iron ore, the Mahoning Mine was finished. The last truckloads came out of the pit and the traditional "clean sweep" broom rode down to Duluth on the last train-load of Mahoning ore. But Hibbing was not finished. While the vast pit filled with silence, a roar and rumble began just beyond the Mahoning's northern rim. In tangled woods bull-dozers were "brushing" a 150-acre site for the Hibbing Taconite Company plant, a joint enterprise of Bethlehem Steel and Pickands Mather. With full production in 1976 the plant will surpass the fabulous Mahoning, producing an annual 5½ million tons of pellets for many decades to come. Over the route that carried the Mesabi's first open pit iron ore an endless flow of pellets will move to the Duluth-Superior lakehead.

THE LONG SHIPS PASSING

Among the French and Indian names on the map of upper
Michigan are some stolid English names—Gladstone, Arnold,
Brampton, names chosen by railroad promoters who were
selling stock to British investors. At the turn of the century
the most resounding British name was Rudyard Kipling, poet
of the empire, and both Kipling and Rudyard got onto the
map: Kipling on Escanaba Bay and Rudyard in the woods
near Sault Ste. Marie. Informed of his two offspring in the
wilderness Kipling sent an impromptu rhyme to the railroad
man who had named the stations.

> *. . . They do not make me walk the floor*
> *Nor hammer at the doctor's door;*
> *They deal in wheat and iron ore,*
> *My sons in Michigan.*

Ten years later, recalling that in European folklore iron
could exorcise demons and witches (hence the horseshoe over
the stable door—to protect the animals), Kipling wrote the
ballad "Cold Iron."

> *"Gold is for the mistress—silver for the maid—*
> *Copper for the craftsman cunning at his trade."*
> *"Good!" cried the baron, sitting in his hall,*
> *"But Iron—Cold Iron—is master of them all."*

In the Labrador wilds in the 1890's, gold prospectors
cursed the iron ore that bewildered their compasses. Half a
century later, when a new iron ore technology was ready to
meet the world's unending demand for steel, Labrador became a luring name. Iron was the master that sent geologists,
explorers and construction crews into the subarctic wilderness, that built railroads through the Labrador bush and loading docks on the Gulf of the St. Lawrence.

One of the pioneer geologists in that never-never land was

Stephen Royce from Crystal Falls, Michigan, on the Menominee iron range. The son of a Harvard philosopher, Royce went to the Lake Superior region as a young mining engineer and spent years as an explorer for iron companies. He was an ardent collector of firearms, a voracious reader, a prodigious eater, a tireless swimmer, a furious driver of automobiles, a lover of the northern woods and waters. Once at Gogebic Lake some men found his car at the end of the road and footprints in the sand, but the big cold lake was empty. They sent for the sheriff to report a drowning. When the officer arrived, hours later, something appeared far out on the lake. It came nearer—a big head and a powerful pair of shoulders. Out of the water strode dripping Stephen Royce, ready to eat, drink and argue.

Royce had strong opinions about religion, medicine, food, automobiles and air travel. He loved poetry and knew Kipling by heart. In 1936 Steve Royce and a friend were sent to Labrador to make a preliminary survey of iron lands. They had to fly in, though Royce had strong views, with statistics to support them, about the hazards of air travel. Informed that they would be furnished $100 parachutes, he found that there were better parachutes at $200 and he demanded them. The two men were landed at Knob Lake and they spent a season in that empty country wading swamps, hacking through thickets, and fighting black flies and mosquitoes. With gasoline hand drills probing the muskeg they got a glimpse of the immense Labrador Trough of iron ore. Back in civilization, his parachute still untested, Royce remarked that he had stood on a range of iron that could become a new Mesabi.

At that time world conditions argued against a huge financial risk, and low cost iron ore was still available on Lake Superior. The mining industry was not drawn to a remote and difficult source of supply. Stephen Royce went on geologizing in upper Michigan until his death in 1954. But he had seen iron lands that in time would dwarf the ranges of Lake Superior.

Iron is one of the earth's most common elements. Nearly 5 percent of the earth's crust is iron. But almost never is pure metallic iron found in nature, and it is not commonly found in sufficient concentration to warrant mining and refining. Where iron is mined depends upon the quality of the ore, its accessibility to men and machines, and the means of transporting it to the world market. A map of the earth showing major iron deposits has a speckled look. The iron locations are mostly dots, some larger than others as though marked by a freshly wetted pen. But the largest marking is much more than a dot; it is a fishhook shape, a thick-shanked fishhook, in a remote and forbidding province of Canada. This is the great Labrador Trough.

The Labrador Trough, rich in many minerals, extends 400 miles from the Quebec-Labrador border to Ungava Bay. The lower portion of it, closest to the waterways of the world, is designated the Quebec-Labrador iron field. This segment of the trough is 90 miles long, 30 to 40 miles across, with ore beds just beneath the surface. Setting up their drills twenty-odd years ago, the geologists bored in. From each hole came hundreds of feet of test core. Laid out on the ground like varicolored macaroni, it was a kind of x-ray of the buried strata. Rubbing their iron-reddened hands over an oil lamp under a pitch of dripping canvas, the explorers mapped the ore body that had waited for aeons under the muskeg. In a single deposit they reported more than a billion tons of high grade ore. Thousands of miles away, in Frankfurt, Hamburg, Milan, Toronto and New York financiers began selling $235 million of mortgage and trust bonds to create a mining industry in the wilderness.

In a terrain carved by the Pleistocene ice sheet, scraping off hilltops and filling valleys with boulders, gravel and sand, the dense spruce forest spreads northward to subarctic barrens. The bush is broken by countless unnamed lakes, sere prairies of muskeg and the scars of forest fires. Through unmeasured time it was a silent realm, but in the 1960's came the drone of airplane and helicopter, the rumble of bull-dozers, the grinding of trucks. Tent houses were hauled over corduroy roads. Track-laying began on a 360-mile railroad. To light the town and heat the houses and drive the machines in ore-processing plants, hydroelectric power flowed through high tension lines from the falls of the Unknown River. Then came the whistle of a locomotive and the clatter of railroad cars. The first trainloads of ore went down to Port Cartier, Sept-Iles and Pointe Noire on the St. Lawrence, where American and foreign freighters would carry it away.

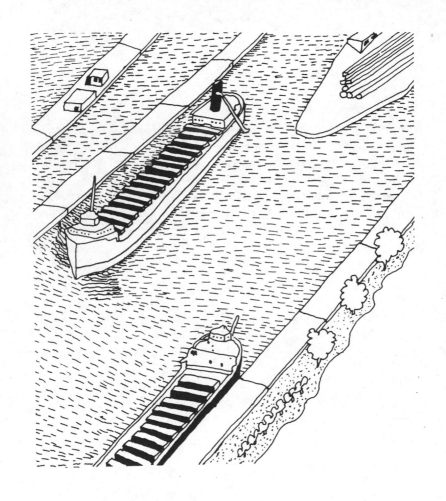

CHAPTER TWENTY-SIX

Overlook at the Locks

Until 1957, when the great bridge spanned the Straits of Mackinac, upper Michigan was sundered from the South. Then, with a four lane-highway, the world found Sault Ste. Marie. For the stream of visitors the town reclaimed its history with markers, memorials and museums. Now its Tower of History offers a seagull's view of the surroundings, a tourist boat transits the canal in the shadow of great freighters, and observation platforms rise beside the busy locks.

Freighters are always in view at Sault Ste. Marie, and one of them is on view to multitudes every season. Moored in the City Dock on permanent station, the 550-foot S.S. Valley Camp looks like a working vessel until you see the line of people filing up the gangway. After fifty years of hauling bulk cargo it is a museum boat, now listed in the National Register of Historic Places as an example of the long ships that have implemented the age of steel.

A guided tour from engine room to pilot house includes an exhibit of photographs and relics in the Number Three cargo hold. The oldest and most arresting artifact is a Chippewa canoe, the first means of transport on the lakes. Sturdy and graceful, strong enough to carry heavy loads yet light enough for portage, it is a native product that white men would imitate but could not improve. Under the sewn birchbark is the old tension the Chippewa builders gave it, stout crosspieces bowing out the rim, curved ribs shaping the bow and stern. That worn and dented craft made long journeys—to Grand Portage, Moose Factory, Winnipeg, James Bay. Most of its travels were in the wild north country, but once it went to Windsor to welcome the Prince of Wales (Edward VII) on his visit to Ontario. After a trip on the Detroit River and Lake St. Clair, the Prince gave each of his ten Indian paddlers a barrel of crackers. With that cargo they pushed up the wide waters of Lake Huron and through the wooded straits of the St. Marys. Now the canoe is berthed in a freighter's hold while the big bulk carriers steer past.

THE LONG SHIPS PASSING

A hundred and fifty years ago tribesmen gathered at the Sault, pitching their camps beside the loud, white water. Every spring they came, following dim trails through the great woods, paddling over the Big Sea Water. Sap was running in the maple groves, fish swarmed in the river. With whoops and cries the Chippewas ran the rapids, a bow man netting fish from swirling waters, a stern man steering through the spray. There was fabulous fishing then; the Indians traded a hundred pounds of whitefish for four fingers of tobacco. They boiled maple sugar in smoky kettles and roasted fish in the coals. They feasted after the hungry winter. All night campfires twinkled on the shore.

This was the ancient Chippewa capital, and there was a Chippewa name for the water racing down from Gitchee Gumee: *Paiwating* ("shallow cataract") they called the mile of wild water falling twenty feet from the level of Lake Superior to the level of Lake Huron. But the French had been there a long time too—this is the oldest white settlement west of Montreal—and the priests gave it their most cherished name. Along with bark chapels and burial crosses they planted in the wilderness the name of the gracious Virgin.

Surrendered (on paper) to the United States in 1783, the Soo region continued to be occupied by the British. Even after the War of 1812 they retained a fort on Drummond Island and controlled the entire St. Marys waterway. British merchants, often with French factors and voyageurs, held on to the Indian trade despite the terms of international treaty.

Now Sault Ste. Marie has a million visitors a year. In 1819 it had one. That summer the pioneer lakes steamer Walk-in-the-Water left its regular run on Lake Erie for a voyage to the Straits of Mackinac. Among its passengers was Alexander Macomb, colonel of engineers in the United States army. From Mackinac he made a side trip to Sault Ste. Marie, which was then only a French mission station. With Chippewa paddlers Macomb explored and mapped the intricate St. Marys waterways. On his map—two miles to an inch—he noted: "The land not good, trees mostly spruce and Canada balsam." The Little Neebish Channel he labeled "a communication for boats and canoes," and of the Great Neebish he warned: "ships cannot go up this way but boats drawing 2 feet." On the site of Sault Ste. Marie he merely drew a dotted line and wrote "Portage 1 mile." It must have galled this soldier—he held a Congressional medal for his defense of Plattsburg in 1814—to mark a "British Post" on the United States territory of Drummond Island.

Called to Washington in 1821 as head of the Corps of Engineers, Macomb became commanding general of the United States army seven years later. He did not live to see the St. Marys channel dredged to twelve feet in the 1860's, or the twenty-seven-foot channel of today with separate traffic lanes around Neebish Island.

No American flag flew over Sault Ste. Marie before 1820. In May of that year Territorial Governor Lewis Cass ("Big Belly" the Indians called him) was preparing an expedition to Lake Superior. On the Detroit riverfront lay three big canoes—*canots du maître*—thirty-six feet long and seven feet across, fitted with mast and sail. Into them went all kinds of goods and gear, Indian presents, scientific instruments and military supplies. In 1820 Detroit, with its ribbon farms lining the river, its timbered fort and log stockade, was the outfitting place for the northern wilderness.

On May 24 the canoes were loaded. Ten Canadian boatmen and ten Indian guides and hunters (at sixty cents a day) paddled up the river. Twenty soldiers and scientists followed in carriages, accompanied by half the townspeople, past Windmill Point to Lake St. Clair. At the Grosse Point landing they embarked. To shouts of the villagers the canoes pushed into Lake St. Clair—"as if a new world was about to be discovered."

After that fine send-off, a gale lashed Lake St. Clair and

the canoes were forced ashore. Two days later they were under way again, through the St. Clair flats, past Fort Gratiot and into vast Lake Huron. Paddling from dawn to starlight they made seventy miles a day along the wild lake shore. At each new camp the world lay farther behind them.

On a June evening a band of swarthy children were playing beside the St. Marys River, their shrill voices almost lost in the roar of the rapids. Suddenly a boy pointed down the river and the voices ceased. In silence they watched the approach of three canoes. Sunset gleamed on rifle barrels and a strange flag blew in the wind. When the craft came into the landing, the whole village gathered.

The Cass expedition had arrived to plant the first American flag at strategic Sault Ste. Marie. While the Indians watched— wearing their British coats and medals—the Americans made camp on the green riverbank.

Next morning, while the Indians ringed the camp in a somber silence, Cass announced that the United States would build a fort there, on land ceded by the Treaty of Greenville in 1795. Chief Sassaba, wearing eagle feathers and a red coat given him by the commandant at Fort Drummond, kicked away the American presents and raised a British flag. Cass drew up his twenty soldiers and pulled down the Union Jack. Through his interpreter he told the chief that no foreign flag could fly on United States soil; the Indians must understand that the United States was in control here; if they resisted, a strong foot would be placed upon their necks and they would be crushed.

After a day of smoldering hostility, Sassaba paddled down the river and tension relaxed. The other chiefs accepted the Americans, acknowledging their claim to a tract beside the river. In a changed atmosphere Indians swarmed around the American presents, and the expedition moved on to Lake Superior.

In 1823 army troops built a stockade—the original Fort

Brady—beside the river rapids. The American flag has been there ever since. Now it flies from a tall steel skeleton mast between the second and third locks of the canal.

What brought this place a future was not the rocky land but the rushing water. On his 1819 map General Macomb made an arresting drawing of "The Entrance into Lake Superior," with Gros Cap and Point Iroquois framing a square-rigged sailing vessel. During the next thirty years, schooners, built above the falls, coasted the wild Superior shores and explorers mapped the rough land for minerals and timber. In 1840 geologist Douglass Houghton uncovered veins of copper on rugged Cape Keweenaw, and in 1844 surveyor William Burt found an iron outcrop in the old worn hills that became the Marquette range.

In 1837 two English visitors left records of the Soo. One was Captain Frederick Marryat, who habitually traveled in bad humor. Journeying from Mackinac to Sault Ste. Marie in a canoe driven by five sweating voyageurs, he described his toiling paddlers as "lazy, gluttonous scoundrels." At the rapids he found about fifty houses, mostly of logs, inhabited by halfbreeds. He was as much interested in the horses as the humans; the horses, he said, fed upon fish, seizing trout from unguarded canoes and running off with it in their mouths. Returning by canoe to Mackinac, Marryat and a couple of other travelers camped on a river meadow heaped with new-mown hay. To soften the beds they carried armfuls into their tent, and then found that the hay was swarming with mosquitoes. Trying to smoke them out, the travelers set fire to the hay and nearly burned down their tent. So, itching and smarting, Marryat left the north country.

A more cheerful visitor was Mrs. Anna Jackson, wife of the Attorney General of Upper Canada. At the Sault she was the guest of the Rev. William MacMurray, missionary to the Indians on the British side. She became the first white woman to run the rapids in a canoe. As she described it:

I went to the upper end of the portage and we launched into the river. . . . In a minute we were within the verge of the rapids, and down we went with a whirl and a splash!—the white surge leaping around me, over me. With astonishing dexterity the Indian kept the head of the canoe to the breakers, and somehow or other we danced through them. . . . I had not even a momentary sensation of fear, but rather a giddy, breathless, delicious excitement. I could even admire the beautiful attitude of a fisher, past whom we swept as we came to the bottom. The whole affair, from the moment I entered the canoe till I reached the landing place, occupied seven minutes, and the distance is about three-quarters of a mile.

After that morning ride the Chippewa called their visitor *Wahsahge-wahnoqua*—"woman of the Bright Foam."

In 1850 Sault Ste. Marie was still a remote and lonely place. Its single road bordered the river and its paths ended in dense spruce and balsam. The mile-long portage street ran into restless water. Above the rapids began the vast cold lake. The town straggled along the river—two hotels, a trading post, a few shops and a hundred dwellings lining Water Street.

Two streams of commerce met there. Out of the North came bales of beaver, otter, mink and marten skins, barrels of whitefish, bars of copper. Up from Lake Huron came tobacco, flour, whisky, traps, knives, axes, gunpowder and blasting powder. All went over the portage. In the summer of 1847 after a River and Harbor Meeting in Chicago a party of delegates visited Sault Ste. Marie. An Eastern editor described the little portage town in the big wilderness, the heaped platters of whitefish in the hotel, and the thrill of shooting the rapids in a Chippewa canoe—though three visitors had drowned in that sport a few weeks earlier. He watched the portage cart hauling goods between vessels within sight of each other and inevitably he thought of a canal. So did some Congressmen in the party.

OVERLOOK AT THE LOCKS

But the Soo was a long way from Washington, and Congress took no action. However, in his annual message of 1851 President Fillmore observed that "a ship canal around the Falls of St. Mary of less than a mile in length, though local in its construction, would be national in its purpose and benefits." Construction began in 1852, and after two strenuous years America had its first ship canal. Its commerce commenced in 1855.

The first annual report of the canal superintendent was issued in 1857. It recorded the freight shipped through the locks: including 3,219 railroad spikes, 27 pumps, 1 steam sawmill, 1 locomotive and tender, 82 car wheels and axles, 32 wagons, 502 thousands of bricks, 259 barrels of fish, 132 barrels of sauerkraut, 88 barrels of onions, 37 barrels of pickles, 600 picks and shovels, 7 ox yokes, and 1 church bell—in addition to 4,400 tons of copper and 26,000 tons of iron ore. All of that year's manifest could be carried in a single freighter now.

In its first ten years the canal's annual tonnage swelled to 284,000. By 1865 most of the cargo was grain, copper and iron ore. In 1875 the annual commerce had reached 1½ million tons and a second lock was needed. Under direction of General Godfrey Weitzel the Army Engineers built a single-lift lock 515 feet long and 80 feet across. Shipping men then agreed that lake freighters would never exceed 200 by 38 feet; the lock was designed to accommodate four such vessels.

Two years later General Orlando M. Poe, a bulky man with iron gray hair, steady dark eyes, and a firm mouth softened by gray mustache and goatee, predicted that traffic would outgrow the Weitzel Lock within a decade. His forecast was realized. With development of new mines in the Gogebic and Vermilion iron ranges, canal traffic kept on growing. In 1887 work began on the site of the old tandem locks, now obsolete. Nine years later the Poe Lock, 800 by 100 feet, began operation. The canal tonnage was then, in

1896, 16 million. Eleven years later, with the giant Mesabi range in huge production, it was 58 million, with more growth ahead. Mines, mills and freighters could not keep up with the ravenous demand for iron and steel.

In 1914, the year of the opening of the Panama Canal, a third lock, named for General E. L. B. Davis of the Army Engineers, was completed. Stretching 1,350 feet, it was the longest lock in the world. War requirements of grain and iron ore called for another lock of the same dimensions. The fourth lock, named for Louis C. Sabin, canal superintendent, first opened its gates on September 1, 1919.

For the next twenty years, a period of "normalcy" followed by depression, the engineers' projects were confined to dredging of the lake harbors and river channels. But with World War II steam shovels bit deeper into the mine pits and twenty-one big new freighters went into the lakes trade. Now the Weitzel Lock was obsolete. In its place the engineers, working night and day, built the MacArthur Lock, 800 feet long, 80 feet across, and a significant 31 feet deep. In 1942 a record 120 million tons of commerce passed through the canal. During the war years Great Lakes vessels delivered 889 million tons of cargo, four times the volume carried by the United States Merchant Marine on salt water.

Although far from the scenes of combat, the Soo was sealed in security. Troops from the enlarged Fort Brady patrolled the canal reservation, gun emplacements guarded the approaches, antiaircraft balloons hovered over miles of the channels and the locks. For a decade after the war, restrictions were retained, but they were ended with the Soo Locks Centennial celebration in 1955. Cascades of fireworks arched over the river from both Canadian and American shores. In a festive marine parade great heavy duty freighters were decked like pleasure craft in flags and pennons. Bands played in the government park and a multitude of visitors thronged the riverfront. For the first time in fifteen years

cameras recorded the rise and fall of huge carriers in the
canal, the opening and closing of lock gates, the procession
of long ships passing.

Inside the De Tour entrance, with Lake Huron astern,
ships steer for sixty miles through the intricate St. Marys
channel. The route was first marked in 1863 by day buoys;
then by kerosene lamps, lit and extinguished every dusk and
dawn by a nearby caretaker; finally by gas buoys burning
night and day and serviced by the Coast Guard. In 1946 the
Pittsburgh Steamship Company's freighter A. H. Ferbert
made the first use of radar—moving safely through twenty-
two miles of tortuous channel in a heavy fog. That miracle
spread quickly; by 1950 most of the lake vessels were
equipped with radar.

The radar screen gave a navigator a clear view in all kinds
of weather, but it created problems too. Some trusting captains, running in blinding fog or snowfall, brushed other vessels or bumped the canal locks. A few wholly lost their bearings. One notorious shipmaster, down-bound, steered into
the Electric Company's power canal (no traffic in sight, he
said cheerfully), believing he was headed into the MacArthur
Lock. It was then decided to close the locks in times of poor-
est visibility. Two days of thick weather in early November,
1973, created a backup of ships waiting in Whitefish Bay. On
November 10, thirty-seven freighters locked through the Soo
with 814,000 tons of cargo. Two super-carriers, the Roger
Blough and the Stewart J. Cort, were in the waiting line.

The smoke of forest fires is an almost forgotten hazard in
the St. Marys, but fog is as menacing and unpredictable as
ever. Academic analysts have discussed the problems of bad
weather and the subsequent slowed passage through the canal.
"The locking operations," they explain heavily, "may be
viewed as a queuing process not dissimilar to the queuing
phenomenon at a supermarket checkout counter or a bank

window. If the lock is busy, they undergo a certain amount of waiting time." The captain says it better. Peering through the narrows and scanning the radar screen, he rings the engines to DEAD SLOW. "Five or six ahead of us. There goes the record on this run." Clocks are ticking in the company offices in Cleveland and Chicago. Computers show how many millions of dollars are tied up in a 700-foot vessel and its cargo, and how many thousands are lost with each delay. Lake men balance that with another reality. "Sometimes you just have to wait. The weather has been here longer than we have."

In recent years the Mackinac Bridge and Interstate 75 have brought parking problems to Sault Ste. Marie. For visitors a viewing platform was built in the upper park, beside the Mac-Arthur Lock. As the locks have been enlarged, so has the observation space. Now a million visitors a year survey the canal and its commerce.

In the 1960's the lakes fleet was changing. The older vessels, plodding at ten miles an hour, made about thirty trips a season in the ore trade. The newest ships, at sixteen miles an hour with three times as much cargo, made forty trips at least. A modern vessel with a smaller crew could replace three of the older freighters. Economics dictated the building of still larger carriers, and that prospect called for a larger lock to replace the Poe Lock of 1896.

For four years the old lock was sealed off in a huge cofferdam. While work went on—blasting, razing, dredging, pouring massive masonry and installing the great gates—commerce flowed around it, ships creeping in to the locks on either side. This was the first time, anywhere, that a canal lock was constructed between streams of endless traffic. The new lock was opened in June, 1969, on the tenth anniversary of the St. Lawrence Seaway. Its dimensions—1200 feet between the gates, 110 feet across, and 31 feet deep—brought a new challenge to the shipping men. One revolution, the replacing of two 10,000-tonners with one 20,000-tonner, was succeeded by another: they could now replace five 10,000-tonners with one great freighter holding 50,000 tons. When the new Poe Lock was given the old name, it was recalled that General Poe, watching the parade of ships from his office window eighty years ago, declared: "The wildest expectations of one year seem absolutely tame the next."

From the overlook visitors watch the procession of ore-carriers: the weathered old steamers trailing coal smoke and the smokeless new motor vessels with bright brass and paint-work. Interspersed among them are the varicolored ocean ships flying the ensigns of Norway, Sweden, the Netherlands, France, England, Germany, Russia, Greece, Japan. On the decks, raising a hand for tourist cameras, are seamen from Buffalo, Cleveland, Port Huron and Milwaukee; and from Oslo, Göteborg, Glasgow, Liverpool, Piraeus, Hamburg, Helsinki, Odessa and Yokohama. European vessels may have African or Oriental crews, drawing a fraction of the pay of United States seamen. Two centuries ago the Soo was cosmopolitan—Algonquin, French, British, Canadian, American. Its commerce is more cosmopolitan now.

From the ship's rail seamen watch the passing town. For lakemen it is a familiar but still satisfying sight; after wide water and wilderness shores here is life, movement, color and variety. For the crews of ocean ships this is a close and lei-surely look at the United States, like strolling through the street. The shops, cafes and filling stations are strange to them, the signs inscrutable and exotic. At weathered old St. Marys, the Lascars, Pakistanis and Nigerians are half the world from home.

Upbound, at the edge of Sault Ste. Marie, a ship swings westward into the broad river. The Canadian Soo spreads over the north shore. It is a commercial and industrial city four times the size of Sault Ste. Marie, Michigan; but the

American town has more features. After the green fairways of the Country Club comes a stretch of wharves and mooring basins. Welch's Dock, alive with tourists, houses a historic reproduction of the town in 1852—miniature vessels at the quays, toy wagons on a miniature Portage Street, tiny replicas of the Johnston House and the Old Indian Agency as it was when Schoolcraft lived there with his half-Chippewa bride. There are Lilliputian Indians mending canoes, smoking fish over a slow fire, prudently hanging presents on a pencil-size Manitou pole. Neat little Fort Brady is enclosed in 700 whittled pickets, and the toy brig Columbia is loading six barrels of iron ore, the first ever to go down the lakes.

Lake seamen, unaware of this diorama, know the full-scale present—the 1300-foot electric plant powered by swift water in its own canal, and beyond it the city dock where the museum freighter Valley Camp is on permanent station. Government Park, once the military reservation, is a green waterfront graced by a 20-jet fountain. Sparkling on a sunny day, at night it becomes a color spectacle with changing lights and music timed to the rise and fall of the water. At this point, passing the Coast Guard station and the Engineers' depot, a ship enters the canal approach.

Portage Avenue, the old bypass road around the rapids, bends with the river and borders the canal. This part of it is tourist street: the Ojibway Hotel, Seven Seas Motel, Sugar Island Fudge Shop, Soo Souvenir Shop, Long Ships Motel, Northview Lounge and Tavern, and, to jar a vacationer, H & R Block Income Tax. The North Land Museum, a commercial venture, occupies the old Soo Railroad station.

Over roofs and treetops is a glimpse of Lake Superior State College, the town's newest institution. Its students and athletic teams are called The Lakers. Their campus displays a century-old nautical iron anchor with some links of chain, a relic removed from the famous wooden freighter V. H. Ketchum, which in 1905 caught fire, was beached and burned

OVERLOOK AT THE LOCKS

at the water's edge near Ile Parisienne in Lake Superior. The Ketchum, 1,660 tons, was built at Marine City on Lake Huron in 1874.

To camera-clicking visitors the great vessels move casually into the locks. Actually there is a dispatching system as carefully operated and controlled as one found at an airport. The procedure begins in a ship's pilot house before it is in sight of the Soo. At three points, both up- and down-bound, the vessel reports by radio phone to the Coast Guard station, and the Coast Guard ("Soo Control") transmits to the lock master. Nearing the approach the navigator has a final exchange:

"Calling W U D 31, the lock tower. This is the John Sherwin, sir. We're just down at Big Point, drawing twenty-seven feet."

"You take Poe Lock, John Sherwin."

"Thank you, sir."

It is two miles from Big Point to the entrance, which is now in full view. Soon the vessel, hugging the long pier wall, creeps into the lock.

Occasionally a personal message is added to the laconic routine. "Calling W U D 31, the lock tower. This is the Cliffs Victory to the Lock Master. . . . Good morning, sir. We left Marquette just after midnight, and we were short a crew member. He might have got to the Soo. If he's there, will you put him aboard?"

"No seaman has reported here, Captain. But if he comes we'll get him to you."

"Very good, sir. And thank you."

While the ship is in the lock, slowly rising or falling to the new level, mail is handed aboard from the Marine Post Office, and laundry and sundries are delivered. Several times a year a box of books and magazines is brought from the Marine Library in the old Weather Bureau Building at the head of the MacArthur Lock.

Ever since 1915 the American Merchant Marine Library

Association—sailors just call it the Soo Library—has supplied the crews with reading matter. Delivery is quick, simple, and free of charge. At the moment the vessel's deck is flush with the lock's edge, a sturdy woman in a white smock hands a carton of books to a seaman, who lugs it to the crew's quarters. In a handcart the librarian moves four book boxes at a time over the long locks. She could have a dispatcher for that, but she doesn't want one. "This way," she says, "I get to meet our readers."

No one needs a card to use the Soo Library, and if a man wants a special book, he hands over a request. On the next trip the book is there, having been supplied by the Michigan State Library or through Inter-Library Loan. After five years of loan service, the State Librarian wished that other people were as considerate about the care and return of books as are Great Lakes men. The Soo Library is supported by private gift and donation, but since its founding, vessel crews themselves have contributed thousands of dollars.

When the lock gates open, the captain gives a short cast-off whistle and rings the engines to SLOW AHEAD. Past the bascule railroad bridge and under the high span of the International Bridge the vessel moves, between Gros Cap and Point Iroquois, "the Portals," into Lake Superior. With whistle signals an upbound freighter passes one down-bound, loaded to the marks with iron ore pellets. Those pellets make the pig iron that becomes the steel that goes into compass needles and bridge cables, into skyscrapers and subway tracks, into kitchen ware and spacecraft. In the Senate chamber in Washington on April 21, 1840, Henry Clay called the Soo a place beyond the verge of civilization, as remote as the moon. A few tons of its commerce, in the form of the lunar module *Eagle*, was landed on the moon 129 years later. From the overlook a visitor may see that the march of America, from wagon wheel to jet aircraft and space rocket, has come through this place.

OVERLOOK AT THE LOCKS

Now, in 1975, government engineers are making test borings between the fourth lock and the old tail race channel. This work is merely exploratory, but there is room beyond the northeast pier for a new lock, larger than any of the past or present. After 350 years of history, the future still beckons at the Soo.

CHAPTER TWENTY-SEVEN

The Long Ships

BEFORE THE SUNSET LIGHT was gone, Venus, the evening star, gleamed in the fading sky. As darkness deepened, the lookout on the bridge wing saw the brief trail of a meteor—gone in an instant. Meteors are common in the clear lakes air, and "Meteor" was a favored name with captains and shipowners. At one time seven Meteors sailed the lakes: two schooners, two sidewheel steamers, two propellors and a tug. In 1868 the mate of the steamer Meteor was young Alexander McDougall. Pacing the bridge in darkness, he did not wonder about shooting stars but about ships that would carry more cargo than this 340-ton vessel. According to legend, he woke one morning from a dream in which he had watched a cigar-shaped freighter nosing steadily through tossing seas.

Twelve years later McDougall had plans for a new kind of vessel. On his drawing board was a ship of rounded sides and bulbous bow, its forward and after cabins mounted on heavy stanchions above the tubular hull. This lakeman had never seen a whale but he called his ship a whaleback. Eventually, with financial backing in New York, two ends of the first whaleback barge were built in Brooklyn. Shipped to Duluth, they were joined to a center section that McDougall had built there. The first whaleback was loaded with iron ore at Two Harbors in June, 1888. In the next eight years, forty of these novel ships were built at Duluth–Superior. They got more attention than any lake ships before or after them. Cheaper to build and less expensive to run, they carried more cargo than the other freighters. A Chicago editor wrote: "The general introduction of these boats into the lake traffic will mean an enormous reduction in the expense attending the transfer of commodities from producers to the large centers of trade." Yet no whalebacks were built after 1898. The rounded boats were difficult at the docks and their narrow hatches impeded cargo handling.

Eighty years after the whaleback fleet had led the lakes commerce, one of those vessels survives. Built as the ore-

313

carrier Frank Rockefeller, it was renamed the South Park in 1928 and went into the grain trade between Lake Superior and Buffalo; at Detroit it took on a deckload of automobiles for the return run. Converted to oil tanker in 1943, it was renamed Meteor. In 1972 the Meteor was towed into Duluth-Superior harbor where it had been built three-quarters of a century before. On the harborside in front of the Douglas County Historical Museum, a permanent berth was prepared for the last of the whalebacks. Thousands of visitors go aboard every summer. From its glassed-in pilot house they see ships ten times its size passing the harbor entrance.

The last whaleback to be built was the Alexander McDougall, launched in 1898. In that year a writer for the *Marine Review* took a long look ahead, picturing the lake ships of a half-century in the future. "Most of the fleet now," he wrote in a science-fiction vein, "are 1,000-footers, some of them 100 feet wide and 50 feet deep. . . . Electricity is the motive power and most of them have triple screws. . . . A voyage on one of these ships is delightful. You get up in the morning and have a trolley car ride to breakfast aft. After spending the day with the captain forward you put on your dress suit and attend grand opera at the midship theater in the evening, or pass a pleasant time in the 10-story roof garden over the theater."

The *Review*'s artist had a good time with that prediction. His drawing of a "lake ship of the future" showed a navigation bridge at the bow, three smoking funnels over the engine room astern, and a deckhouse island midway on the stretched-out cargo deck. Two electric tramcars shuttled between the midship superstructure and the bow and stern cabins. Over the halfway pleasure pavilion, five flags floated in the wind; long pennants rippled from the foremast and from the mainmast 900 feet astern. Except for the stately pleasure dome and the trolley cars, the science-fiction has largely become fact.

THE LONG SHIPS

With the twentieth century came the first 8,000-ton freighters. Four of them, the John W. Gates, James J. Hill, Isaac L. Ellwood and William Edenborn, began service in 1900. Four years later these giants were eclipsed by the Augustus B. Wolvin, named for a Duluth man who had merged four vessel companies, including the whaleback fleet, into the Pittsburgh Steamship Company, the marine division of the newly formed United States Steel Corporation. Of more than a hundred vessels in that fleet, the Wolvin was the flagship. A little more than 500 feet long, with cargo capacity of 12,000 tons, it was number one on the lakes, briefly. In 1906 came the J. Pierpont Morgan, first of the 600-footers, soon followed by eight similar freighters of deadweight approaching 13,000 tons. These vessels, with red hull, white cabins, and black-and-silver stack, carried record cargoes for the next twenty years. They were surpassed by the Harry Coulby in 1927. On her first voyage the Coulby delivered 14,000 tons of iron ore in Cleveland, and promptly broke that record by loading 14,471 tons of Gogebic ore at Ashland, Wisconsin. This ship was unmatched until the World War II class of freighters appeared in 1942.

The 600-foot carriers, standard for nearly forty years, were coal-burning, steam-driven, gravity-loaded with direct shipping ore from the iron ranges. Ships made the last run at the end of November, racing against winter and the expiration of insurance contracts, with a bonus for crew members who stayed to the season's end. For four months the fleet was laid up in the frozen harbors of Lake Michigan and Lake Erie, only a watchman living like a hermit in the galley while snow drifted over the long decks. Spring brought the fit-out crews. At last, lines were cast off, bells jangled in the wheelhouse and the engine room, and through the vessel went the pulse beat that would not cease until December. As it rounded the breakwater into the open lake the engines pounded out a steady seventy revolutions; dragging a line of hose, the deckhands washed down; and over the wet clean deck came the porter, his white apron blowing, ringing the dinner bell. For all generations of seamen Kipling wrote:

There be triple ways to take, of the eagle and the snake
    And the way of a man with a maid;
But the sweetest way to me is a ship's upon the sea
    In the heel of the North-East Trade.

There were no trade winds blowing on Lake Erie and Lake Michigan, but the air was alive with spring and the horizon was luring.

A Great Lakes seaman logs some 50,000 miles a year, twice the girdle of the earth. In a lifetime he covers the distance to the moon. It looked in 1940 like a settled trade, a commerce that had found its rhythm and dimensions. There were no foreign flags on the inland water, no competition from foreign cargoes, and no end in sight of the prodigal iron ranges of Lake Superior.

But the four years of World War II brought more changes than the forty years past. They brought an insatiable demand for steel and a requirement of new and larger ore-carriers. They brought the end of direct-shipping ore and the beginning of ore-processing. They took over the biggest passenger ships on the lakes; the Seeandbee and the Greater Buffalo were converted to flat-tops for training navy pilots. They brought a new look to the Soo and the dredging of deeper channels in rivers and harbors.

The MacArthur Lock, opened in 1943, is 800 feet long, 80 feet wide, 31 feet deep. In the next twelve years, twenty-five United States vessels with deadweight of 20,000 to 25,000 tons entered the trade. In 1954 came the giant George M. Humphrey, with only inches to spare as she locked through. By then plans were developing for freighters of 40,000 tons and a Soo lock of unprecedented proportions. In

1968 the new Poe Lock, 1200 x 110 x 32 feet, was ready for giant new carriers.

As it had developed in a century and a half, the Great Lakes commerce was largely self-contained. But after 1959 the lakes were no longer an inland waterway. When the St. Lawrence Seaway opened these waters to the shipping of the world, foreign competition became a new concern in that commerce. Foreign insurance and construction costs are half of U.S. costs, and foreign seamen's wages are less than a quarter of the pay scale on U.S. and Canadian vessels.

One man who saw opportunity in the heart of North America was a Greek tobacco merchant who began a career in Canada as a wholesale stamp dealer. The Seaway gave him larger projects. In the 1960's Phrixos Basil Papachristidis built five big freighters with the name Papachristidis Co. Ltd. almost lost on their long hulls. With a base in Montreal, Papachristidis enjoyed the Canadian subsidy for shipbuilding. That subsidy, now reduced, spurred the building of a score of maximum-size Seaway freighters, while American shipyards were mostly idle.

By 1960 the U.S. fleet on the Lakes was growing old. The assumed life of a bulk freighter is fifty years, and many of the three hundred American vessels were older than that. Year by year, old familiar names dropped out of the lists. Some retired ships were used for storage, a few became breakwaters, many were broken up for scrap metal—some towed across the Atlantic to breaking yards in Spain and Italy. Eventually the ore-carriers themselves went into the blast furnaces.

All last voyages are lamentable, but the final trip of the Arcturus was a calamity. After forty-eight years with the Interlake fleet, the 540-footer was retired in 1961. Towed to Port Colburne, she was loaded with 6,000 tons of scrap iron for delivery in Norway, where the old carrier would join her cargo in the breaking yard. Heavy seas in mid-Atlantic sprang a bulkhead and the Arcturus had no pumps to combat sea water. The towboat got her, badly listing, to the Azore Islands, where she was repaired. A few days after Christmas they began the final 2500-mile haul to Oslo. On January 11, battered by a storm in the Bay of Biscay, the old laker sank off the northern coast of Spain.

Fifty years ago any vessel that could load 5,000 tons of ore was profitable. Often they had return cargoes of coal, pay loads each way. But the coal trade has diminished, and what there is goes in older freighters; the big, fast carriers cannot afford the relatively long time at the coal docks. The newest freighters cruise a hundred thousand miles a season, half of the time with empty holds. They must make a profit with a one-way commerce. Half a century ago the crews had some time ashore at each end of the trip. In the 1920's freighters spent a third of their time in port, but today's vessels are too expensive to lie idle. Generally the crews remain aboard, with TV in the recreation room and a harbor bumboat bringing tobacco, razor blades, magazines and newspapers alongside. Lake seamen get postal service at the Soo, where mail comes aboard from the Marine Post Office on the locks; and again at Detroit, where 14,000 times a year, in all hours and all weather, the mail boat rushes alongside, delivering and collecting a bucket of mail while the ship never slackens. In their quarters the men have books and magazines, pinochle, cribbage, chess and checkers. There used to be marathon poker games above the throbbing engines and sporadic crap games on the fantail. Pseudo-sailors came aboard in November, working a trip as deckhand or coal-passer while they cleaned out the crew's wages from the last pay day. Now, supported by a marine mail-savings plan, men end the season with money on deposit.

Loss of time is a modern master's worry, as loss of the ship haunted captains a century ago. A recent Interlake captain was so time-conscious that he bought a two-wheeled scooter, powered by a one-cylinder motor, for quick trips ashore; it was put onboard and off by the pantry tackle. On the dock he would scoot between power shovels and railroad cars, missing them by inches. In fact, Inches was his name. After retirement, less in a hurry, Captain H. C. Inches became curator of the Great Lakes Historical Museum at Vermilion-on-Lake Erie.

Although the crews have limited time ashore, bars and taverns in the harbor districts still buzz with talk of lakes shipping and lake seamen. A favorite place is the Iroquois Club on Ashtabula Harbor's raffish Bridge Street. Unlike the Rusty Anchor and the Ship Aground, this place has a polished brass doorknob and a doorbell. It is a membership club, open to seamen only. Founded in 1937 by Frank Cragan, now a white-haired ex-sailor with sea-blue eyes and a foghorn voice, the Club gives an impression of stained glass, dark woodwork and accumulating tradition. It has a ladies' parlor, billiard tables, card and checkers tables, a writing desk, lounge chairs and a reading rack, and a curved bar as long as a mooring line. A familiar story there concerns Moses Cleaveland and the naming of the Ashtabula River. In 1796 Cleaveland's surveying party camped at the rivermouth, where Cleaveland offered his men two gallons of wine if they would agree to name the river for his daughter Mary Esther. It bore her name until the jug was empty. Amid pictures of old and new lake freighters, old steamboat schedules, fleet houseflags and insignia is a framed letter that came to Frank Cragan on January 2, 1974, his eighty-second birthday—a message from the Interlake Steamship Company conveying congratulations and the Company's appreciation of his help and hospitality to crews of bulk freighters for nearly forty years.

In the rivers and canals lakemen watch the ocean ships with little curiosity and comment. But they can call a lake freighter by fleet and by name while it is miles away, and they probably know some members of its crew. In passing, the two ships exchange a whistle greeting—one long and two shorts. As they come abreast, the mate of a Reiss self-unloader steps out of the wheelhouse and calls across two hundred feet of water: "Taking coal to Charlevoix!" In his wheelhouse doorway the mate of the straight-decker cups his voice: "To Conneaut, then to Duluth!" They could talk on radio telephone, but this is more like a meeting.

The old Poe Lock, a wonder when its gates first opened in 1896, was obsolete in 1950, and the Army Engineers began planning a new lock to replace it. Through the new Poe Lock in 1972 passed the new carrier Roger Blough, 850 feet long, with 45,000 tons of iron pellets. The Blough, 128 feet longer and 30 feet wider than any predecessor, retains the traditional freighter symmetry, with raked masts and funnel and the long cargo space framed in a four-decked superstructure, bow and stern. From any angle it has poise and balance; on the horizon it makes a graceful silhouette against the sky. Its diesel engines deliver 13,600 horsepower (lined up nose to tail those horses would make a parade twenty-seven miles long). Its cargo-hold conveyor belts can discharge 10,000 tons an hour.

In 1973 came the self-unloader Charles E. Wilson, with only a deckhouse astern. That seven-story superstructure rises from an operating deck through the second deck, main deck, C, B, and A decks that comprise ship's quarters, to the bridge deck. Twin diesels drive the seventeen-foot propeller and power the generator for electric heat in the quarters and for hot water to de-ice the cargo deck and hatch covers. Another generator powers the bow-thrusters, for aid in canal and harbor steering, and the unloading boom. The engine room, once a hot realm clanging with shovels and furnace doors, is a bright white maze of pumps, tubes, tanks, valves, casings, rods and couplings. Gone are the coal-passers shoveling out the bunker, raking the fires, shooting ashes into the lake. No sweating stokers heave coal through the fire doors; no wipers tread the catwalk above the great driving arms. This engine room is equipped for one-man operation.

Cumbrous-looking, with its broad bow and rounded stern, a model of this freighter was tested in the Ship Model Basin at Wageningen, Netherlands, beside a model with sheered bow and transom stern. The bulbous lines of the Wilson showed 14 percent less resistence. The testing basin reveals surprising hydrodynamics.

In the new freighters, diesel engines have replaced the reciprocating engines and Scotch boilers that for seventy years powered the lakes commerce. Diesels are economical of space, fuel, maintenance and man power. They have many advantages over the ponderous old triple-expansion engines with fire tubes passing through horizontal boilers to the smokestack. But veteran engineers sometimes recall with a sigh the throbbing old engine room. There was something satisfying about a reciprocating engine: steam, created in the boilers, passing through the separator and into the high-pressure valve chest, expanding in the cylinder to drive the heavy piston, then led to the low-pressure cylinder for a reciprocating stroke; so to the condenser and, as water now, pumped back to the feed tank and delivered again to the boiler; the cycle ready to repeat once more. In place of that rhythmic power and order there is the din of the big diesels, as an engineer turns a valve and watches a needle on a gauge. The newest prospect is the unmanned engine room with robot controls, a never-sleeping electric monitor and an automatic alarm.

When the gates of the Poe Lock first opened on June 26, 1969, there were no vessels requiring its 1200- by 110-foot basin. But that summer, 500 miles away at Erie, Pennsylvania, men in a new shipyard laid the keel of Hull 101—which became the first 1,000-foot freighter on the lakes. The new ship was built by a new method. In an assembly shop, workmen formed 48-foot sections of the massive hull. Into a huge graving dock the finished section was floated; then the dock was pumped dry while a new section was assembled and attached. By these 48-foot additions the hull grew out from the assembly plant until it extended as long as three football fields. Meanwhile a thousand miles away, at Pascagoula, Mississippi, on the Gulf of Mexico, the bow and stern units were constructed. The two were joined together—navigation bridge welded to engine room. Using a fraction of their massive power the diesels drove this odd craft—"Stubby," the men called it—around the Florida keys, up the coast to the Gulf of the St. Lawrence, and by Seaway to Lake Erie. There the fore and aft sections, parted, were joined to the 818-foot cargo hull. On May 1, 1971, the new carrier was christened Stewart J. Cort. After outfitting and trial runs, the longest ship with the shortest name passed through the Poe Lock and loaded 50,000 tons of pellets at Taconite Harbor. This great vessel evoked the same superlatives that had greeted her nonpareil predecessors, all the way back to the wooden V. H. Ketchum and the iron Onoko. The Cort's crew of twenty-eight is smaller than the crews that manned the old 500-footers and carried one-tenth the Cort's cargo.

On this giant freighter everything is powerful—the broad, blunt bow; the square lines of the deckhouses; the massive twin propellers; the retractable loading booms with belts like a moving highway pouring out 20,000 tons an hour. The funnel is gone and there is no fleet insignia except the house-flag fluttering. In place of tapered mast is a stubby steel tower supporting radar scanners.

A year after the Cort made news the lakes saw another 1,000-foot freighter, the integrated tug-barge Presque Isle. It too was built at Erie, Pennsylvania, a place first known as Presque Isle ("Almost an Island") when in 1813 young

THE LONG SHIPS

Oliver Hazard Perry built from native timber the flotilla that wrested Lake Erie from the British. In size and power the Presque Isle is a virtual twin of the Cort; otherwise the two carriers are radically different. The Presque Isle is a 150-foot tug locked into the notched stern of a 975-foot barge. The combination makes a craft 1,000 feet long with 105-foot beam. Like the Cort, it was built for the pellet commerce between Lake Superior and the steel mills at the southern end of Lake Michigan.

Fifty years ago the owners christened a new ship, put it into service, and began breaking records for cargo volume, time of passage, and rates of loading and unloading. In 1974 analysts ran masses of data through computers to compare the economics of tug-barge and self-contained ship. One argument for the tug-barge is reduced crew costs. The huge Presque Isle carried sixteen men; the Cort, twenty-eight. Reasons for the Cort's larger complement are union requirements, crew satisfaction, and the traditional fleet concern for ship maintenance. A minimal crew means minimal upkeep of the vessel, which will require shore-based maintenance at additional cost. The Presque Isle crew is fed by cafeteria line rather than by the table service that is traditional on the lakes. That austerity reduces the steward's department to a single cook against the cook, second cook, and two porters on the Cort. (Nobody, now, on any vessel, makes the ship's rounds with dinner bell at mealtime; that homely touch went out with World War II.) A more important difference between the two carriers is deadweight displacement. The deep notch in the barge stern, housing the rigidly connected tug, is lost cargo space. The tug-barge is like a loaded ship burdened with ballast in the engine room; on each trip the Presque Isle can carry 3,000 tons less cargo than the Cort.

While owners and managers ponder these concerns—acquisition cost, operating cost, carrying capability and the "required freight rate sensitivity to crew size and capital cost"—

the big ships lock through the Soo, round Point de Tour, and glide under the great Mackinac Straits Bridge. In the sunset they steer past the radiant flashing, four times a minute, of the lofty White Shoal Light. The ship's clock chimes the half-hours and in the autumn sky the Pleiades glitter over vast dark water. Even in an age of headlong technology, some things are unchanging.

Concluding an exhaustive study, a team of designers found "little reason, economically, to choose an ITB (integrated tug-barge) over a ship when considering maximum-sized vessels." In November, 1973, following announcement of the new taconite project at Hibbing, Minnesota, to produce 5½ million tons a year of iron ore pellets, came word of a related project. With a $70 million contract the Interlake Steamship Company had ordered from the American Shipbuilding Company's Lorain yard two 59,000-ton self-unloading freighters. On its long deck each will have thirty-six 65- by 11-foot hatches. For unloading, three belts will convey cargo to a 250-foot boom that can discharge 10,000 tons an hour. Diesel engines delivering 16,000 horsepower will glide the huge ship over the lakes at sixteen miles an hour loaded, seventeen light. Four diesel generators will supply electrical power.

The first of the twin vessels will be commissioned in June, 1976, when the Hibbing plant begins full-scale operation. The other vessel will go into service a year later. On these ships it will be a long walk from the stern cabins to the forepeak. But no one will rig a lifeline over those thirty-six hatches, and there will be no need to cross the icy deck in punishing weather. Everything will be controlled from the six-story superstructure at the vessel's stern.

On the cloudless June morning of June 1, 1974, a white and blue liner, flying the blue and white ensign of Greece, rounded the Chicago breakwater and was met by a big red fireboat arching plumes of spray. When the Stella Maris II eased into a berth at Navy Pier, reporters and photographers jostled up the gangway and a mayor's deputy brought the city's greetings. Foreign ships are commonplace at Navy Pier, but this was different. With the Stella Maris, passenger cruising had returned to the Great Lakes.

In Piraeus, 5,000 miles away, the Stella Maris had been equipped with sanitation and navigation devices for river, canal and lake cruising. Half a century ago some fifteen steamship lines operated passenger schedules on the lakes. In the 1960's the last Canadian and American liners succumbed to highway travel and jet air schedules. Now the appeal of rest, recreation, and the changing shores of the American heartland had brought a yachtlike vessel with 200 passengers to the Great Lakes navigation routes. From June 1 to the end of October the Stella Maris made 14-day cruises between Chicago and Montreal, with shore excursions at Toronto, Niagara Falls, Detroit, Mackinac Island and Holland, Michigan. With it another era of Great Lakes cruises may be beginning.

Long before history began in the lakes country, winter besieged the Indian camps. While wind wailed through the forests and snowstorms dimmed the straits, the tribesmen huddled around their fires. In intervals of bright weather they made hunting trips—men, women and children dragging sleds through the snow. At night they unrolled their mats of bark and rushes and built shelters in a trampled place. At morning the children, knee-deep in snow, called: "Come porcupine, come beaver, come elk and deer." When hunting was good the sleds were heaped with smoked venison and bear meat. Often the hunters went home hungry.

When civilization changed the country, winter still brought silence to the lakes. At the end of November most navigation ceased. Spring might come, fitfully, and yield again to winter. On March 13, 1852, Lake Erie's harbors were reported clear of ice; on April 22 they were sealed tight again. In May of that year seven steamers and more than twenty schooners were frozen in near Buffalo. Ten years later the St. Clair River lights were extinguished December 1, but the channel remained open. On January 1 the propeller Montgomery arrived in Chicago after an easy run from Buffalo. That mild winter tempted other captains, and in February a sudden severe freeze caught a fleet of schooners in Lake Erie. One of them, the Badger State, was loaded with grain. Drift ice held the vessel fast, but was not solid enough to let the men walk ashore. When they had eaten all the galley stores, the crew turned to their cargo. They lived on boiled oats till the ice broke up in April.

Captains with late-season cargoes ran the risk of uncertain arrival or no arrival at all. Winter can come suddenly, temperatures diving far below zero and blizzards swirling. Blown spray freezes quickly; soon a ship is sheathed in ice. The connecting rivers freeze solid, with steamers locked in the channel.

One of these onsets came at the end of November, 1926, trapping 153 vessels in the St. Mary's River. The W. E. Fitzgerald, upbound to Fort William with hard coal screenings, shared its cargo with other freighters that had run out of fuel; to the marooned ships, men trundled wheelbarrows over the frozen channel. A fog frost, followed by temperatures of 35° below zero, encased the ships in ice. When the Fitzgerald's wheelhouse turned into an igloo, seamen chopped ice from doors and windows while the radio called for help. Crunching through the channel came the car ferry St. Marie, followed by six Canadian and American tugs. The rescue boats made little difference until a change of weather released the helpless fleet.

As freighters grow in size and cost, the length of the navigation season becomes an increasing concern. In 1972 the Great Lakes-Seaway system carried 224 million tons of commerce, nearly twice that of the Panama Canal. This tonnage moved between mid-April and early December. For more than a century the iron ore trade has been halted in winter because the natural ores, with inherent moisture, could not be handled in cold weather. Even before the lake channels were frozen, ore turned solid in railroad cars and on the loading docks. The fleets lay idle for a third of the year.

But taconite pellets are dry. They flow through the conveyors as freely at 50° below zero as at 50° above. What remains is the problem of ice-bound channels and harbors. In collaborated efforts the shipping industry, the Coast Guard and the Army Engineers have extended the season by changes in vessel structure and lock operation and by augmented ice-breaking and escorting through frozen channels. Until 1967 nothing moved on Lake Superior after mid-December, and the Soo was sealed in ice and silence until mid-April. But during the next five years the Soo locks operated into the winter season, each year a little longer—until January 3, January 8, January 15; then, to the industry's surprise and gratification, till February 2, February 4, and February 11. In 1973 shipping continued into mid-February, 3½ million tons of cargo being moved in severe winter weather. "Home for Christmas" was but a memory for hundreds of lake seamen. A summer-leave program now provides July and August vacations for winter-sailing crews.

The lakes themselves rarely freeze over, but by January the St. Mary's River is ice-bound, and in Whitefish Bay and the Straits of Mackinac the ice is thick and hardening. In the past a Coast Guard ice-breaker battered through to marooned vessels. Now the procedure is "preventive breaking" —ice-breakers, ice tugs and buoy tenders keeping the channels open. Navigation has been helped by the dredging of broader channels, the use of ice-resistant buoys, and the development of radar and laser guidance signals. Further assistance comes from the Ice Central Station in Cleveland, which receives information from the Weather Bureau, the Coast Guard, and vessels en route. Reports by radio telephone guide ships through bewildering ice fields.

Near the lower end of the St. Mary's River lies the 1,000-acre island that the Indians called Pahgahduhwahmanis. It took a shorter name from white men who built a kiln to burn its dense limestone. That business is totally forgotten, but for many years freighters have stopped at Lime Island to replenish bunker fuel. At the latest census Lime Island had a population of fifty-three, including thirteen schoolchildren and a teacher. Deer and foxes are more numerous. Each year the island's fuel service supplies hundreds of vessels with coal and oil. Coal, brought up from Lake Erie, is stockpiled on a dock; oil tanks hold $3\frac{1}{2}$ million gallons of bunker fuel. In thirty minutes a ship can refuel and be under way again—except in wintry weather when the Lime Island channel is notorious for ice packs; many vessels imprisoned there have called the Coast Guard for deliverance. Now the Lime Island channel has a pioneer bubbler device, air lines on the bottom bringing up warmer water that retards the surface freezing. With that new technology the notorious Lime Island ice packs may melt into memory.

In several other locations bubbler systems have provided effective ice control. After a test installation at Duluth in 1971 a Coast Guard commander reported: "Transit of the bubbler area was much easier . . . and the sole reason was the bubbler system. [That] transit was non-stop as compared to the continual backing and ramming necessary in the adjacent area." Since then enlarged bubbler systems have been developed in Duluth-Superior harbor and are being installed at Escanaba, Marquette, and in the ship channels of Whitefish Bay and the Straits of Mackinac. Some success has come from a further experiment: warm air pumped through a girdle of perforated tubing has retarded ice formation on the bow and hull of freighters.

In the final decades of the twentieth century that old devil ice will lose his hold on lake shipping. Already the season has been lengthened to ten months, and lake men foresee year-round operation for the great new ships that move cargo at less cost in money and fuel energy than any other means of transportation.

Lake freighters used to trail a web of fluttering gulls, watching for galley refuse. But gulls could not cleanse the harbors of industrial waste or wipe up oil slicks on the water. Pollution is as old as commerce on the lakes. Nearly a century ago a writer in the Chicago *Record* rhymed it in the words of a tugboat hand on the grimy Rebecca Nye.

> *With my pipe a-lit and puffin', and the bridge lights shinin' red*
> *And the black smoke hangin' heavy as a rain cloud overhead,*
> *And the garbage in the river bobbin' up and down, you see*
> *There's a heap of satisfaction to a homebody like me.*
>
> *This is home, the greasy water and the sulphur and the smoke,*
> *And the smell that comes a-floatin' up the river till you choke,*
> *And the tootin' of the whistle, and the crashin', splashin' sound*
> *As the whizzin' old propeller swings some passin' boat around.*

But what was tolerable, even amusing, in the 1880's became hazardous and repulsive ninety years later.

Waste material cannot endlessly be poured into the lakes without destroying them as a natural resource. In recent years ecologists have found serious pollution in all the lakes, with Erie, Ontario and Michigan in more critical condition than Huron and Superior. The worst areas are those of dense population, where municipal wastes are added to industrial contamination. Reports tell of a mat of algae two feet thick and twenty miles across that drifts over Lake Erie in midsummer. This may be something of a Loch Ness monster; vesselmen who cross Lake Erie by various routes have seen only occasional mats of grass smaller than a hatch cover. However, the lake's critical condition is undisputed. Oxygen is wholly lacking in some areas of the lake bottom. Scavenger fish replace the indigenous species, and many beaches are contaminated by municipal sewage. Other threatened areas are the southern end of Lake Michigan, the western end of Lake Ontario, Saginaw Bay on Lake Huron, and the extreme upper reach of Lake Superior.

In 1857 the Army Corps of Engineers began dredging harbors and channels, with a project depth of twelve feet. Every year since then the dredging has gone on—powerful dippers, clam shells, ladder and suction dredges moving millions of tons of material from the channel floor. The present depth is twenty-seven to thirty feet in main channels and major harbors. Until recently masses of muck and slime were dumped in the open lake, but the 1960's brought reform. At Toledo the Corps used three separate diked areas, two landsites and one island-site, in Maumee Bay. At Detroit the River Rouge dredgings were deposited on Grassy Island. During 1967 confined disposal sites were constructed at Buffalo, Cleveland, Indiana Harbor and Green Bay. The Rivers and Harbors Act of 1970 required approved disposal for all polluted material. Now at a cost of $272 million, seventy-two disposal projects are underway. Generally the diked areas will permit the return of filtered water into the lake.

While cities have exerted increasing control of municipal and industrial wastes, the Great Lakes fleet has developed its own sanitation program. A 1970 regulation required that all vessels, domestic and foreign, install retention or treatment systems for sewage and garbage. In 1972 a demonstration of shipboard treatment was conducted on the steamer Cliffs Victory. This 18-miles-per-hour ship, fastest on the lakes, was the first to install flow-through devices for secondary treatment of waste water. Even the water from drinking fountains goes into the works, along with sewer, galley, engine room and bilge tank wastes. Automatically monitored, the system sounds an alarm when effluents exceed the established standards. As John Horton of the Cleveland-Cliffs Steamship Company reported: "The goal was to demonstrate that a ship is a self-contained unit and can effectively supply means to control pollution the same as a shore-side city." The use of incineration, filtration and chemicals in place of the old lake-dumping was bad news for the gulls but good for millions of people.

Amid the current voices of doom come some words of purpose and hope. Shallow Lake Erie pours a vast outflow down the Niagara River. If pollution were ended today, it would take but six years to flush 90 percent of the dissolved nutrients into Lake Ontario, where great depth diminishes the immediate crisis and allows time for redemption. Environmentalists generally agree that the condition of Lake Erie has not worsened since 1970. Commerical fisherman and divers are more positive: they say Lake Erie's waters are steadily improving, that it now supports more and better fish than it did five years ago, that its beaches are cleaner and its rivers more clear. Vesselmen say simply that the lake looks and smells better every season. Lake Erie, written off as dead a decade ago, may be coming back. If public desire is determined enough, the technology that built the great commerce will redeem the lakes as a natural resource. Just 3 percent of the earth's water is fresh, and four-fifths of that is frozen in glaciers. The seas of sweet water are a public asset beyond calculation.

CHAPTER TWENTY-EIGHT

The Harbor Lights

In THE TOWN OF ELLINGTON, Connecticut, nine-year-old Alva Bradley, driving the cows to their stony pasture, could look north to Soapstone Mountain, east to Crystal Lake, and west to Broad Brook, which found its way to the Connecticut River. When the Bradley family moved to Vermilion, Ohio, in 1823, he looked at white sails on Lake Erie and his mind followed them to Canada, Buffalo, Cleveland and Detroit. Like all the Yankees in New Connecticut he found a wider world.

At fifteen Alva Bradley sailed as cook's helper on a Vermilion schooner. Within a decade he was master of his own vessel, loading fish, salt, pork and wool, carrying goods and people over Lake Erie. At Port Burwell in 1839 a young Canadian woman came aboard with four small children. Her name was Nancy Edison. Captain Bradley helped her to join her husband in Milan, Ohio, near Vermilion, where Edison had set up a shingle mill. To the mill in following seasons Bradley brought deckloads of Canadian lumber. Sam Edison's youngest son, born in 1847, was christened Thomas Alva Edison for Captain Alva Bradley. He was known as "Al."

In 1840 in Vermilion Captain Bradley had built a house for his own growing family. From the rivermouth came the clang of saws and the thud of axe and hammer, where Vermilion men were building schooners. Bradley's shipyard launched the 104-ton South America in 1841 and the Birmingham, 135 tons, three years later. The South America was lost in a Lake Erie storm in 1843; the Birmingham foundered off Buffalo in 1854. But with wheat, pork, hides and wool consigned to Buffalo for transshipment on the Erie Canal, and manufactured goods moving to Ohio's lake ports, a schooner earned its cost in a few seasons. Bradley went on building. He named his vessels for far places—Oregon and London. Then came the Ellington, a graceful two-master of 190 tons burden; for twenty years it carried a Connecticut name along with cargoes of fish, cheese, butter, crockery and assorted hardware. By that time the boy from Ellington knew every harbor between Buffalo and Detroit and all the capricious weather of Lake Erie.

As business grew, Captain Bradley moved to Cleveland, buying a small farm on the eastern edge of the city. His neighbors there were John D. Rockefeller, Stephen Harkness, Henry Flagler and Samuel Andrews, men who talked of Pennsylvania oil wells, Cleveland refineries, and a cooperage factory that would produce 10,000 barrels a day to supply kerosene for the lamps of America. Indifferent to that promise, Bradley kept on building lake vessels. In Cleveland in 1870 he launched the Alva Bradley, a 934-ton schooner that paid for itself in a season. But the era of sail was ending; lake commerce of the future would be bulk cargo from the north country to the industrial Midwest. In 1874 Bradley ordered two steamers, the first of a new fleet that brought iron ore to Ohio's furnaces and mills.

As president of the Vessel Owners' Association, Alva Bradley was a leader on the lakes. He died in 1885 in a Euclid Avenue mansion. The mansion is gone, but in Vermilion the old Bradley house still stands, as sturdy and trim as the schooners that sailed out of Vermilion harbor.

Vermilion was named for the red clay of the riverbank, where daubed Indian warriors once whooped and stamped around the Wyandot fires. Now it is a tranquil town with leafy branches mirrored in lagoons. As the site of the Great Lakes Historical Society's Marine Museum, it is a hearthstone of memories and tradition.

On the Great Lakes the future has always had more pull than the past. While he mapped scattered Indian camps on the wild lake shores Father Hennepin foresaw "an infinite number of scattered towns which might have communication one with another by navigation for five hundred leagues together, and by an inconceivable commerce which would establish itself among them." Now that his prophecy is realized, the past acquires increasing interest and appeal. In 1944 the Great Lakes Historical Society was organized in Cleveland. The late Alva Bradley, grandson of the Vermilion captain, was its first president. Its first collection of books and papers was housed in a room of the Carnegie West Branch of the Cleveland Public Library.

In the early 1900's yachtsman Fred W. Wakefield of Cleveland sometimes put in to Vermilion, where he enjoyed the drowsing old town and its sheltered harbor. In 1909 he moved his electrical lighting business there and built a handsome house, called "Harbor View," above the rivermouth. Commodore Wakefield died in 1934, while dredges were opening lagoons in the low ground east of the river. After his widow's death in 1951 the mansion above the lagoons was empty. A year later the Wakefield sons created the Vermilion Foundation, which granted "Harbor View" to the Great Lakes Historical Society, with funds to convert the old mansion into a marine museum. A new wing, added in 1968, greatly enlarged the museum space and increased its appeal. Like the lakes commerce of Commodore Wakefield's time, every year brings record numbers of visitors.

Through the stone gateway visitors step into a nautical surrounding. On the lawn, under rustling oak and buckeye trees, is an old-fashioned anchor, leaning on its crosspiece with one fluke in the earth and the other in air. Beyond it stands a barrel-shaped capstan that once weighed a vessel's ground tackle ("ground taykle" a schoonerman soon learned to say). Across the entrance walk, under a 95-foot flagpole, are a 4-bladed propeller and a 12-spoked steering wheel. A museum picture window frames a sloop with spread canvas.

Inside the vine-covered house a ship's clock chimes sea watches, and the windows look at lake and sky. Beyond walls lined with photographs of lake freighters, the room opens into a full-scale ship's bridge fitted with old and new navigation equipment—pelorus, gyro-compass, steering wheel and binnacle, whistle pull, engine room signal, and a live radio tuned to a weather station. Below the pilot house stands a

high-pressure steam engine that once delivered 500 horsepower for a Duluth tugboat. The engine room stairwell is
framed in a pair of gilded greyhounds, relics from the old
excursion steamer that loped between Detroit, Toledo and
Put-in-Bay in the early 1900's. One of her Sunday passengers
has remembered her homeward-bound in a Lake Erie rain
squall. "Dusk and a scud of clouds darkened the west, lights
flashed out along the shore, and far in the blackness Toledo
lay, a city of stars. With the first gust of rain the decks
cleared, uneasy people crowding into the lounge. Through
the mist the Greyhound snuffed her way; the brass rocker-
arms amidship moved up-down, up-down, like the pulsing
heart of a live creature. That steady throbbing quieted all
fears. She shook herself slightly as she scuffed the quay,
safely home again."

On the museum's lower level the eye goes to a mural paint-
ing that covers the east wall. Under the words "Great Lakes
Shipping 1869-1969" is a seascape busy with lake vessels of
all types and periods: mackinaw fishing boat, lumber schooner with deckload, wooden lumber steamer with a barge in
tow; sidewheel passenger steamer, wooden iron-ore freighter,
harbor tug, three-stacked passenger steamer, self-unloading
bulk freighter, whaleback steamer, a 500-foot bulk carrier of
1900, and a 700-footer of 1969. This striking composite, picturing two centuries of marine evolution, was done by Alexander B. Cook of Cleveland. On one wall it conveys the
theme and the feeling of the whole museum.

The exhibit rooms are rich in relics—timbers from Perry's
flagship Niagara, name boards from vanished vessels, wooden
rudders, sea chests, ships' bells, whistles and life rings. Out of
sight, in the library room, are files of papers, records, log
books, maps, charts, and light lists. A recent gift from the
Wakefield family is a bill of lading from the lakes' first
steamer, Walk-in-the-Water, that sank near Buffalo in 1821.

In the museum's entrance hallway stands the great many-
prism lens of the old Two Harbors Light from the historic

iron-ore port on Lake Superior. One wall of a lower room is covered with pictures of Great Lakes lighthouses in all seasons and in all weather. Another wall shows fifty paintings of schooners, brigs, passenger steamers, dredges, ferry boats, tug boats, and bulk freighters. On display in the ship-model room are forty scale models of famous sailing vessels and steamships; each one is a product of knowledge and crafts-manship. The Inter-Lake Yachting Association Room con-tains records, trophies, pictures and mementos of nearly a century of Great Lakes pleasure sailing. Adjoining it is the Vermilion Room's display of local history, from stone imple-ments of the Indians through the schooner era to the modern marina.

The museum drew 12,000 visitors in 1972, 21,000 in 1973, nearly 40,000 in 1974. Its appeal has surpassed all expectations.

Outside the museum, on Huron, Ferry and Washington streets, the past survives in the homes of nineteenth-century lake captains—Captain Bradley, Captain Gilchrist, Captain Horton, Captain Bell, Captain Minch and a score of others. The old sail loft, where fishermen sewed canvas and mended their gill-nets, has been converted into a famous restaurant with a unique Vermilion flavor. Its windows watch an end-less procession of yachts, sloops and cruisers from the serpen-tine lagoons.

From the rivermouth, twin entrance piers extend into the lake. An outer breakwall was added in 1974. On a summer evening the lake lies vast and tranquil, giving back the amber sunset. With dusk the entrance lights begin their gleaming, green on the east pier, red on the west; a strong white flash-ing marks the end of the long breakwall. Through the harbor lights the last pleasure boats come home to their moorings, and out in darkness the long freighters pass under the summer stars.

At Vermilion the past has been assembled and recon-structed. Five hundred miles north, on Mackinac Island, it simply accumulates. "Things stay, we go," reflected Henry Rowe Schoolcraft, Indian Agent on the Northwestern Frontier. The Agency House, in gardens stretching back from the white limestone road that bordered the little port, burned down on New Year's night in 1873. But the Indian dormitory that Schoolcraft built for visiting tribesmen still stands under the gun platforms of Fort Mackinac on the hill.

In 1833 the Indian agencies of Sault Ste. Marie and the Mackinac Straits were combined under Schoolcraft's direction. Leaving a sub-agent at the Soo, he put his family, his Indian servants, his books, papers and household goods aboard the schooner Mariner for removal to Mackinac Island. The rambling Agency House stood amid orchard trees and arbor vines in the east garden of the fort. It was surrounded by a log stockade, with a heavy gate defended by loopholes. Schoolcraft never closed the gate.

After the remoteness of Sault Ste. Marie, Mackinac Island seemed a crossroad. "Here," Schoolcraft wrote in his journal, "the great whirl of lake commerce from Buffalo to Chicago continually passed. The picturesque canoe of the Indian was constantly gliding, and the footsteps of visitors were frequently seen to tread the 'sacred island,' rendering it a point of contact with the busy world." In the long northern winter he studied Indian languages and legends. With the help of his wife—the daughter of an Irish trader and granddaughter of a Chippewa chief—he compiled the native mythology that other writers would later use in romantic portrayals of the red man. Schoolcraft knew both the poetry and squalor of savage life.

To the island came Indian tribesmen from all directions. Beaching their canoes, ragged and hungry with their dogs beside them, they made straight for the Agency. Their standard greeting was "Kitte-mau-giz-ze Sho-wain-e-min"—"I am poor, show me pity and charity." Mrs. Schoolcraft always gave them something from her pantry while her husband issued kettles, blankets, garden seeds and requisitions on the Agency storehouse.

After the greedy fur harvest the tribes were destitute. Game was depleted throughout all of lower Michigan. The Chippewa and Ottawa were in debt to the traders, and their only livelihood was the sale of cordwood to the steamboats—some of which, they said, was never paid for. Settlement was encroaching on their lands, for which they had no compensation. It was time for a treaty council.

In the fall of 1835 Schoolcraft went to Washington to prepare for an intertribal conference. Next spring the chiefs—some in boiled shirt and stovepipe hat, others in Indian blouse and headdress—were assembled in the old Masonic Hall in Washington. They ceded all the land in the lower peninsula north of Grand River and west of Thunder Bay, and in the upper peninsula from Point Detour through the Straits of St. Mary, west to the Chocolate River and south to Green Bay. For about two million dollars in annuities they gave up sixteen million acres. An incidental clause in the treaty called for construction of an Indian dormitory on Mackinac Island where chiefs could be housed on official visits. When an Indian boardinghouse went up where warriors once danced in the firelight, the old wild ways were past.

Late that summer of 1836 four thousand Indians, led by 143 chiefs, came to the island for their first payment. They feasted on rations from the Agency while soldiers patrolled the village streets. "So large an assemblage of red and white men," Schoolcraft noted, "probably never assembled here before." Tribal campfires smoked and flickered on the shore all the way from Arch Rock to the steep west bluffs. At the end of September, when the hills were turning gold and scarlet, wagonloads of corn, rice, flour, pork and tobacco were piled on the tramped beach, and agents doled out $150,000 worth of implements and clothing. In Indian summer weather the canoes pushed off, laden with that bounty.

A year later the chiefs asked for some of their allotment in cash. Schoolcraft's men counted out 42,000 half-dollars, throwing the coins onto the Indians' greasy blankets, and the braves whooped off with jingling burdens. Island merchants would lessen those loads, and traders would be waiting with whisky and trinkets when the tribes reached home.

In 1841 Schoolcraft ended his stay on Mackinac Island. Concerned with his wife's health, his children's education, and his own literary pursuits, he moved to New York. He had outlived the northwestern frontier. During his first season on the island, on November 13, 1833, he had marveled at a display of northern lights—the *Jebiung Nemeidewaud* of the Ojibways—ghostly banners shimmering across the midnight sky. It was a sight of mysterious grandeur, touching the ancient dread and wonder of the tribes. Now the wonder was gone and the once-magical island was becoming real estate. "An opinion arose," he wrote in his journal, "that Michilimackinac must become a favorite watering place, or refuge for the opulent and invalids during the summer; and lots were eagerly bought up from Detroit and Chicago."

That prediction soon came true. By 1850 Fort Mackinac was a tourist attraction. Summer visitors admired the morning dress parade, and dignitaries were entertained in the officers' mess. Carriage roads took pleasure-seekers past places that were feared and hallowed by the Indians.

The fort that had seen the traffic of Indians, voyageurs and traders now watched the arrival of excursion boats, and the village overflowed with vacationists. The old buildings of the fur company were converted into the John Jacob Astor House, with rocking chairs on the veranda and card and billiard tables in the public rooms. The Mission House, once filled with Indian and half-breed children, offered "good accommodations for 200 guests." The Miners' Arms Hotel was patronized by copper and iron men who waited at Mackinac for boats to Lake Superior.

THE HARBOR LIGHTS

In 1895 the island was granted by the federal government to the State of Michigan to be preserved as a state park. The old landmarks remained—Chimney Rock, Lover's Leap, Pontiac's Lookout—and century-old French lilacs blossomed around the white stone fort above the halfmoon harbor. Through the straits passed the great twentieth-century commerce, but the years brought little change to Mackinac Island. When the Straits Bridge was opened in 1957 the state of Michigan began a historical restoration of Old Fort Michilimackinac at Mackinaw City on the mainland. Fort Mackinac, built in 1779 of island stone and timber, has never crumbled.

Winter locks the island in a long stillness, but summer brings crowded ferry boats from Mackinaw City and St. Ignace at either end of the great bridge. Thousands of visitors take the carriage drive past the Grand Hotel to Arch Rock, Sugar Loaf and the old Post Cemetery with its weathered gravestones. Back at the village they climb the long ramp to Fort Mackinac. In the blockhouses, the barracks and the officers' quarters, historical displays review three centuries at the Straits.

In long evening shadows the ferry boats fill up again and the village streets grow quiet. Dusk brightens the beacons in the Round Island channel and the fort stands dark against the stars. At Mission Point the lake murmurs as it did before history began there. Beyond the harbor lights the long freighters pass where Jean Nicolet, in a bark canoe, peered westward over unknown waters.

ACKNOWLEDGMENTS

FOR HELP IN acquiring information about the Great
Lakes I am indebted to several institutions and a number of
persons. I am particularly grateful for the aid received, through
conversation and correspondence, from Miss Alice B. Clapp of
the Carnegie Library of Sault Ste. Marie which houses the late
Judge Joseph H. Steere's collection of books and monographs
pertaining to Lake Superior and the Soo, and to George A.
Marr and Oliver T. Burnham of the Lake Carriers' Association
for free access to the Association's records and reports; the
office of the Association, overlooking Cleveland harbor and
the wide sweep of Lake Erie, is an appropriate place to work
on the lakes story. I am indebted also to H. F. Rook, General
Superintendent of the St. Mary's Falls Canal, Isaac DeYoung,
General Superintendent, retired, of the Canal, Fred S. Case of
Sault Ste. Marie, Otto E. Wieland, president of the St. Louis
County Historical Society in Duluth, and Frank H. Kahle
of Ashtabula, Ohio, for various information. Members of the
staffs of the St. Louis County Historical Society, the Marquette Historical Society, the Michigan State Library at
Lansing, the Peter White Library, Marquette, the Hoyt Public Library, Saginaw, the Cleveland Public Library, the Burton Historical Collection of the Detroit Public Library, and
the Miami University Library have all aided me in finding
materials. I want to acknowledge my debt to the excellent
State Guides of Michigan, Wisconsin and Minnesota, to which
I turned for a good deal of detailed geographical and historical information. Ivan H. Walton's valuable essays on "Marine

ACKNOWLEDGMENTS

Lore" in the Michigan *Guide* and the Michigan History Magazine I drew upon for a number of details of the life aboard lakes vessels in the era of sail. I found myself turning frequently to the illuminating collection of photographs and records in Dana T. Bowen's current *Lore of the Lakes*. In addition to the books listed in my bibliography I used the files of the Michigan History Magazine, the Wisconsin Magazine of History, the Great Lakes News, the *Daily Mining Journal* of Marquette, the Michigan Pioneer and Historical Collections, the Annals of Cleveland (an extremely useful digest and index of Cleveland newspapers made by the Works Progress Administration of Ohio), the Publications of the Buffalo Historical Society, the *Papers and Records* of the Ontario Historical Society, and the *Great Lakes Pilot* published by the United States Hydrographic Office.

To this point my acknowledgments pertain to the 1942 edition of *The Long Ships Passing*. In bringing the book up to date, as of 1975, I was particularly concerned with new developments in the mining and processing of iron ore, with the construction of larger locks at Sault Ste. Marie and of larger freighters, and with the St. Lawrence Seaway traffic that has more than doubled since the waterway was opened in 1959. For generous assistance I am indebted to Mr. John Horton of the Cleveland-Cliffs Steamship Company, to Mr. E. J. Mapes of Pickands Mather & Co., to Captain John T. Packer and other officers of the steamer Cliffs Victory, and to Captain Elmer Strong and Chief Engineer B. H. Reid of the steamer V. W. Scully. For various courtesies and information I am grateful to Mr. Arthur N. O'Hara and Mr. Arthur D. Copeland of the Great Lakes Historical Society Marine Museum at Vermilion, Ohio; to Mr. Alexander B. Cook of Cleveland; to Mr. Joseph Jenkins, manager of the B&O Dock at Lorain, Ohio; to Mr. Bill Muloin, Mr. Bill Brandon and Mr. Perry Briand of Wabush Mines at Pointe Noire and Sept-Iles, Quebec; and to Mr. Frank Kahle, man-

ACKNOWLEDGMENTS

ager of Far East Operations of United States Lines, Tokyo. Over a number of years I have accumulated obligations to Ms. Janet Coe Sanborn, editor of *Inland Seas*, and to Mr. Oliver T. Burnham, a long-term executive of the Lake Carriers' Association.

Walter Havighurst
Oxford, Ohio

BIBLIOGRAPHY

Bald, F. Clever. *Michigan in Four Centuries*. New York, 1954.
——. *The Sault Canal Through 100 Years*. University of Michigan, 1954.
Barry, James P. *Georgian Bay*. Toronto and Vancouver, 1968.
——. *Ships of the Great Lakes*. Berkeley, California, 1973.
Bayliss, Joseph and Estelle. *Historic St. Joseph Island*. Cedar Rapids, 1938.
——. in collaboration with Milo M. Quaife. *River of Destiny: The St. Mary's*. Detroit, 1955.
Beard's Directory and History of Marquette County, with Sketches of the Early History of Lake Superior. Detroit, 1873.
Beasley, Norman. *Freighters of Fortune*. New York, 1930.
Beston, Henry. *The St. Lawrence*. New York, 1942.
Bowen, Dana Thomas. *Lore of the Lakes*. Daytona Beach, Florida, 1940.
——. *Memories of the Lakes*. Daytona Beach, Florida, 1946.
——. *Shipwrecks of the Lakes*. Daytona Beach, Florida, 1952.
Bowyer, Dwight. *Ghost Ships of the Great Lakes*. New York, 1968.
——. *Great Stories of the Great Lakes*. New York, 1966.
——. *True Tales of the Great Lakes*. New York, 1971.
Burnham, Guy M. *The Lake Superior Country in History and Story*. Boston, 1930.
Burton, James L. *Commerce of the Lakes and Erie Canal*. Buffalo, 1851.
Catlin, George B. *The Story of Detroit*. Detroit, 1923.
Channing, Edward, and Lansing, Marion Florence. *The Story of the Great Lakes*. New York, 1912.
Corps of Engineers, U.S. Army. *The Vital Links—Great Lakes Connecting Channels*. June, 1959.
Curwood, James Oliver. *The Great Lakes*. New York, 1909
Cuthbertson, George A. *Freshwater*. Toronto, 1931.

345

BIBLIOGRAPHY

DeKruif, Paul. *Seven Iron Men*. New York, 1929.

Disturnell, J. *The Great Lakes, or Inland Seas of America*. Philadelphia, 1871.

——. *Sailing on the Great Lakes*. Philadelphia, 1874.

Elliott, James L. *Red Stacks over the Horizon*. Grand Rapids, 1967.

Ellis, William D. *The Cuyahoga*. New York, 1966.

Fowle, Otto. *Sault Ste. Marie and Its Great Waterway*. New York, 1925.

Gjerset, Knut. *Norwegian Sailors on the Great Lakes*. Northfield, Minnesota, 1928.

Hall, J. W. *Marine Disasters on the Western Lakes*. Detroit, 1872.

Hatcher, Harlan. *A Century of Iron and Men*. Indianapolis and New York, 1950.

——. *The Great Lakes*. New York, 1944.

——. *Lake Erie*. Indianapolis and New York, 1945.

——. *The Western Reserve*. Indianapolis and New York, 1949.

——, and Walter, Erich A. *Pictorial History of the Great Lakes*. New York, 1963.

Hedrick U. P. *Land of the Crooked Tree*. New York, 1948.

Henry, Alexander. *Travels and Adventures*. Edited by Milo M. Quaife. Chicago, 1921.

History of Bay County, Michigan. Chicago, 1883.

History of the Upper Peninsula of Michigan. Chicago, 1883.

Hodge, William. *Papers Concerning Early Navigation on the Great Lakes*. Buffalo, 1883.

Holbrook, Stewart H. *Iron Brew*. New York, 1940.

Holmes, Fred L. *Badgers, Saints and Sinners*. Milwaukee, 1939.

Horwood, Harold. *Newfoundland*. New York, 1969.

Hubbard Bela. *Memorials of Half a Century*. New York, 1887.

Inches, C. H. *The Great Lakes Wooden Shipbuilding Era*. Vermilion, Ohio, 1962.

Inland Seas. January 1945—.

Interstate Port Handbook *The St. Lawrence Seaway—Fact and Future*. Chicago, 1959.

Ireland, Tom. *The Great Lakes–St. Lawrence Deep Waterway to the Sea*. New York, 1934.

Jameson, Anna. *Winter Studies and Summer Rambles*. New York, 1839.

Johnson, Edwin F. *The Navigation of the Lakes*. Hartford, Connecticut, 1866.

BIBLIOGRAPHY

Josephson, Matthew. *Edison.* New York, 1959.

Kellogg, Louise Phelps. *The French Regime in Wisconsin and the Northwest.* Madison, 1925.

Lake Superior Iron Ores. Cleveland, 1938.

[Lanman, Charles]. *Life on the Lakes.* New York, 1936.

Limnos. Spring 1968—.

Livingstone, W. A. *The Great Lakes Problem.* Detroit, 1891.

Longyear, John M. *Landlooker in the Upper Peninsula of Michigan.* Marquette, Michigan, 1960.

Mabee, Carlton. *The Seaway Story.* New York, 1961.

MacLennon, Hugh. *The Rivers of Canada.* New York, 1961.

Malkus, Alida. *Blue Water Boundary.* New York, 1960.

[Mansfield, John Brandt]. *History of the Great Lakes.* 2 vols. Chicago, 1899.

Marquette, Michigan. Marquette, 1891.

Mills, James Cooke. *History of Saginaw County, Michigan.* Saginaw, 1918.

———. *Our Inland Seas.* Chicago, 1910.

Muir, John. *The Story of My Boyhood and Youth.* Boston, 1913.

Murdoch, Angus. *Boom Copper.* New York, 1943.

Nute, Grace Lee. *Lake Superior.* Indianapolis and New York, 1944.

Oliver, David D. *Centennial History of Alpena, Michigan.* Alpena, 1903.

Parkman, Francis. *The Jesuits in North America.* Boston, 1895.

———. *LaSalle and the Discovery of the Great West.* Boston, 1907.

Peckham, H. H. *Old Fort Michilimackinac at Mackinaw City.* Ann Arbor, Michigan, 1938.

Peterson, Eugene T. *Michilimackinac: Its History and Restoration.* Mackinac Island 1962.

Pound, Arthur. *Lake Ontario.* Indianapolis and New York, 1945.

Ratigan, William. *Straits of Mackinac.* Grand Rapids, 1957.

St. Lawrence Seaway Manual. United States Senate Document, No. 165. 83rd Congress, 2nd Session. Washington, D.C., 1959.

Sawyer, Alvah H. *A History of the Northern Peninsula of Michigan.* Chicago 1911.

Schoolcraft, Henry R. *Narrative of Travels from Detroit Northwest Through the Great Chain of American Lakes.* Albany, 1821.

———. *Oneota, or The Red Race in America.* New York, 1844.

347

BIBLIOGRAPHY

——. *Personal Memoirs of a Residence of Thirty Years with the Indian Tribes on the American Frontiers.* Philadelphia, 1851.

Seaway Review. Spring 1970–.

Souvenir of the Lakes. Detroit, 1831.

Swineford, A. D. *History and Review of the Copper, Iron, Silver, Slate and Other Material Interests on the South Shore of Lake Superior.* Marquette 1876.

Terrell, John Upton. *Furs by Astor.* New York, 1963.

Thwaites, Reuben Gold, ed. *The Jesuit Relations and Allied Documents.* Cleveland, 1898–1901.

Waldron, Webb. *We Explore the Great Lakes.* New York, 1923.

Williams, Ralph D. *The Honorable Peter White.* Cleveland, 1907.

Woolson, Constance F. *Castle Nowhere.* New York, 1875.

INDEX

A. H. Ferbert, steamer, 305
Agassiz, Louis, 44
Alaska, 139
Albany, N.Y., 127; *Evening Journal,*
    29
Alexander Holly, barge, 233
Alger-Smith Logging Company, 118
Algic Researches, 47
Algonquin, schooner, 163, 165, 169,
    172
Algonquin tribes, 6, 10, 18; language,
    12–13, 15, 92, 233
Allegheny Mountains, 25
Allers, Captain Charley, 147, 154
Allouez, Claude, 11, 13, 14
Alpena, Mich., 92–94, 98, 107–108,
    118; lumber barons, sawmills of,
    93; old-time lumbermen still liv-
    ing in, 93–94
Alpena, steamer, 241
Alva Bradley, schooner, 334
Ambassador Bridge, 29
Amelia, schooner, 239
American Fur Trading Company, 35,
    162
American Merchant Marine Library
    Association (Soo Library), 309–
    310
American Shipbuilding Company,
    324
Amherstburg, 66
Anchor Line, 261
Andrews, Samuel 334
Angelique, Indian woman, 163, 169–
    172
Apostle Islands, 31–32, 100, 169, 176
Arcturus, steamer, 317–318
Arkansas, 9
Arkansas River, 15

Artois, 17
Ashland, Wis., 25, 31, 36, 39, 99, 100,
    177, 213, 270
Ashtabula, Ohio, 26, 27, 39
Atlantic, steamer, 140, 141
Atlantic Ocean, 20, 23, 66, 70, 83,
    128, 135, 240, 260, 269, 270, 271
Au Gres River, 91
Augusta, schooner, 67–71, 204
Augustus B. Wolvin, steamer, 221,
    315
Au Sable, Mich., 117
Au Sable River, 92
Averill, Capt., 175, 176, 177

Babcock, W. I., 222
Badger State, schooner, 326
Baltimore, Md., 70, 274
Baltimore, steamer, 204
Baltimore & Ohio R.R., 39
Bancroft, 11
Bancroft House, 90
Bannockburn, 241
Bar Point, 28
Barclay, Capt., 62
Baron-Humboldt Mine, 285
Bathurst, Lord, 63
Bay City, Mich., 87, 89, 95, 106–107,
    140, 187, 221, 251
Bay de Noc, 109, 131, 212
Bayfield, Capt. Henry Wolsey, 161
Beauharnois Lock, 278
Beaver Falls, 24
Beaver Islands, 147–154, 240
Bela Hubbard, schooner, 187
Bell, Captain, 337
Bell, John, 67
Belle Isle, Detroit, 29
Bernard's Light, 232

349

INDEX

Bessemer steel, 212
Bete Grise Bay, 49, 177
Bethlehem, Pa., 271
Bethlehem Steel Corp., 291
Bethune monastery, 17
Big Sable Point, 116
Bird Island, 77
Black Hawk War, 80, 125, 127
Black River, 92
Black Rock, N.Y., 65, 77, 79, 88, 123
Block, Miss Babette, 265
Blue Water International Bridge, 29
Bob-Lo Island, 28
Bois Brule, 49
Bonga, Stephen, 35, 215
Book of the Law of the Lord, The,
  150, 153
Boston, 51, 100, 168, 273, 274
Boston Mining Company, 163, 175
Bourke-White, Margaret, 279
Bowen, Mrs. E., 239
"Boy" boats, 106
Brace, Capt. C. S., 239
Bradley, Alva, 335
Bradley, Captain Alva, 333-334, 337
Breckenridge, John C., 67
Brulé, Etienne, 10
Brule River, 99
Bryant, William Cullen, 159
Buena Vista, steamer, 91
Buffalo, N.Y., 26, 38, 64, 65, 66, 69,
  73, 77-79, 81-83, 87, 88, 95, 101,
  116, 118, 124, 125, 126, 128, 134,
  136, 137. 140, 141, 221, 235, 240,
  241, 243, 252, 271, 273, 274;
  Morning Express, 51
Buffalo Light, 142
Burch, Jonathan, 92
Burlington, Wis., 148, 154
Burt, John, 201
Burt, Wellington R., 90
Burt, William A., 9, 51, 181, 182,
  301
Burton, Capt. William, 83
Byers, Ed, 111

Cadillac, 61
Cadotte, Achille, 163, 165
Calais, 17
Callan, Bill, 90

Calumet, Mich., 31, 51, 168
Calumet Mining Company, 168
Campau, Louis, 87
Canada, 24, 30, 31, 36, 135, 223, 260;
  Board of Grain Commissioners,
  235
Canfield Capt. Augustus, 201
Cape Horn, 269
Carnegie, Andrew, 181
Caroline, steamer, 105
Carp River, 51, 100, 181
Carus, Capt. Edward, 74, 247
Cass, Gen. Lewis, 32, 44, 123, 299-
  300
Cass River, 89
Cayuga Creek, 57
Champlain, 5, 6, 10
Charity Islands, 59
Charles E. Wilson, diesel, 320, 321
Charles F. Price, steamer, 251, 256
Charlevoix, Mich., 91
Chatauqua, N.Y., 148
Cheboygan, Mich., 25, 91, 94, 95,
  251, 265
Chequamegon Bay, 13, 169
Chesapeake, steamer, 140
Chesapeake & Ohio R.R., 39
Chicago, 5, 10, 23, 25, 26, 38, 39, 66,
  68, 73, 80-81, 82-83, 94, 95, 97,
  98, 118, 121, 125, 126, 128, 129,
  140. 147, 175, 224, 240, 241, 243,
  252, 261, 269, 270; great fire of,
  99, 107, 108, 115; Grain Market,
  236
Chicago & North Western Railway,
  212
Chicago River, 16, 80, 81, 108, 126,
  142, 269
Chicora, steamer, 240
China, 5, 6
China, steamer, 141, 261
Chippewa, schooner, 164
Chippewa, steamer, 124
Chippewa Indians, 8, 9, 13, 14, 15,
  19, 43-49, 63, 87, 123, 129, 147,
  159, 188, 190, 191, 202, 203, 204,
  205, 229, 242, 297-302, 339-340;
  language, 30, 45, 47, 49, 215;
  legends, 8, 31, 46-49, 203
Cholera, 82, 125-126, 188, 203

INDEX

Christopher Columbus, steamer, 141
Church, Philetus, 229
Church Hill Weather Tower, 153
Cicero, Paulette, 94
City of Cleveland, steamer, 127
Civil War, 92, 98, 140, 209, 270
Clarion, steamer, 242
Clason, Lewis, 92
Clay, Henry, 36, 200, 201, 310
Cleaveland, Moses, 319
Clermont, steamer, 260
Cleveland, Ohio, 10, 25, 26–27, 37, 38, 39, 64, 66, 73, 74, 79–80, 81, 94, 105, 118, 122, 127, 131, 140, 163, 184, 221, 222, 239, 240, 251, 256, 263, 264, 269
Cleveland-Cliffs Iron Company, 189, 191
Cleveland-Cliffs Steamship Company, 331
Cleveland Mine, 182, 189
Cleveland sawmill, on Lake Superior, 100
Cliff Mine, 51, 164, 176
Cliffs Victory, steamer, 331
Clinton, De Witt, 77–78
Cloquet, Minn., 119
Coburn, steamer, 116
Colonel Cook, schooner, 69–71
Columbia, brig, 209, 308
Columbia, steamer, 94
Columbia River, 40
Columbia Transportation Company, 279
Commodore Perry, steamer, 164
Conestoga wagons, 40
Confederated Islands, 32
Conneaut, Ohio, 26, 27, 220
Constellation, steamer, 127
Cook, Alexander B., 336
Cooke, Jay, 36–37
Coolidge, Calvin, 272
Copper Harbor, Mich., 164, 167, 176, 254, 255
Coppermine Point, 255
Cornish miners, 38, 209, 210–211
Coulby, Harry, 261, 263
Coulee, steamer, 235
Cragan, Frank, 319
Crimean War, 83

Cross Village, 115
Crystal Falls, Mich., 212
Cuba, 70
Cuyahoga River, 27, 79, 80, 127, 222, 239, 263, 264, 265
Cuyuna Iron Range, 215

D. G. Kerr, steamer, 220
Dablon, Father, 50
Dalton, Henry G., 261, 264
Davenport, Iowa, 35
Davenport, Capt. James, 115, 243
Davidson, James, 221, 222, 261, 262, 263
Davis, General E. L. B., 304
Davis Lock, 205, 304
Dead River, 51, 100
Dean Richmond, steamer, 81, 269
Death's Door, 259
Delaware, steamer, 133
De Pere, Wis., 49
Des Plaines River, 15
De Tour, Mich., 30, 52, 74, 123, 227, 228, 229, 231, 234, 251
Detroit, Mich., 25, 26, 28, 29, 50, 52, 61, 63, 64, 65, 73, 74, 88, 94, 116, 117, 118, 121, 122, 123–124, 125–126, 127, 131, 141, 167, 168, 169, 170, 187, 197, 202, 203, 240, 269
Detroit River, 25, 59, 65, 87, 122, 162, 242, 271
Dickens, Charles, 127
Diesel engines, 321
Discovery, schooner, 161
Dispatch, steam tug, 115
Dollar, Robert, 273
Door Peninsula, 24
Douglas, Stephen A., 67, 68
Douglass Houghton, steamer, 233
Drummond's Island, 49
Duddleson, Capt., 253
Dulhut, Daniel de Grosolon, Sieur, 18, 60
Duluth, Minn., 24, 26, 32, 36–41, 60, 74, 119, 163, 214, 216, 221, 223, 234, 235, 241, 243, 245–247, 252, 261, 271
Duluth & Iron Range R.R., 37, 39, 100, 290

INDEX

Duluth, Mesabi & Northern R.R.,
39, 216, 290
Dunkirk, 17
Dutch settlers, 26, 129, 130–134

Eagle Harbor, Mich., 254
Eagle River, Mich., 164, 167, 169,
176, 177
Ecorse, Mich., 29
Edenborn, steamer, 245
Edison, Thomas Alva, 285, 286, 333
Edwin N. Ohl, steamer, 234
Eisenhower Lock, 277, 278
Eldred, Anson, 92
Eldred, Julius, 50
Eliza Ward, schooner, 200
Ellington, schooner, 333
Ellwood, steamer, 245–246
Ely, H. B., 184, 209
Emerson, Curt, 90–91
Empire, steamer, 29, 127
Enterprise, steamer, 124
Erie, Lake, 9, 10, 23, 25, 26, 28, 31,
38, 58–59, 61–63, 65–67, 74, 82,
84, 88, 105, 118, 121, 124, 125,
128, 129, 140, 183, 235, 239, 240,
242, 248, 252, 269
Erie, steamer, 105, 128, 241
Erie Canal, 24, 26, 40, 65, 77–78, 81,
121, 127, 148
Erie Mining Company, 290
Escanaba, Mich., 36, 39, 66, 99, 212,
223, 242
Eureka, barque, 269
Evans, Edwin Townsend, 141, 221
Evening Star, steamer, 106
Everett, J. D. H., 178
Everett, Philo, 9, 51, 181–182
Extenuate, schooner, 147, 154

Fairbanks, E. T., & Company, 202
Fairchild, Charley, 113
Fairport, Ohio, 131
Farmer's Ridges, 230
Field, Elvira, 150, 152
Fifield, Wis., 119
Fillmore, President Millard, 303
Finnish settlers, 30, 38, 227
Firelands, the, 28
Firestone, Harvey, 285

Fish, Capt. Job, 121, 122
Fisher Tower, 29
Fitz-Herbert, Mrs., 45
Flagler, Henry, 334
Flint, Mich., 87
Flint River, 89
Florence, schooner, 164
Ford, Henry, 182, 285
Forest fires, 107–119
Forest Queen, steamer, 94
Forestville, Mich., 116
Forrester, Mich., 116
Fort Brady, 197, 199–200, 228, 300–
301, 308
Fort Dearborn, 10, 80, 125
Fort Drummond, 300
Fort Erie, 62, 63
Fort Frontenac, 59
Fort Gratiot, 125
Fort Mackinac, 62, 204, 338, 340, 341
Fort Malden, 61
Fort Michilimackinac, 341
Fort St. Joseph, 232
Fort St. Louis, 60
Fort Wilkins, 176
Fort William, 31, 49, 223, 235, 236,
254, 255
Fox River, 7–8, 15; portage, 7, 8, 9,
15
Frank Rockefeller, steamer, 314
Franklin, Benjamin, 215
French River, 9, 61
Frontenac, Count, 57
Frontenac, steamer, 121
Fur trade, 18–20, 87
Fur Trader, schooner, 164, 188

G. P. Griffith, steamer, 105
Garden Island Shoal, 151
Garden River Indians, 229
Geerlings family, 130
General Taylor, steamer, 165
George IV, 45
George, Lake, 228, 229
George F. Baker, steamer, 233
George M. Humphrey, steamer, 316
Georgian Bay, 9, 10, 11, 40, 63, 260
German settlers, 23, 26, 38, 82, 129,
134, 188, 203
Gilchrist, Captain, 337

INDEX

Gitchee Gumee, 31, 47, 298
Giwideonaning, 30
Glanville, Joseph, 288
Gogebic iron range, 212–214, 216
Good Tidings, gospel ship, 247
Goose Island, 232
Gooseberry River, 18
Grain trade, 66, 81–84, 136, 270–271
Grand Marais, 49
Grand Portage, 19
Grand Rapids & Indiana R.R., 98
Grand River, 239
Grand Sable Banks, 167
Grant Park, 23, 25
Graveraet, Robert J., 187, 188
Grays Reef Light, 142, 151
Great Freeze, 235–236
Great Lakes Historical Museum, 319
Great Lakes Historical Society, 334–335
Great Lakes News, 265
Great Lakes-Tidewater Association, 271
Great Northern Railway, 39
Great Western, steamer, 127
Greater Buffalo, steamer, 142, 316
Greater Detroit, steamer, 142
Green Bay, 6–7, 9, 15, 17, 19, 38, 59, 99, 109, 122, 190, 259
Green Bay, schooner, 239
Green Bay, Wis., 13
Greenough, William, 228
Greyhound, steamer, 336
Griffin, first commercial vessel on the lakes, 17, 57–60, 231, 239
Groseilliers, Médart Chouart, Sieur de, 9, 18
Groundwater, John, 251, 256
Gull Island, 100

Halley, Myron, 78
Hancock, Mich., 31, 51, 168
Harbor Beach, Mich., 251
Harding, Warren G., 272
Harkness, Stephen, 334
Harrison, Gen. William Henry, 62
Harrisville, Mich., 107, 108
Harry Coulby, steamer, 315
Harvey, Charles T., 201–204
Hayes, John, 163

Hayes, Rutherford B., 212
Hecla, steamer, 37
Hennepin, Rev. Louis, 9, 16–18, 20, 23, 24, 57, 58–59, 60, 334
Henry, Alexander, 44, 50
Henry Clay, steamer, 124, 125, 228
Henry of Navarre, 14
Herman, Eugene, 265–266
Hiawatha, 48
Hibbing, Frank, 288
Hibbing, Minn., 216, 289–291
Hibbing Taconite Company, 291
Hill, Jim, 141
Hillman, Mich., 107
Hinckley, Minn., 119
Holland, Mich., 38
Hoover, Herbert, 272
Horton, Captain, 337
Horton, John, 331
Horvath, George, 112
Houghton, Douglass, 9, 50, 116, 163–164, 167–169, 187, 301
Houghton, Mich., 31, 51, 66, 168
Hubbard, Bela, 116
Hudson Bay, 58, 215
Hudson River, 24, 78, 81, 121, 124, 136, 260, 269
Hudson's Bay Company, 63, 161
Hull, Gen. William, 61
Humphrey, Capt. Jasper, 69–71
Hurley, Wis., 212, 213, 214
Huron Indians, 5, 6, 10, 11, 13

Icelandic settlers, 38
Ile au Galets, 102
Illinois, 23, 68, 81, 121, 128; Lake of the, *see* Lake Michigan
Illinois, steamer, 68, 204
Illinois and Michigan Canal, 80
Illinois Indians, 14, 16, 18, 60
Illinois River, 15, 17, 269
Illinois Waterway, 269
Immigrant boats, 26, 67, 81, 121, 124–139, 141–144
Inches, Captain H. C., 319
Independence, steamer, 164 165, 175–178
India, steamer, 141, 261
Indian treaties, 44, 87, 181, 204
Ingalls, Charlie, 109–115

INDEX

Interlake Steamship Company, 264, 319, 324
International Deepwater Commission, 270, 271
Invincible, schooner, 161
Irish settlers, 23, 26, 38, 82, 134, 203, 209
Iron Age, steamer, 212
Iron City, steamer, 165
Iron Cliff, steamer, 212
Iron Duke, steamer, 212
Iron King, steamer, 212
Iron King Mine, 214
Iron Mountain, Mich., 212
Iron Ore Company of Canada, 283
Iron ore trade, 71-73, 183-185, 275-276
Iron River, 99
Iron River, Wis., 119, 212
Ironwood, Mich., 212, 213
Iroquois Club, 319
Iroquois Indians, 9, 18
Ishpeming, Mich., 182, 209, 210, 211
Isle Royale, 8, 31, 161, 163, 169-172, 215
Isaac L. Ellwood, steamer, 315
Itasca, Lake, 44

J. Pierpont Morgan, steamer, 315
Jackson, Anna, 301-302
Jackson, Mich., 181
Jackson Mine, 182
James B. Eads, steamer, 236
James Carruthers, steamer, 254
James Davidson, steamer, 279
James J. Hill, steamer, 315
Japan, steamer, 141, 261
Jesuit Relations, 11-16
Jesuits, 5-16, 31, 49, 197, 227
John Fritz, steamer, 233
John Jacob Astor, schooner, 162
John W. Gates, steamer, 315
Johnson, Capt., 199-200
Johnson, Levi, 79-80
Johnson's Lives of the Poets, 44
Joliet, Louis, 9, 15
Jones, Herbert, 256
Julia Palmer, steamer, 164, 175
Juneau County, Wis., 35

Kalamazoo, Mich., 124
Kaskaskia, Ill., 16
Kewaunee, Wis., 243
Keweenaw Peninsula, 13, 31, 50-52, 162, 164, 167-169, 175, 176-177, 219, 241, 253
Kichiwiski, Chippewa chief, 24, 37
Kilbourn, Byron, 80
King Strang Hotel, 153
Kingston, Ont., 81, 136
Kingston, Wis., 137
Kipling, Rudyard, 278, 292
Knudson, Martin, 259

L. C. Waldo, steamer, 253
L. G. Mason, steamer, 106
Labrador Trough, 282, 293, 294
La Branche, 160
Lady Elgin, steamer, 67, 68-69, 205
Lake Carriers' Association, 118, 232, 233-234, 259
Lake Erie and Ohio Canal, 27, 64, 79
Lake George, in St. Mary's River, 49
Lake Huron, 1, 9, 20, 23, 25, 59, 63, 74, 87, 88, 90, 92, 95, 107, 108, 116, 117, 118, 123, 125, 131, 143, 160, 161, 228, 240, 241, 243-245, 248, 251-252, 256, 261, 265
Lake St. Francis, 279
Lake Superior & Ishpeming R.R., 39
Lake Superior Copper Company, 175
Langford, Joe, 27
L'Anse à la Bouteille, 49
Lansing, Mich., 108, 152
Lapeer County, Mich., 116
La Pointe, 13, 14, 49, 169, 176
La Salle, Robert Cavelier, Sieur de, 58-60
Laurentian Mountains, 30, 183, 197
Lawrence, flagship of Commodore Perry, 62
Leafield, 239
Leavitt, B. F., 244
Les Chenaux Islands, 231
Lexington, schooner, 242
Liberty, schooner, 133
Lime Island, 328
Limestone trade, 93
Lincoln, Abraham, 67

354

INDEX

Little Cedar River, 99, 115
Little Silver River, 169
Liverpool, 220, 269, 270, 271
Livingstone, William, 233
Long Point, 140
Lorain, Ohio, 26, 223
Lucia A. Simpson, schooner, 74
Ludington, Mich., 16, 91, 97
Lumber trade, 73, 87–102

MacArthur Lock, 304, 305, 306, 309, 316
McDougall, Alexander, 260–261, 313–314
Mack, Andrew, 125
McKay, Capt. George Perry, 164–165, 172, 177
McKenney, Thomas, 234
Mackenzie, Alexander, 9
Mackinac, Straits of, 5–8, 9, 11, 14, 16, 38, 46, 59, 131, 162, 189, 235, 297, 306, 324, 327, 341
Mackinac Island, 16, 19, 23, 52, 61, 88, 122, 123, 125, 129, 137, 150, 152, 160, 197, 229, 232, 251
Mackinaw City, Mich., 9, 107, 341
McKnight, Sheldon, 160–161, 168, 184, 200
MacMurray, Rev. William, 301
McNutt, Betsy, 152
Macomb, Alexander, 298–299, 301
Madeira Pet, steamer, 269
Madeline Island, 31
Mahoning Pit, 216, 289, 291
Maine, 90
Majji Gessick, Chippewa chief, 181, 182
Major Barbara, barque, 115
Manhattan, steamer, 175
Manistee, Mich., 91, 97, 98, 108
Manistee Rivers, 98
Manistique, Mich., 49, 99, 243
Manitou Islands, 147, 242
Manitowoc, Wis., 74, 99, 131, 133, 240, 247
Marine City, Mich., 39
Marine Salvage Company, 279
Marquette, Jacques, 9, 11, 14–16, 97
Marquette, Mich., 31, 36, 39, 66, 71,

72, 100, 172, 175, 183, 184, 187–191, 209, 210
Marquette iron range, 51, 181–185, 201, 209–212
Marryat, Captain Frederick, 301
Marshfield, Wis., 119
Mason, Stevens T., 199
Massachusetts, 9
Mataafa, steamer, 245–247
Mattawa River, 9
Maumee River, 28, 62
Mears, Charlie, 97–98
Medford, Wis., 119
Menard, Father, 12
Mennonites, 98
Menominee, Mich., 99, 100, 109–115, 223
Menominee iron range, 212, 293
Merchant, schooner, 164, 175
Merchant, steamer, 221
Mesabi iron range, 37, 214, 215–216, 222, 285–291
Meteor, steamer, 165, 244
Miami Indians, 18
Miami Rivers, 28
Michigamme, Mich., 212
Michigan, 5, 20, 97, 98, 107, 116, 121, 129, 135, 199, 200, 229
Michigan, Lake, 6, 8, 9, 13, 14, 16, 23, 24, 31, 38, 44, 59, 63, 65, 68–70, 74, 80, 82–84, 95, 100, 105, 108, 109, 114, 115, 125, 126, 129, 130, 132–134, 139, 140, 147, 149–154, 182, 204, 212, 236, 239, 240, 241–242, 243, 252, 259, 269, 273
Michigan, schooner, 63–64
Michigan, U.S. gunboat, 151, 152
Michigan Northern Power Company, 30, 43
Michilimackinac. See Mackinac Island
Michipicoten, 49
Milwaukee, Wis., 26, 38, 67–70, 81, 82, 101, 121, 133, 134, 135, 136, 137, 147, 214, 252, 265, 269
Milwaukee River, 80, 82, 129
Minch, Captain, 337
Mineral Rock, steamer, 165, 231
Mink, schooner, 161
Minneapolis, 60

INDEX

Minnesota, 20, 84, 98, 123, 216
Minnesota, steamer, 71
Mississippi River, 7, 8, 9, 17, 18, 20, 32, 35, 40, 44, 63, 98, 123, 126, 148, 167, 215, 269; discovery, 15
Mobile, Ala., 70
Mohawk valley, 77, 78
Monaghan, John, 93
Monongahela River, 180, 222
Montezuma Hall, 91
Monticello, steamer, 175
Montreal, 15, 18, 45, 61, 70, 272, 274
Montreal River, 213
Moose Lake, Minn., 119
Mormons, on Beaver Island, 147-154, 231
Morse, Rev. Jedediah, 123
Morse, Samuel F. B., 123
Mott, Charlie, 169-171
Mountain Iron Company, 215-216
Muddy Lake, 228
Muir, Daniel, 134-138
Muir, John, 134-139
Munising Bay, 48
Munuscong Lake, 230
Muskegon, Mich., 97, 98, 147
Muskegon River, 91, 97

Nancy, schooner, 63, 231
Napoleon, steamer, 184, 190
Nasmuth, barge, 245-246
Nauvoo, Ill., 148
Neebish Cut, 25
Neebish Island, 30, 63, 101, 219, 227, 228, 230, 232, 233, 234, 236
Negaunee, Mich., 182, 210, 212
Negro deckhands, 72
New Brunswick, 90
New Orleans, 63, 126, 140, 273
New York City, 24, 32, 51, 63, 70, 78, 94, 100, 136, 168, 203, 263, 271, 273, 274
New York State, 78, 95, 147
New York State Barge Canal, 269
Newberry & Dole, commission merchants, 81
Newport Mine, 214
Newton, Isaac, shipbuilder, 260
Niagara, flagship of Commodore Perry, 336

Niagara, packet boat, 78
Niagara Falls, 9, 24, 57, 64, 105
Niagara River, 17, 59, 61, 77, 95, 121
Nickerson, Nate, 111
Nicolet, Jean, 5-8, 9, 20, 59, 341
Nipissing, Lake, 9
Nipissing Indians, 6
Noah's Ark, packet boat, 78
Nokomis, 48
Nolan, Louis, 181-182
Norfolk & Western R.R., 39
Norman songs, 19
Norrie Mine, 214
North American, steamer, 142
North Channel, 5
North Star, steamer, 233
North West, steamer, 141
North West Fur Company, 19, 63, 161, 198
Northern City, steamer, 111, 114, 115
Northern Islander, The, 150
Northern Lake Company, 163
Northland, steamer, 141
Northwest Passage, 8
Norwegian immigrants, 141

Ocean, schooner, 164
Oconto, Wis., 99, 110
Oconto River, 107
Odd Fellow, steamer, 106
Ogdensburg, steamer, 140, 141
Oglebay, Norton & Company, 216
Ohio, 26, 28, 39, 40, 79, 81, 95
Ohio River, 28, 79, 121, 180, 222
"Old Mont Line," 71-72
Oliver Mining Company, 216
Onoko, steamer, 221, 222, 322
Ontario, Lake, 9, 23-24, 57, 61, 81, 121, 135, 240, 269, 271
Ontario, steamer, 121, 269
Ontonagon, Mich., 49, 99, 100, 178
Ontonagon Boulder, 50
Ontonagon River, 49-50
Ord, James, 45
Orlando M. Poe, steamer, 205
Osborn, Chase, 219
Osceola, brig, 81
Oscoda, Mich., 117
Oshkosh, Wis., 119
Oswego, N.Y., 81, 136, 269

INDEX

Ottawa Indians, 147, 339–340
Ottawa–Lake Nipissing route, 10, 11, 18, 57, 61
Ottawa River, 9
Otter, schooner, 161

Pacific, brigantine, 269
Pacific Ocean, 63
Paddington, Capt., 254–255
Paint River, 99
Panama Canal, 273
Papachristidis, Phrixos Basil, 317
Papachristidis Co., Ltd., 317
Parmenter, E. L., 113
Partridge Point, 230
Passenger cruising, 325
Peach Island, 28
Pease & Allen, shipping firm, 131
Pelee Passage, 142
Pembine River, 99
Peninsula, steamer, 184
Pennsylvania R.R., 39
Penobscot Tower, 29
Pentwater, Mich., 97
Pepin, Lake, 17
Pere Marquette Railway, 16
Perrot, Nicholas, 18
Perry, Oliver Hazard, 25, 28, 62, 323, 336
Persons, Capt. John D., 244
Peshtigo, Wis., 108, 110, 112, 114–115, 119
Peshtigo River, 107
Pewabic, steamer, 244
Philadelphia, 36, 37, 271, 274
Phillips, Wis., 119
Phoenix, steamer, 105, 130
Pickands, Mather, shipping firm, 264, 291
Pictured Rocks, 48
Pigeon River, 215
Pike River, 99
Pilot, schooner, 79–80
Pilot Island, 259
Pioneer, steamer, 124
Pittsburgh Steamship Company, 223, 245, 305, 315
Plymouth Rock, steamer, 139, 260
Poe, Gen. Orlando M., 222, 232, 303, 307

Poe Lock, 205, 264, 303, 306–307, 317, 320, 321, 322
Point Abino, 123
Pointe Aux Barques Reef, 115
Polish settlers, 38
Pollution, 329–331
Populism, 264
Porcupine Mountains, 100
Port Arthur, 31, 49, 223, 235
Port Huron, Mich., 39, 66, 88, 107, 117, 125, 253
Portage River, 167
Porte des Morts passage, 259
Porter, Gen., 77
Portland cement, 93
Portsmouth, Ohio, 79
Posey, North Albert, 215
Poverty Island, 242
Presque Isle (Erie, Pa.), 62
Presque Isle, tug-barge, 322–232
Prince Shoal Light, 280–281
Prince of Wales (Edward VII), 297
Put-in-Bay, 25, 28, 62
Pyramid Point, 240

Quebec, 7, 10, 11, 15, 18

R. J. Hackett, steamer, 221
R. W. England, steamer, 245
Racine, Wis., 82–83, 147
Radisson, Pierre E., 9, 18
Rains, Owen, 228
Rainy Lake, 215
Randall, Governor Alexander W., 67–68
Recollets, 11
Recovery, schooner, 161
Red River carts, 40, 160
Regina, steamer, 256
Reserve Mining Company, 290
Revolutionary War, 61
Richardson, Hugh, 223
Rider, Capt. Redmond, 177
Riel, Nicolas, 228
River Rouge, Mich., 29, 223
Rivers and Harbors Act of 1970, 330
Rochester, N.Y., 78
Rock of Ages, 25
Rockefeller, John D., 222, 334
Roger Blough, diesel, 305, 320

INDEX

Rogers, Capt. Jedediah, 123
Rogers City, Mich., 93
Roosevelt, Franklin D., 272
Roosevelt, Theodore, 139, 205
Root River, 82-83
Rough, Capt. James, 64
Roulleau's Light, 232
Round Island, 5
Rouse Simmons, schooner, 243
Royal Geographic Society, 45
Royce, Stephen, 293-294

Sabin, L. C., 233, 304
Sabin Lock, 205, 304
Saginaw, Mich., 87-92, 98, 106, 108, 214, 261; loggers' resorts in, 89; lumber barons of, 90
Saginaw Bay, 59, 89, 90, 107, 116, 118
Saginaw River, 64, 87, 88, 90, 106, 187, 221
Sahgonahkato, 107
Sailors Encampment, 228, 231-232
St. Anthony, Falls of, 9, 60
St. Catherine Lock, 278
St. Clair, Lake, 29, 59
St. Clair, Mich., 64
St. Clair River, 29, 65, 107, 125, 256, 260, 271, 326
St. Croix River, 36
St. Ignace, Mich., 9, 14, 16, 25, 49
St. James, on Beaver Island, 149, 153, 154
St. Joseph, Mich., 240, 269
St. Joseph River, 17
St. Joseph's Island, 49, 227, 228
St. Lambert Lock, 278, 280
St. Lawrence River, 5, 9, 11, 18, 19, 23, 24, 57, 58, 61, 70 126, 221, 240, 269, 270, 271, 273, 274, 275
St. Lawrence Seaway, 20, 206, 220, 269-277, 306, 317
St. Louis, Mo., 98, 121, 126
St. Louis Bay, 36
St. Louis River, 32, 123, 215
St. Marie, steamer, 326
St. Mary's, Ga., 45
St. Mary's Falls Canal, 31, 43, 67, 68, 84, 101, 142, 165, 177, 197-206, 220, 222, 228, 229, 232, 233, 264, 271

St. Mary's River, 5, 8, 30, 43-47, 52, 57, 199-200, 219, 227-236, 251, 259, 263, 271, 327, 328; rapids of, 10, 159, 161-162, 184
St. Paul, Minn., 98
Sam Ward, steamer, 184
Sandusky, Ohio, 24, 26, 27, 39, 127
Sandy Hook, 78
San Francisco, 269
Sargeant, General George B., 35-36
Sassaba, Chippewa chief, 300
Saterlee, Capt. Charles, 233
Sault Ste. Marie, Mich., 9, 13, 14, 19, 23, 25, 30, 38, 43-47, 63, 159-161, 164-165, 187, 189, 190, 197-206, 227, 228, 229, 233, 260, 264, 265, 297-311, 327; portage trail, 43, 50, 57, 163, 164-165, 168, 175, 183, 184
Sausaukee River, 99
Savannah River, 215
Saxon, Oscar, 113, 114
Scandinavian settlers, 23, 26, 38, 98, 141
Schoolcraft, Henry Rowe, 32, 43-52, 123, 167, 228, 234, 308, 338-340
Scott, brig, 269
Scott, Walter, Alpena pioneer, 92
Scottish settlers, 38, 134-139, 260
Seeandbee, steamer, 142, 316
Seligman, "Little Jake," 91-92
Selkirk, Earl of, 123
Seneca Chief, packet boat, 78
Seneca Indians, 10, 57
Seneffe, battlefield of, 60
Seney, Mich., 99
Sept-Iles, 282-283, 295
Sheboygan, Wis., 99, 132-133
Shegud, Chippewa chief, 203
Sheldon Thompson, steamer, 125
Shiawasee River, 89
Shingle Point, 30
Shipmasters' Association, 259
Shipwrecks, Great Lakes, 74, 239-256
Simpson, Capt. Jerry, 264
Sioux Indians, 14, 17, 20, 60
Sir William Siemens, steamer, 233
Skilling, woodcarver, 63
Slavic settlers, 26

INDEX

Sleeping Giant, 31
Smith, Joseph, 148
Smith, Milton, 251, 256
Smith, Moses, 148
Smith, Capt. W. W., 233
Smithsonian Institution, 50, 150
Snell Lock, 278
Snyder, William P., 261
Soo. *See* Sault Ste. Marie
Soo Canal. *See* St. Mary's Falls Canal
Soo Library. *See* American Merchant Marine Library Association
Soo Line (railroad), 39, 197
Soo Locks Centennial, 1955, 304
South American, steamer, 142
South Park, steamer, 314
South Street, New York waterfront, 70
Spalding & Bacon, Soo freighters, 184
Sparrows Point, 271
Spectacle Reef, 25
Speed, Col., 129
Stannard brothers, mariners, 162–163
Stannard Rock, 163
Starved Rock, Ill., 60
Stella Maris II, diesel, 324–325
Stevens, Moses, 159
Stewart J. Cort, diesel, 305, 322, 323
Strang, James Jesse, 147–154, 240
Stuntz, George, 32–38, 40, 215
Sturgeon Bay, 74, 115, 243
Sugar Island, 30, 197, 227, 228, 230, 263
Sulpitians, 11
Superior, Lake, 5, 8, 9, 13, 14, 18, 23, 25, 30–32, 35, 38, 39, 40, 44, 47–52, 71, 72, 100, 101, 119, 123, 160–178, 182, 183, 184, 204, 205, 210, 211, 214, 215, 216, 219, 222, 234, 235, 240, 245–247, 251, 252, 253–256, 274
Superior, steamer, 88, 123–124, 228
Superior, Wis., 32, 99, 100, 216, 256, 261
Superior City, steamer, 221
Sutter, John A., 51, 168
Swallow, schooner, 164
Swan Creek, 27, 164

Sweet, Capt. G. B., 130–131

Taconite, 287, 327
Taconite Harbor, 291, 322
Taft, Lorado, 23
Tanner, John, 45
Tate, David, 229
Tawas River, 92
Teal Lake, 181, 182
Telegraph, steamer, 240
Templeton, steamer, 242
Theriault, Frenchy, 112
Thomas A. Scott, steamer, 261
Thompson, Capt. Edward, 71
Thorson, John, 269
Three Rivers, Que., 11
Thunder Bay, 87, 93, 94, 118, 140, 165, 277
Thunder Bay Island, 243–244
Thunder Bay River, 92, 107
Thunder Cape, 31, 235, 236, 240
Tilden, Samuel J., 212
Tittibawassee River, 89
Toanchi, Huron village, 11
Tobacco River, 91
Toledo, Ohio, 24, 26, 27, 39, 40, 118, 164
Tom Dowling, steam tug, 101
Tomlinson, George Ashley, 261, 262–263
Tonawanda, North and South, on Niagara River, 95, 118
Tonty, Henry de, 58, 60
Topsail Island, 230
Toronto, 61, 223
Tower, Charlemagne, 37
Traverse Bay, 24
Tregarthen, steamer, 220
Turret Chief, steamer, 254–255
Two Harbors, Minn., 37, 39, 215, 253

United States Hydrographic Service, 118
United States Steel Corporation, 216
Upper Lakes & St. Lawrence Transportation Company, 222

V. H. Ketchum, steamer, 221, 308–309, 322
Valley Camp, steamer, 297, 308

359

INDEX

Van Anden, Joshua, 159
Vandalia, steamer, 127
Vermilion iron range, 37, 214–215
Vermilion Foundation, 335–336
Vermilion, Lake, 36, 37, 215
Vermilion, Ohio, 333, 335, 337–338
Vessel Owners' Association, 232, 234
Victoria, Mich., 100
Victory, steamer, 221, 222
Vistula, 27
Voree, Wis., 148, 149, 152
Vulcan, Mich., 212

W. E. Fitzgerald, steamer, 234
Wabush Mines, 283
Waboojeeg, Chippewa chief, 45
Wakefield, Fred W., 335
Wakefield, Mich., 212, 213
Walk-in-the-Water, steamer, 88, 121–123, 298, 336
Walworth County, Wis., 148
War of 1812, 61, 161, 199
Ward, David, lumberman, 91
Ward, Capt. Eber, 72, 91, 201, 205
Washington, D.C., 24, 50, 201
Washington, steamer, 105
Washington Island, 38, 239
Watson, Jonas, 178
Waugoshance Reef, 102, 115, 243
Webster, Daniel, 200, 201
Weed, Thurlow, 29
Weitzel, General Godfrey, 303
Weitzel Lock, 205, 206, 303, 304
Welland Canal, 24, 81, 271, 277
West Virginia, 39
Western Metropolis, steamer, 139
Western Reserve, 28
Western Star, steamer, 247
Western World, steamer, 139, 260
Westmoreland, steamer, 241–242
Wexford, steamer, 239
Whaleback steamers, 74

White, Peter, 187–189
White Rock, phantom city, 116–117
White Shoal Light, 324
White Shoals, 115
Whitefish, 43–44
Whitefish Bay, 31, 46, 74, 161, 165, 167, 175, 198, 241, 255, 327, 328
Whiting, J. T., 168
Whitman, Walt, 102
Wilkeson, Capt. David, 27
Wilkeson, Samuel, 77–78
William A. Irvin, steamer, 220
William Edenborn, steamer, 315
William Nottingham, steamer, 255–256
Williams, Harvey, 88
Wilson, Capt. Jack, 68, 204
Wilson, Thomas, 261, 263
Winchell, Horace, 288
Winchell, N. H., 287
Windmill Point, 25
Windsor, Ont., 25
Winnebago, Lake, 7
Winnebago Indians, 7
Winnetka, Ill., 69
Wisconsin, 17, 23, 35, 59, 80, 81, 98, 119, 121, 128, 129, 135
Wisconsin River, 7, 8, 9
Wolvin, Augustus B., 261
Woodward, Judge Augustus, 122
Woodworth, "Uncle Ben," 122
Worcester, Mass., 187
World War II, 275, 304
Wright, Phoebe, 152
Wright, Sarah, 152
Wyandotte, Mich., 29

Yangtze River, 274
Yosemite Valley, 139
Young, Brigham, 148
Young Lion of the West, packet boat, 78